GREAT WAR BRITAIN

GREAT WAR BRITAIN
THE FIRST WORLD WAR AT HOME

LUCINDA GOSLING

First published 2014

The History Press
The Mill, Brimscombe Port
Stroud, Gloucestershire, GL5 2QG
www.thehistorypress.co.uk

British Library Cataloguing in Publication Data.
A catalogue record for this book is available from the British Library.

ISBN 978 0 7524 9188 2

Typesetting and origination by The History Press
Printed in India

CONTENTS

The TATLER

Vol. LVIII. No. 756
London, December 22, 1915

REGISTERED AT THE GENERAL POST OFFICE AS A NEWSPAPER Sixpence.

"WE ARE FED UP WITH WAR NEWS—SEND US 'THE TATLER.'"

And somebody evidently has complied with this very frequent request in the case of these hardy gunners, who were snapshotted "somewhere in France" reading the Christmas Number of this paper. Whilst people at home eagerly devour the war news, the men who are actually doing the business are glad to get away from it—which is understandable if you live in a daily and even hourly atmosphere of battle, murder, and sudden death

b

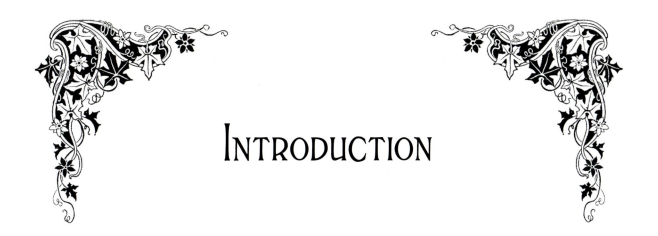

INTRODUCTION

If there was anything to distinguish the summer of 1914 from any other it was the exceptional heat. As the mercury rose, *The Tatler* magazine's staff worked through the suffocating heat. 'With the thermometer at goodness knows what, these lines are grudgingly contributed by a perspiring and waistcoatless staff,' it informed readers. 'The office cat is undergoing a course of ice massage; life is very trying.' But despite the uncomfortable working conditions, the magazine continued as usual, and it being the height of the 'Season', there was plenty on which to report. There were the usual preoccupations and highlights of that time of year – speech day at Harrow; centenary cricket at Lord's attended by the King, and Children's Day at the exclusive Ranelagh club. Advertisements reflected the hot, lazy days of high summer – golf balls from J.P. Cochrane, Whiteway's famous Devon Cyders, Colgate's Talc Powder available in violet and cashmere bouquet ('delightful after bathing in the sea') and the Casino at Dieppe reminded potential customers that it was just five hours from London. Ostend, 'Queen of the Sea-Bathing Resorts', in Belgium was publicised as easily accessible by motor car from Paris or Brussels. The sensational murder trial of Madame Caillaux in Paris, accused of killing the editor of *Le Figaro*, was the talk of smart society, while the equally sensational 'ravishing' Russian Ballet was performing at Drury Lane.

In its 8 July issue, there was a ripple of concern over the news that in Sarajevo, the heir to the Austrian Empire, Archduke Franz Ferdinand, had been assassinated along with his 'brave wife'. Under the heading, 'Flutter and unrest in the diplomatic circle of the near-eastern powers', a page of pictures showed various ministers and ambassadors flitting from embassy to embassy in London. But it was one story of many, given as much space as the forthcoming boxing match between the French idol Georges Carpentier and 'Gunboat' Smith or the tragic death of Sir Denis Anson, who had fallen overboard and drowned in the Thames during a nocturnal riverboat party, also attended by Lady Diana Manners and the eldest son of the Prime Minister, Raymond Asquith. In its Small Talk section, At Wimbledon, the American Norman Brookes had beaten four-times champion, the dashing Anthony Wilding, to win the championship while Mrs Lambert Chambers slugged her way to a seventh victory beating Mrs Larcombe in the final. *The Tatler* ran photographs of the two 'Titans of Tennis' exhibiting remarkably similar jaw lines.

Opposite: Although *The Tatler* catered for an upper-class readership, it was keen to emphasise its popularity with all classes of society, including, as here, troops at the Front. (Illustrated London News/ME)

By the end of July, 'Gay and Glorious Goodwood … the last great gathering of society swallows before dispersing to the sea, the stream and the moors, or the cure' marked the end of the Season. Eve, *The Tatler*'s gossip columnist, worried what she would wear in the heat, as 'Goodwood frocks get smarter and smarter, and really now they're very much the same as the Ascot ones.' Some 'Pictorial Consolation for the Perspiring Londoner' was offered in the form of a page of pretty women in swimsuits, including 'a charming young German lady in a quaint costume pour la plage.' Further on, a fashion spread suggested Burberry for ladies heading to the grouse moors of Scotland that August.

Due to being a weekly magazine, *The Tatler* was at a disadvantage when it came to reporting immediate news and when Britain declared war on Germany at midnight on 4 August, the Wednesday issue had already gone to press. Thus, inappropriately, its first issue of the war featured the benign subject of Princess Mary on its front cover, looking awkward and a little frumpy, but, significantly, with her hair up for the first time, prompting the caption to read, 'Our Grown Up Little Princess.' Perhaps the only hint of the cataclysm about to erupt was a portrait of the popular Count Mensdorff-Pouilly, the Austro-Hungarian Ambassador in the same issue – 'a great sportsman and a prominent member of the Jockey Club' – and two small sketches in the 'Letters of Eve' column which commented on the 'growing military influences on fashion', though Eve seemed to think that if young men were to be called up for military service then it would more likely be to deal with the situation in Ireland.

It is only fair to point out that *The Tatler* was not alone in this blinkered view. Not far from *The Tatler* offices in Milford Lane, off the Strand, were those of *The Sketch* magazine, in Great New Street, on the north side of Fleet Street. *The Sketch* was a friendly rival and senior by eight years (launched in 1893; *The Tatler* in 1901). It also had the newly mature Princess Mary as its cover girl on 5 August, and its enthusiasm for girls in bathing costumes was even greater, with four whole pages of comely bathing belles shared with readers. Elsewhere, the actresses Phyllis Monkman and Eileen Molyneux were featured wearing a strapless gown and shockingly short skirts respectively, in photographs entitled: 'Costumes to be Recommended in Hot Weather.' 'The Clubman' column on the

No. 681, JULY 15, 1914]   THE TATLER

THE TRAGEDY OF THE THAMES
Familiar Faces at Sir Denis Anson's Inquest.

SIR HERBERT TREE AND HIS DAUGHTER, MISS IRIS TREE—(INSET) MR. RAYMOND ASQUITH (LEFT)
AND COUNT BENCKENDORFF
The famous actor-manager and his charming daughter are seen leaving the coroner's court at Lambeth, where the inquest was held over the tragic death of Sir Denis Anson and Mr. William Mitchell, the gallant bandsman who tried in vain to rescue the young baronet who dived recklessly into the Thames during a midnight cruise. The details of the sad ending to a young man's career and the midnight supper party on the river, at which so many well-known people were present, need no further elaboration. The deepest sympathy is extended to the relatives of Sir Denis Anson, who only quite recently succeeded to the baronetcy, and of the brave bandsman, and also to the friends who participated in a jaunt which ended so tragically.

Notable members of society, including Sir Herbert Tree and his daughter Iris, attending the inquest into the tragic death of Sir Dennis Anson and Mr William Mitchell during a nocturnal riverboat trip on the Thames. Other members of the party had included Lady Diana Manners and Raymond Asquith, eldest son of the Prime Minister. (Illustrated London News/ME)

The Sketch

No. 1123 —Vol. LXXXVII.　　　WEDNESDAY, AUGUST 5, 1914.　　　SIXPENCE.

HER FIRST HAIR - UP STUDIO - PORTRAIT : PRINCESS MARY, THE GROWN - UP.

Princess Mary, it is, of course, unnecessary to remind our readers, is the only daughter of the King and Queen. She was born on April 25, 1897. Her full names are Victoria Alexandra Alice Mary.

Photograph by Campbell-Gray, London.

As weekly magazines, both *The Sketch* and *The Tatler*, were at a disadvantage when it came to reporting immediate news. Their first issues of the war featured a photograph of Princess Mary on their covers, wearing her hair up for the first time. (Illustrated London News/ME)

29 July commented, somewhat petulantly, how the London Season had been spoilt by a combination of court mourning (for the Austrian Archduke), troubles on the stock exchange and militant suffragette activity. The Royal Horse Show a few weeks previously had been disrupted by protests, and museums and galleries were closing their doors to visitors in fright because of the potential damage that might be wreaked by the troublemakers. The previous week, the same columnist had written about the current shortage of men in the Regular Army, 'should any national emergency come suddenly upon this country.' The next week, a photograph of the baby son of the Duke and Duchess of Brunswick (the daughter of the Kaiser) was published with the news that he, and any future children, would be styled 'Highness' and designated a Prince of the United Kingdom of Great Britain and Ireland. His uncle, described as 'our very friendly Crown Prince, the Kaiser's heir,' was pictured at a tennis tournament in Zoppot. Elsewhere, *The Sketch* ran a page of pictures on the lavish party held by Mrs Keiller, aka the artist Doll Phil-Morris, at her home, No. 13 Hyde Park Gardens. The theme of a Venetian masquerade required everyone to dress in masks and eighteenth-century gowns, and her commitment to authenticity led her to flood the terrace of her garden to replicate the Grand Canal and have a miniature Bridge of Sighs constructed to traverse the water.

This was the world of *The Tatler* and *The Sketch*; a world of ballrooms and bazaars, duchesses and debutantes, royal babies, engagements, marriages, fashions from Paris and polo at Hurlingham. As the country's social compasses, they reported on the smartest functions and the cream of society, casting a spotlight on those who had talent, influence, pedigree, power or simply a pretty face. In an entertaining blend of theatre, society gossip, royal doings, sport, fashion, motoring, travel and irreverent writing and opinion they paint a portrait of a gilded and glamorous elite, whose privileged lives were about to be shaken, damaged and, in some cases, destroyed by the outbreak of war. *The Tatler* and *The Sketch* had chronicled Edwardian society at play through a golden era for the upper classes. In August 1914, they turned to depicting society at war.

The Tatler and *The Sketch*, at 7*d* and 6*d* respectively, pitched themselves as quality magazines aimed predominantly at a middle- and upper-class market. They were part of a small group of titles known as the 'mid-weeklies' due to the fact they were published each Wednesday) or 'sixpenny weeklies', designed to 'appeal to cultivated people who in their leisure moments look for light reading and amusing pictures with a high artistic value' (the *Illustrated London News*, 1928). These were magazines rooted in the tradition of the illustrated press. *The Sketch* had been launched by the *Illustrated London News*, the world's first illustrated newspaper when it was first published in 1842. *The Tatler* was the younger sibling of *The Sphere* (though only by eighteen months) and its editor, Edward Huskinson, pioneered what was described at the time as 'personal journalism', determining to 'yoke the snapshot, ephemeral as it appeared, to the lasting quality of the printed word. In this way, *The Tatler* may be said to have begun to speak in a new language and to record the appearance of people in what was generically spoken of as Society, with a capital "S".' It was a complementary arrangement. The *Illustrated London News* (ILN) and *The Sphere* concentrated on event-driven news reporting which during war meant battles, political changes and overseas developments, leaving *The Sketch* and *The Tatler* free to be more eclectic, gossipy and, occasionally, frivolous.

To this duo should be added a third title, catering to a similar audience. *The Bystander* launched in 1903 as a protégé of *The Graphic*, claiming to be 'Everything About Everybody Everywhere' and to look at the lighter side of life with a satirical touch. Early on, it concentrated on political satire (though this decreased after the war), along with cartoons, sport, travel, motoring and, again, society news, all carried out with a characteristic, tongue-in-cheek humour. Tailored perhaps to a slightly more masculine audience, *The Bystander* trumped both *The Sketch* and *The Tatler* in terms of popularity with the troops when it began to publish the cartoons of Bruce

Bairnsfather in 1915, an unexpected golden goose for the magazine as Bairnsfather rapidly became the most popular cartoonist of the war. *The Bystander* was humorous and opinionated and, although it supported the female contribution to the war effort (albeit as a novel temporary arrangement), it had been an unabashed critic of the suffragette movement in the preceding decade.

The Tatler in particular, which had increased in price to a shilling by the end of the war, positioned itself as the unofficial organ of the smart set, frequently picturing persons of note engrossed in the magazine, reading about their friends, acquaintances and

Marthe Troly-Curtin, who, under the pen name of Phrynette, wrote a similar column to Eve in *The Sketch*. The magazine wrote of her way with words during wartime: 'it is the gift of laughter and of tears which has won for her such favour…' (Illustrated London News/ME)

perhaps themselves. In 1915, the Aga Khan was photographed by Sarony reading a copy; the theatre and film actress Jessie Winter was pictured reading it two years later; Queen Sophie of Greece, sister of the Kaiser, was photographed on the beach at Eastbourne absorbed in a copy of *The Sketch*. The magazines also proved essential reading at the front. Not only were officers occasionally pictured with *The Tatler*, but humble Tommies too. In December 1915, *The Tatler* ran a photograph showing four members of the Royal Artillery perched on their gun, engrossed in

the magazine's Christmas number. Keen to demonstrate it could have widespread appeal, it published a request from one anonymous soldier on its cover:

I have wondered if one of your very generous readers would care to send me their copy after they have finished with it. It does not matter how old or dirty it may be so long as the inside is there. I would not trouble you, but my folk at home are not in a position to send it … It would do your eyes some good if you could only see our boys crowding around the one book, and on some occasions, it may only be a few pages someone has found. I expect some lucky officer had it sent to him.

The Sketch, which would always have a slightly risqué streak, became another favourite of soldiers when it exclusively published a series of illustrations by Raphael Kirchner in 1915. The 'Kirchner Girls', with their faint whiff of eroticism, were the first illustrated wartime pin-ups, as soldiers at the front literally pinned them up to decorate the walls of their dug-outs, bringing a little feminine allure to an otherwise unappealing environment. In fact, illustration and cartoons constituted a significant and popular proportion of each magazine. *The Sketch* particularly (whose by-line was 'Art and Actuality') championed the work of a number of illustrators who would go on to become household names, William Heath Robinson and George Studdy (who drew the cartoon dog Bonzo in the 1920s) among them.

By 1928, *The Tatler*, *The Sketch* and *The Bystander* would all have become part of the

Olivia Maitland Davidson, the journalist who was the voice of Eve pictured with her Master Tou-tou and Miss Bing, both of whom were also fictionalised in her columns. (Illustrated London News/ME)

same group owned by Illustrated Newspapers known as the 'Great Eight'. Together they tell a lively and compelling story of the First World War. Another magazine whose war issues provide us with a particularly interesting narrative of the home front experience is *The Queen*. First launched in 1861 as the brainchild of entrepreneurial journalist Samuel Beeton (husband of the more famous 'Mrs', Isabella), *The Queen* magazine was named after Queen Victoria with her blessing. Therefore it was staunchly royalist and set out to inform and engage its female readers on a whole range of topical issues and domestic matters. It would always be a standard bearer for women's issues both in the home and on the subject of child rearing, but also on women's education and employment. *The Queen* in wartime was a force to be reckoned with, picking up the baton of voluntarism without hesitation and spurring its readers to do whatever they could for the war effort. A week into the war, on 12 August, the magazine was already asking, 'What Can We Do?'

This country is now passing through what is perhaps the gravest crisis of its history, a crisis which every one of us, great and small, will have to combine to render less acute. For young men there is the one and easiest course of action and that is to respond to the appeal for recruits, which has been issued by the Government at the instance of Lord Kitchener. For women there is an equally clear course of conduct and that is to assist in some small way in alleviating the condition of the injured in some form or another. Even if they are not versed in the science of nursing they can readily obtain employment in minor capacities by enrolling themselves under the services of the Red Cross League or other allied societies.

Yevonde

A "TATLER" PICTURE FOUND IN THE GERMAN TRENCHES

The above picture of Miss Phyllis Elaine was published in "The Tatler" of June 14, 1916, and the page was found in the German trenches with the inscription on it of which the following is a translation: "May victory soon come. We must see more of such beauties. England is indeed the home of true beauty. Karl Tipzer (Captain)." Miss Elaine is appearing in "The Nut" at the Prince of Wales' on the 20th

The Tatler's popularity spread even beyond the British trenches. The magazine was delighted to report that this picture, of Miss Phyllis Elaine, originally published on 14 June 1916, was found in a captured German trench along with the hopeful inscription:'May victory soon come. We must see more of such beauties. England is indeed the home of true beauty. Karl Tipzer (Captain).' (Illustrated London News/ME)

This was *The Queen*'s style; dutiful, practical, tenacious. It was not a magazine to take no for an answer. It was convinced, quite rightly, that Britain's women could rise to the challenge of war and assaulted its readers with advice on training courses, identified avenues of employment, guidance on voluntary services and charities that needed help. It featured knitting patterns for soldiers' comforts as well as sewing patterns for clothing for Belgian refugee children, a myriad of war savings ideas were offered and food shortages were tackled by a weekly food column, 'Le Ménage', written by an old hand of women's magazine journalism, Constance Peel (Mrs C.S. Peel). Alongside all this practical advice were the latest fashions from Paris, Court news and the usual round of weddings and society engagements. In comparison to *The Tatler*, *The Sketch* and *The Bystander*, *The Queen* seems rather staid and worthy – lots of words, fewer pictures – a magazine for bluestockings, middle-class mothers and philanthropic spinsters. If *The Tatler* et al. are the frivolous and glamorous younger siblings, then *The Queen* is the sensible older sister. But though it may lack wit and revelry, it more than compensates with a detailed depiction of women and their role in the war.

Despite a delayed reaction in some quarters, by the middle of August, the mid-weeklies had entirely turned their attention to the war. It was a rapid transformation, but one that reflected the frenetic activity across the country as people and resources were galvanised and prepared for what lay ahead. *The Tatler* featured Lord Kitchener on its cover, and inside, portraits of national icons – the Prince of Wales, Admiral Jellicoe and First Lord of the Admiralty, Winston Churchill, under the title 'Bravo Winston!' in admiration for the rapid mobilisation of the Navy. In the 'Letters of Eve' column, Eve commented, 'It's rather awful and frightening, isn't it, the sudden way things happen? It seems hardly possible – does it? – that scarcely two weeks ago those of us who live to be amused were, well, just amusing ourselves, and that with such an amazing volte face all the things don't matter, all the non-essentials have been swept away.'

Coverage of the usual subjects continued but in some cases, adjustments were necessary. After a hesitant start, wartime theatre thrived and fashion remained a dominant interest, not least because it kept people employed. Weddings, if anything, increased in number –

'Cupid also busy mobilising in this sad period', wrote *The Tatler* in its report on a cluster of nuptials – but many were quieter affairs than they might otherwise have been. Sport limped on in reduced circumstances as many of its protagonists left the playing fields for what was to be dubbed 'the greater game'. War ensured there were plenty of alternative news stories to report. 'Adversity makes strange companions and war is a great leveller of class and caste. In these times of stress, Society is finding things of all kinds to do, and is doing it with all its might', reported *The Sketch* in its 26 August issue. Replacing balls and parties were countless charity events; and instead of debutantes in their court gowns, well-known young women were photographed in nursing uniforms. The mid-weeklies never ignored the fundamental issues affecting the nation, but they reacted in their own way and from the unique perspective of the beau monde. Taxes on luxury goods sent a shiver of anxiety through fashionable Mayfair dressing rooms

Above: 'A Topping Tonic after taking Turkish Trenches – some officers of the gallant Lancashire Fusiliers enjoying a short respite with an old and valued friend.' Officers at Gallipoli reading several issues of *The Tatler* magazine during a break in the fighting. (Illustrated London News/ME)

Opposite: Eve of *The Tatler* was introduced in May 1914 and is imagined here at her writing desk, quill poised, by Annie Fish. Her column entertained and amused readers throughout four years of war. (Illustrated London News/ME)

Annie Fish at the time of her marriage to Walter Sefton of the well-known textile manufacturing firm of J. R. Sefton & Co. Her illustrations for the 'Letters of Eve' column were fresh, modern and reflected Eve's joie de vivre. (Illustrated London News/ME)

while the government restrictions on drinking and licensing hours saw nightclub society making do with ginger beer after hours at Ciro's and Murray's. The upper classes found ways to reconcile the pleasures and pastimes of the old world, with the urgent requirements of the new. By September, *The Tatler* reported that the Countess of Wilton had accepted presidency of a war fund to be organised by the women golfers of the Empire, and Lord Tredegar was converting his luxurious steam yacht, *Liberty*, into a hospital ship. Lady Beatty, wife of Admiral David Beatty and fabulously wealthy thanks to her father, the Chicago department store founder Marshall Field, was doing the same with her yacht, *Sheelagh*. Aristocratic and wealthy women offered the two things they could easily spare – time and money. Distinguished ladies, among them the Marchioness of Salisbury and Mrs Asquith, the Prime Minister's wife, were heading branches of Queen Mary's Needlework Guild after an appeal by the Queen herself on 10 August, 'to organise a large collection of garments for those who will suffer on account of the war.' Lady Lovat was providing forty beds for the wounded at her home, Beaufort Castle, while Mrs Waldorf Astor (Nancy Astor) was lending her riverside house at Taplow for hospital purposes. Mrs Anthony Drexel, wife of the American millionaire, was 'a prominent worker on the American Ladies' Fund organised by the Duchess of Marlborough', and Lady Sarah Wilson, the aunt of Winston Churchill who had turned war correspondent during the Siege of Mafeking, was pictured with news that she was appealing for funds to equip a stationary base hospital somewhere on the Continent. The details were sketchy but, being posed with a bulldog and a resolute expression, nobody was about to question her patriotic credentials. In the world of the stage, the actresses Lena Ashwell, Eva and Decima Moore were seen hard at work in the Little Theatre as members of the Women's Emergency Corps.

As the war began to take its unforgiving toll on the officer classes, *The Tatler* in particular found the very core of its social sphere dramatically eroded. Many of the personalities gracing magazine pages during those final heady days of the summer of 1914 did not survive the war. That July, *The Tatler* had celebrated such well-known personalities as Captain Leslie Cheape, the polo supremo who had helped England to a historic win over America in the Westchester Cup that year. By 1916, he had been killed in Egypt. Tennis heartthrob Tony Wilding died on the Western Front, killed by a shell explosion on top of a dug-out during the Battle of Aubers Ridge. The latest portraits of the Grand Duchesses of Russia, the beautiful daughters of the Tsar, featured on the front cover of *The Sketch* magazine's 29 July 1914 issue. By July 1918, they would be dead, executed along with the rest

of their family by Bolsheviks in the cellar of a house in Yekaterinburg. At the Chaloner-Benyon wedding in July 1914, one photograph featured Mrs Dubosc Taylor, 'one of the most beautiful women in society', leaving the church. She threw herself into nursing work during the war but four years later, the same magazine was reporting her death due to the influenza epidemic. Lady Victoria Pery (later Brady), who garnered admiration with her aviation exploits, including looping-the-loop with the French airman, Gustav Hamel, was cited as living proof by *The Sketch* in September 1914 that there should be a R.F.F.C. (Royal Feminine Flying Corps). She too was another victim of flu in 1918. In its 2 September issue, *The Sketch* suggested reprising the stage play *An Englishman's Home*, which, when written in 1909, predicted the consequences of an enemy invasion. Its author, Guy du Maurier, brother of the actor Gerald du Maurier, was a Lieutenant Colonel in the Royal Fusiliers and killed by shell fire near Kemmel in March 1915. Lord Desborough was pictured in *The Sketch* arriving at the Eton and Harrow match at Lord's with his youngest son, Ivo. He would lose his two elder sons, Julian and Billy Grenfell, in the war, two bright and promising men who very much symbolise the 'lost generation' of the First World War. Magazines such as *The Tatler* and *The Sketch*, which delighted in reporting on bright and promising people, must have found the job of informing their readers that so many flames had been cruelly and prematurely extinguished a poignant task.

Quality magazines called for quality writers and *The Tatler*, *The Sketch* and *The Bystander* could boast plenty, among them Richard King, author of 'Silent Friends' in *The Tatler*, and Keble Howard who wrote 'Motley Notes' in *The Sketch*. But the voice that is most audible of all is that of Eve, *The Tatler*'s inimitable gossip columnist who each issue shared with readers the 'Correspondence between the Hon. Evelyn Fitzmaurice and Lady Betty Berkshire'. 'Letters of Eve' was written by Olivia Maitland-Davidson and first appeared in the magazine on 20 May 1914, continuing on through the war and out the other side. It was an instant hit and was copied with some success by a similar column in *The Sketch*, 'Phrynette's Letters from London', authored by Marthe Troly-Curtin and illustrated by Gladys Peto.

Eve is a chatty, light-hearted society girl, flirtatious, vivacious, fun loving, fond of fashion and 'frivol' (frivolity). To her fictional friend Betty she confides all her thoughts, grumbles and views on wartime life using an odd but endearing form of upper-class slang. As a tour guide to Great War Britain, she is enormous fun. Eve plays up her shallow concerns and superficiality but deep down she is sincere; occasionally indiscreet but never cruel. Best of all, Eve is a master – or mistress – of self-deprecation, fully aware of her flaws and that her own activities and daily concerns are petty and minor in comparison to bigger issues at stake. But by mocking herself, she also holds up a mirror to the society she is part of. Eve, as the representative of *The Tatler*'s readership, never allows society to get above itself and is fully aware that to those outside her tribe, the upper classes promoted so enthusiastically in the magazine could be little more than indulgent show-offs. It is a self-awareness that is perfectly expressed in a scheme she tells Betty about in 1916; to star in a film along with her nursing society chums:

I'm always being asked for new ideas, but I'm being horribly selfish and not giving any away, 'cos I want all I've got for my own parties. Still, there was one I just flung 'em in passing, so to speak. It was cinema films of us doing war work, which I thought'd be awf'ly amusin'. You know, pictures of the Duchess of X giving the wrong man the wrong medicine in her hospital of Y – Z__. The Princess B waking an insomnia case out of his first sweet natural slumber to give him his sleeping draught, and Lady Ermyntrude Blank scrubbing the floors with best Pears' soap at Pompom-sur-Mer. Jolly good idea, don't you think so? Most people'd simply love it – the people film'd, I mean – and if the rest of the world didn't rush to it it wouldn't matter, there'd be such a rush of us to see what we looked like on the movies in those fascinating Red Cross head-dresses that we do so dearly love assuming with, or without, excuse.

While Ms Maitland-Davidson gave Eve her voice, equally important was her image. Annie Fish, whose stylised linear drawings soon became synonymous with the character, illustrated the 'Letters of Eve' column. They felt modern and fresh, far more akin to the 1920s than the 1910s. Eve, through the drawings of Fish, became a celebrity beyond the confines of the magazine. She was the subject of an exhibition, books and appeared in human form on stage (in the revue, *Tina*) and screen (in *The Adventures of Eve*, starring Eileen Molyneux). Her image was used on a range of costume jewellery and as a design on fabric by the firm Sefton, whose owner was Annie Fish's husband. When the actress Isobel Elsom posed for some publicity photographs with a stuffed toy dog, everybody knew it was Tou-tou, based on Eve's – and the author's – Pekingese dog. Such was Eve's renown that Olivia Maitland-Davidson even took *The Sphere* and Tatler Ltd to court over ownership of the pseudonym. She had previously threatened action against Annie Fish when the latter held an exhibition of drawings under the name of Eve and when a new magazine entitled *Eve* appeared in 1919, with articles within by an Eve who was not Ms Maitland-Davidson, the judge ordered the proprietors to desist from using the name and to choose an alternative *nom de plume*.

Olivia Maitland-Davies had a busy and successful journalistic career during wartime. Not only was she the woman behind 'Eve', she also wrote the weekly 'In England Now' column by Blanche in *The Bystander*, but her career was cut tragically short when she died suddenly after an operation in 1920.

After the passage of almost one hundred years, it is surprising how easily Eve and her imitators are still able to fascinate and amuse. War can be a dry subject in the wrong hands but their writing brings alive a fascinating cast of characters living through a tumultuous time. Through them we learn of the preoccupations of the time, the coping mechanisms, the minutiae, discomforts and joys of daily lives. Certain individuals emerge repeatedly; names such as Lady Diana Manners, Lady Drogheda, Elizabeth Asquith and the dancer Irene Castle, Gladys Cooper, Elsie Janis and the adorable Gaby Deslys. These were the celebrities of the day, at the fulcrum of London life, and their personal experiences of the war can be pieced together through the gossip columns, society notes and theatrical reviews in the mid-weeklies.

There are aspects that grate against our twenty-first century sensibilities; in many ways the magazines of the war period did little to dilute the deeply driven class distinctions of British society. Cartoons of the time played up to class stereotypes, the highlighting of those from society who got their hands dirty in munitions factories or scrubbing hospital floors shows just what a novelty it was and the officers-only policy in the weekly rolls of honour seems a gross misrepresentation of those who served and gave their lives for their country. But we must be careful to apply a rational perspective and not to dismiss the contribution of the upper classes and aristocracy to the war. It is well known that officers from the educated middle and upper classes, the subalterns who were expected to lead from the front during an attack, proportionately suffered more losses during the war than any other rank. *The Tatler* and other weeklies were simply reporting, with dignity, on those who were part of the social class it represented. And there were many women who used their rank, wealth and status to help and comfort those less fortunate – not just wounded soldiers and sailors, but refugees, the unemployed, widows and orphans. Though the roles of both warrior leader and lady philanthropist continued to follow the expected feudal patterns, the upper classes could not be accused of fiddling while Rome burned.

It has been a pleasure and a privilege to turn the pages of these volumes and see the war through the eyes of those who lived during an exceptional period in British history. In the course of my research, I've discovered a society that worked as hard as it played, and through the pain and anguish of loss on an unprecedented scale, still found room to laugh as well as cry. War transformed Great War Britain, a transformation recorded with skill, elegance and style in the magazines forming the heart and soul of this book. It is an honour to be able to share it here.

'Your King & Country Want You' by Paul A. Rubens was written as a women's recruiting song and dedicated by special permission to Queen Mary with all profits going to the Queen's Work for Women Fund. The cover, depicting a woman with her arms outstretched, is by John Hassall, the well-known poster artist and illustrator who frequently contributed his artistic skills for free during the war. (ME)

Everybody Should Do His Bit

Recruitment, Patriotism & the War Effort

About halfway along the Strand in central London stands the façade of the old Hotel Cecil, behind which now lie office buildings. When it opened in 1896 it was the largest building of its kind in Europe, with 800 rooms stretching from the Strand down to the Thames Embankment, where its looming outline dominated the riverside vista. The majority of the magnificent structure was demolished in 1930 but it was here in August 1914 that Mrs Cunliffe-Owen, a daughter of the late Philip Cunliffe-Owen, director of the Victoria and Albert Museum, raised the 23rd and 24th Service Battalions, better known as the 1st and 2nd Sportsman's Battalions.

The Sportsman's Battalions worked on the same principles as the Pals Battalions, but instead of recruiting from the same geographical area, they encouraged sportsmen past and present to join up together. The battalions also had the distinction of including men up to the age of forty-five, a dispensation gained by Mrs Cunliffe-Owen from the War Office – her argument being that due to their sporting backgrounds, their health and

fitness was superior to that of the average volunteer. In the early weeks of the battalion's formation, before it was moved to a training camp in Harlow, recruits would drill daily in Embankment Gardens, do physical jerks on the slopes of Savoy Street and route march through the London streets. Police officers would stop the traffic for them as they marched down the Strand, turning into the small alleyway, Carting Lane, by the Coal Hole public house before being dismissed. With few members measuring less than 6ft, the battalions must have been an impressive sight.

Today, the idea of an Army battalion being recruited at a five star hotel and trained and drilled in the heart of central London among public gardens and theatres is incongruous to say the least. But the Hotel Cecil, which would in 1918 become the first headquarters of the newly formed Royal Air Force, was just one of many London buildings requisitioned for the war effort, and the men of the Sportsman's Battalion were just some of those who tolerated makeshift facilities. In December 1914, Eve in *The Tatler* whispered conspiratorially

"There Is Time to Finish the Game"—Drake

Our sketch illustrates a scene last week in the Temple Gardens where the drilling of recruits and the playing of lawn tennis were going on side by side. It also shows that Englishmen rightly believe in the importance at this time of being actively engaged in something—or as "Downwriter" counsels us elsewhere in this issue, of going on doing it—whatever it is. At the time of a similar crisis, it will be remembered, Drake remarked that there was time for him to finish his game of bowls and beat the Spanish Armada, too

BY J. F. WOOLRICH

An impression of new recruits being drilled in Temple Gardens while men play tennis on a court nearby is by J.F.- Woolrich and was published in *The Bystander*. The title references the famous quote of Sir Francis Drake, who insisted on finishing his game of bowls before confronting the Armada. (Illustrated London News/ME)

about the discomfort felt by some of the residents of exclusive Grosvenor Square, which had become occupied by army huts: 'It was the last to go, but now it's gone – the sanctity of Grosvenor Square. I expect you've heard how a thousand 'Terriers' are in residence there – the Queen Victoria Rifles to wit … I did hear it faintly whispered that not all the other residents, those in houses I mean, are quite so pleased about it as they might be. Tommy, you see, is a noisy bird at best, dear thing. And – well, I suppose you don't bargain for a perpetual smell of onioned stew when you scheme – and pay – for a Grosvenor Square residence.'

By March 1917, she described the way in which the war had changed the 'once so delightful and lovely St James' Park' into 'huts, huts all the way, and the very latest, the Ministry of Shipping, almost vies with Buckingham Palace itself.'

The Tatler painted a picture of the rapidly changing scenery in London at the end of September 1914 in a piece entitled 'O Listen to the soldiers in the park':

Regent's Park (or any other park for that matter) on any ordinary autumn afternoon presents an extraordinary peaceful appearance. With the exception of perambulators, children playing in groups, dogs, nurses, and the usual complement of loafers, there is "nothing doing". Now how different it all is. Sitting in that particular corner facing the end (or is it the beginning?) of Mappin Terrace, Regent's Park affords much food for thought. Its grassy expanse is being worn day by day by the tramp, tramp, tramp of a thousand feet. Over by the bandstand on the right a company is marching in motley array to that maddening, monotonous, and apparently unending step that prompted Kipling's lines:-

Boots, boots, boots, boots, moving up and down again.
There's no discharge in war!

At the end of the piece it singled out the 'loafer, [who,] as he grins at these coatless civilian-clad recruits doubling, forming fours, and marking time on this pleasant sunny afternoon, may feel, perhaps, somewhere in himself the call of those hoarse words of command and the everlasting rhythm of the moving feet. If he is wise he will know how to act. Every taxicab in London bears a message that tells him what to do, and the nearest recruiting station is not so far away.'

Not only taxi cabs but advertising hoardings, railway stations – even the Carlton Hotel in Pall Mall draped its entire exterior in patriotic slogans exhorting men to join up for King and Country. The recruitment drive in the autumn of 1914 was a national effort. Mrs Cunliffe-Owen had first been inspired to form the Sportsman's Battalion while buying a uniform for her own son in Bond Street. She had met two acquaintances, renowned big game hunters, who had been unable to enlist due to the upper age limit, and the initial half-joking suggestion that she form a battalion herself where birth certificates were secondary to physical capabilities soon became a reality.

But she was by no means the only civilian to turn recruiting sergeant. *The Tatler* featured a photograph of sisters Ivy and Winifred Mulroney, who spent their days riding around Hyde Park, their horses wearing banners that read: 'Do Not Hesitate – To Arms – for King and Country.' Children in uniform, such as the Master Teddy Benson who could also be found most mornings in Hyde Park angling for recruits, effectively used their diminutive charms to persuade men to take the King's Shilling. The former England cricket captain Archibald Maclaren joined the Army

Service Corps, where he was actively involved in recruitment, giving speeches at theatres and music halls as well as working in his Manchester recruiting office.

Arthur Winnington Ingram, the Bishop of London, was one of the most vociferous supporters of the war and a tireless and effective recruiter in its early weeks. Harbouring a profound belief in the Allies' just cause, he spoke fervently against German atrocities to the point of xenophobia. Asquith commented that Winnington-Ingram's views were 'jingoism of the shallowest kind'. *The Tatler*, writing in September 1914, was more willing to acknowledge his achievements: 'His help and influence are enormous. His popularity with men of all grades of society is exceptional.'

At the London Palladium that month, Phyllis Dare and Evie Greene sang the recruiting song 'Your King and Country Want You', penned by Paul Rubens, donating their fees to

the Queen's Work for Women Fund; over at the Lyceum the play *Tommy Atkins*, starring Jessie Winter and Henry Kendall, was staged, featuring what would be one of the most popular of wartime songs, 'It's a Long Way to Tipperary'. Sheet music for various patriotic songs was sold, with the dual advantage of raising money for war charities as well as conveying the right sentiment to inspire men to enlist. *The Bystander* carried an advertisement for the song 'The Homes They Leave Behind' in October 1914, with profits to be devoted to the National Relief Fund and the Variety Artistes' Benevolent Fund. Rudyard Kipling, the country's leading writer and an a high profile advocate of military preparedness before the war, devoted his efforts to the national cause during this period – mainly through writing, but he used his celebrity too; in February 1915 he spoke at the Mansion House in support of the formation of bands as aids to recruiting and route marching.

The popular music hall comedians George Robey and Harry Lauder were both indefatigable recruiters. Lauder toured his native Scotland and the North of England with a pipe band in tow to stimulate his call for 1,000 men; Robey spent much time amusing wounded soldiers but was one of a number of speakers at Trafalgar Square in September 1915, 'and spoke very seriously, and with an eloquence which had the happy result of bringing forward a few recruits'. Another speaker that day was Horatio Bottomley, editor of *John Bull* magazine, whose levels of journalistic vulgarity were matched by his own oratorical megalomania. *The Tatler* predicted he 'may well be thrown up into a position of

The recruitment campaign of the Great War permeated every area of life. This patriotic Bovril advertisement has a British bull offering his services at an Army recruitment tent. (Illustrated London News/ME)

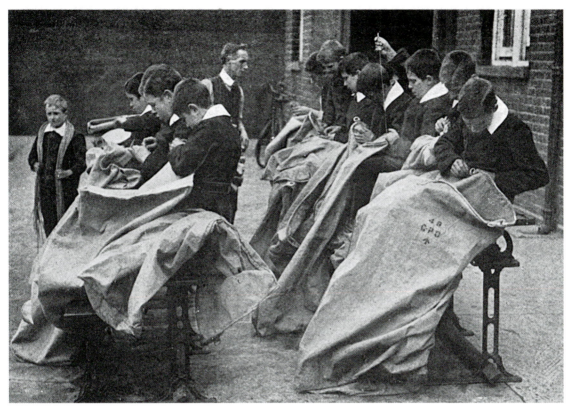

For anyone too young to enlist, there were plenty of ways to help the war effort. Here, children in Farnborough, Hampshire are employed making mailbags for sending Christmas presents to the men in the trenches. (Illustrated London News/ME)

great prominence and power. He knows the working classes and how to appeal to them, and already enjoys a great following amongst them.' In fact, Bottomley was later convicted of swindling *John Bull* readers out of £900,000 worth of Victory Bonds in 1919, a scheme that led to him serving five years in prison.

For magazines like *The Sketch* and *The Tatler*, slogans and jingoism were not their style. *The Tatler*'s distanced appraisal of Bottomley implied that such things were better left to the populist press. Conscientious objectors were barely tolerated but when *The Bystander* printed a photograph of two officers in Trafalgar Square holding the shredded bowler hat of a 'peace crank' orator, it was more concerned that 'the attitude is hardly becoming in officers – and gentlemen' and felt that their actions smacked of 'Prussian-

militarism', adding, 'England is, subject to the war conditions, still a free country, and if a man chooses to make a fool of himself by proclaiming the "brotherhood of man", or anything of that sort, the best course is to leave him to his folly. To make him the victim of organised military attack is to make a small hero of him.' In fact, the magazine was obliged to print an apology the following week when it transpired that the two men were recruiting officers who happened to be holding the hat after it was handed to them following a scuffle, but it still reflected a viewpoint that the English should be above such churlish behaviour. Opinions on war and how the nation could help dominated in *The Bystander* and its contemporaries, but the approach feels more sophisticated. When Scarborough and Hartlepool suffered in a bombardment by the German Imperial Navy on 16 December 1914, an act that brought war to British shores for the first time and inflamed anti-German opinion in Britain, *The Bystander* reported with a double-page spread picturing 'The Havoc Wrought on England's Great East Coast Stronghold'. Not for *The Bystander* pathos or fiery outrage. Instead it appealed to the intelligence of its readers, treating Germany's 'frightfulness' and unsporting brand of warfare with a contemptuous tongue in its cheek. 'The lives of good and brave German soldiers and sailors have been avenged at the expense of English hotel-keepers, shopmen, clerks, artisans, women and children,' it went on. 'For the "Scharnhorst", Germany exacted the price of the Scarborough Grand Hotel; for the "Gneisenau" she has the grocer's shop of Mr Merry Weather … By sheer inadvertence, it must be admitted, some shells fell at Hartlepool, which has since been discovered by the Germans to have forts and a dockyard. But these accidental lapses into fair warfare will occur even in the best regulated Navies.'

Cartoons and satire were *The Bystander*'s forte, and although anti-German illustrations dominated in the first few months of the war, the magazine used humour to address all kinds of wartime issues including censorship, food shortages, and, naturally, recruitment though at times it could rush to judge. Rather unfairly, considering the disproportionate number of Old Etonians who would give their lives in the First World War, the magazine printed a photograph in December 1914 of three 'fine, strapping young fellows' of Eton College and asked why they were not devoting more time to military training than to playing the traditional Wall Game.

Advertisements became war-themed as quickly as editorial content and both Bovril and Johnnie Walker had utilised the jovial figure of the recruiting sergeant in their adverts within weeks. An illustration by Charles Sykes, drawn from life and published in *The Bystander* in early September, pictured men in civilian clothes idly watching through railings as the Inns of Court Rifles, another voluntary battalion, known as The Devil's Own, went through their drilling exercises. The battalion seems to have been one of the few to actually advertise in the society magazines. In 1915, an advertisement in *The Bystander* stated that for 'those desirous of obtaining a commission, public school and university men with some experience of riding and out-of-doors [are] especially eligible'. The following year, Dunlop Tyres ran an advert proudly publicising the fact that 1,500 of their employees had enlisted while the rest were working in shifts, day and night, in order to meet the demands of the war. The message was palpably clear: those who hadn't answered the call to serve should heed the example of those who had.

Nothing spoke more eloquently of this obligation of duty than the stories of those who had already exhibited outstanding bravery or patriotism, setting an example that would inspire others. And so *The Sketch* printed a photograph of Captain Ernest Beachcroft Towse, VC, who had lost sight in both eyes as a result of his Victoria Cross action in the Boer War. In February 1915, he was pictured in full uniform departing for the front where he was to serve as a staff officer, typing letters for wounded soldiers. It was a remarkable episode in a remarkable life; Captain Towse devoted the rest of his life to improving the welfare of the blind and was a founder and trustee of the charity now known as CLARITY. In November 1914, *The Tatler* ran a photograph of a Canadian family in khaki – Captain O. A. Critchley and his three sons – who had all come to Britain to serve at the front, reflecting the whole-hearted patriotism of Britain's colonies. One son, Alfred, was wounded at Ypres, gained the DSO and by the end of the war had

THIS IS NOT A GERMAN FIRM
WE ARE BRITISH AND BELGIAN

£1000 REWARD will be paid to the **QUEEN MARY FUND** if any person can prove otherwise.

The Latest Indisputable Success

"Nature's Grip"

PARTING

Transformation

GIVES

NO POSSIBILITY OF SLIPPING

DEFIES DETECTION in every way.

ALWAYS SMART & BECOMING.

PERFECT FIT GUARANTEED.

A VISIT IS SOLICITED to inspect this wonderful discovery and many others.

Price from **£5 5 0**

Frs. 131.25.

HALF-SIZE from £3 3 0
Ear to Ear, from
Frs. 78.75.

Sent on Approval on receipt of Remittance with Shade of Hair.

GUDA (Regd.) HAIR POWDER, 1/6
THE ORIGINAL AND ONLY REAL DRY SHAMPOO.

HAIR TREATMENT A GREAT SPECIALITY.

To Ladies in trouble with their Hair becoming dull in colour, falling, &c., or going prematurely grey, we strongly recommend them to consult us, either personally or by correspondence. All consultations gratis in Private Saloons.

BRITISH AND BELGIAN ROYAL HAIR SPECIALISTS,
AND EMPLOYERS OF BRITISH LABOUR ONLY.

DUBOSCH & GILLINGHAM

Write for New Illustrated Booklet to— Telephone and Telegraphic Address: Gerrard 6811

285°, REGENT ST. (Oxford Circus End, towards the Polytechnic), LONDON, W.

British firms were anxious to stress their Britishness and used advertising to hammer the message home, particularly companies such as Dubosch and Gillingham, who had the misfortune of a Germanic sounding name. (Hearst Magazines (UK)/ME)

risen to the rank of Brigadier-General. He went on to found the Greyhound Racing Association in Britain. Father of eight Lieutenant Henry Webber overcame the not insignificant obstacle of being sixty-eight years of age when he badgered the War Office into giving him a commission in the 7th Battalion of the South Lancashire Regiment. The *Illustrated Sporting and Dramatic News* reported on his death by shellfire at Mametz Wood on 21 July 1916, the oldest recorded soldier to be killed during the First World War. Notable members of society in khaki were also lionised, from the sons of both wartime Prime Ministers to members of the peerage such as Bendor, 2nd Duke of Westminster, who earned the DSO for leading an armoured car division 120 miles across the desert during the Egyptian Campaign in a daring rescue of imprisoned Royal Navy crews. Earlier in the war, he was credited with rescuing Captain Francis Grenfell V.C. during the latter's heroic rescue of guns under heavy fire at Landrecies. Such courageous action displayed by one of the country's premier dukes embodied the very best of British pluck. Following the news, *The Sketch* ran a picture of him on their front cover, looking dashing in the uniform of the Royal Horse Guards.

In this atmosphere of patriotism and recruiting zeal, being seen to be doing one's bit was imperative. Along the south coast there was a trend for displaying cards in the windows of houses where the male members of the family were serving for their country. Under the title 'No shirkers here', *The Queen* magazine printed a photograph of a cottage window displaying no fewer than six. When the Derby Scheme, calling for men aged between eighteen and forty-one to attest, was launched at the end of 1915, a khaki armlet was given to those who had come forward. 'The khaki armlet will meet the wishes of all those who have for months been asking for some kind of badge to save those who are willing

Advertisement for the famous department store, Gamage's, in London, with war-themed toys dominating in Christmas 1915. (Hearst Magazines (UK)/ME)

to serve in the Army, but are for some good reason not actually in the ranks, from being confused with the mere slacker', wrote *The Queen* in November that year. 'And as it is to be issued also to those who have been invalided out of the Army, it will save many gallant men from the stupid, and in their cases, cruel attention of the 'white feather' people.' Clearly, the magazine did not approve of the ignorant and arbitrary recruitment techniques employed by organisations such as the Order of the White Feather, whose female members offered a white feather to any man found wearing civilian clothes in the street.

There was a myriad of more positive ways that non-combatant Britons could help the war effort. Saving food, buying War Bonds, changing extravagant habits, even cutting down on the amount of paper used in correspondence, as suggested in 1918: 'The Paper Controller tells us that there is still a great deal of needless correspondence, and that paper waste is augmented often by the use of only one side of the note paper or even the enclosure of blank sheets,' wrote M.E. Brooke in her 'Highway of Fashion' column in *The Tatler*. 'This must cease unless we want paper to become as scarce as matches. The sprawling handwriting will have to go, and it is a debatable point whether the neat copperplate writing of our grandmothers' days will be seen again. Many men and women will have recourse to the typewriter as it does save space, and a much commoner kind of paper can be used advantageously.' This was just one of the difficulties of wartime living and bearing such irritations with stoicism and characteristic good humour would all have a positive impact, however small. Weekly messages in *The Queen* magazine encouraged readers to 'Shop Early –

In the Morning If Possible' or confirmed that 'The Lady Who Carries Her Own Parcels Proclaims her own Patriotism'. Shopkeepers often packed goods in bags printed with patriotic slogans; at least until the paper shortages necessitated the recycling of any kind of receptacle. The London County Council installed collecting bags on tram cars to collect tickets, 'by doing so, 200 tonnes of paper will be saved', reported *The Sketch*. In Abbots Langley, Hertfordshire, Lady Kindersley, wife of the Chairman of the National War Savings Committee, set an example by becoming a waste-paper merchant. With the aid of her daughters and a couple of donkey-carts, she collected waste paper locally and sold it in aid of the Red Cross and Fund for Soldiers' Comforts.

General Haig's daughters, Alexandra and Victoria, posed in miniature Red Cross nursing outfits in 1915. (Illustrated London News/ME)

Increasing shortages of fuel also meant that the perambulatory comforts previously enjoyed by the rich were no longer considered patriotic. 'Petrol precious as fine champagne' wrote Eve in September 1917. Ladies who showed an independence of spirit and drove their own cars were given credit for releasing their chauffeurs for service. The Duchess of Marlborough employed a lady chauffeur and the redoubtable Kathleen Pelham-Burn, Lady Drogheda, was frequently seen around London behind the wheel. 'If more people followed this excellent example,' suggested *The Tatler*, 'the National Recruiting Scheme might be given a better chance.' For most people, trains, trams and buses and, if lucky, taxis, were the only option for getting about. Even those wealthy enough to buy petrol could not always procure it, and there was an upsurge in the popular-ity of gas-powered cars, which carried coal-gas in a large, unwieldy looking rubber bag on the roof. Lady Idina Wallace, who would later gain notoriety as a serial monogamist and member of the Happy Valley set in Kenya, owned a 10hp Calcott car fuelled by a Lyon-Spencer gas container so gigantic that it dwarfed the car itself. Eve was admirably accommodating about the transport problem in 1916:

England did very well a hundred, fifty, even twenty years ago before she'd even heard of motor-cars, and we'll just have to get up earlier, that's all, and use Shank's pony for a change, and carry home food ourselves. So tiring, did you say, and heavy? Well, not more tiring than a round or two of golf or an afternoon's lawn tennis. And while so many women are doing munitions and working on the land, or even bus-conduct-ing or ticket-collecting, the others who are doing the easier job of staying at home and looking after their households can surely do a little rough work too?

The eccentric behaviour of Potsdam-born Madame Bertha Trost, who had been a resident of London since 1895, aroused enough suspicion within the paranoid anti-German atmosphere of Great War Britain to have her deported as 'an undesirable' in 1915. (Illustrated London News/ME)

Mrs Cunliffe Owen, founder of the 23rd and 24th Service Battalions, better known as the Sportsman's Battalions, pictured in a bath chair with her husband and son who had just received his commission as a lieutenant. The battalions were raised at the Hotel Cecil in central London and were distinguished by taking men from the sporting world up to the age of forty-five. (Illustrated London News/ME)

The Sketch remarked too, in 1915:

The motors of the rich are mostly at the front, doing more urgent work than dropping ladies in satin slippers at the doors of play-houses. And not only the private motor, but the public taxi-cab, has largely disappeared, and you shall see any night of the week, pretty women diving into the 'Tube' at eleven o'clock or mounting the democratic motor-bus. The fact is, we have all determined to 'keep smiling,' just like our Tommies at the front, and nothing can disturb our general good humour.

Even children could help the war effort. In March 1917, Mr Prothero, the president of the Board of Agriculture, addressed an appeal to teachers throughout the country begging for their help in increasing food production by cultivating school gardens. 'Not only will it give them invaluable training in one of the simplest and best of man's pleasures but it will help them to do work of national importance, and delight them by proving that they, too, can be of use in the general effort,' reported *The Queen*. In July 1918, there was a most unusual request from the National Salvage Council asking for everyone to save fruit stones and nut shells, suggesting that 'Stone and Shell Clubs' should be formed wherever possible. Fruit stones were to be dried out in the sun and packaged separately to the nutshells before being posted off to Captain Ricketts at the Gas Works, Southend-on-Sea. 'We are told that the stones and shells are urgently wanted for some war purposes, at which we can only darkly guess from the address to which they are sent,' wondered *The Queen*, adding that they felt there could be greater coordination in the collecting of valuable waste material (in fact, the boy scouts were engaged to collect sacks of the shells). A few weeks later, the purpose of the mysterious appeal was revealed: 'They are required for conversion into charcoal, which is to be used in the British respirator for the protection of our troops against poison gas … the charcoal thus produced has a power of absorption many times that of charcoal obtained from other material.' A similar scheme to collect conkers for conversion into cordite was launched in the same year.

Children could also display their patriotism through toys, many of which quickly took on a military tone. In December 1914, Holborn store Gamages combined their famous annual Xmas Bazaar with a 'Great War Tableaux', and suggested Dreadnought crackers and a game called 'Britwar', described excitedly as 'The Game of the moment. Makes you feel you are in the wild free country, and is actual warfare. Boys are delighted with it, and soldiers say it is "THE THING".' The following Christmas, the store again combined a 'military pageant' with its bazaar and advertised both Army officer and Royal Flying Corps uniforms for children, a horse-drawn Red Cross wagon and rousing, patriotic books of war adventures among the delights on offer. Elsewhere, war-inspired toys included accurate miniature reproductions of weaponry such as the 'anti-aircraft Maxim Gun', a Dunkirk armoured motor car or Kill Kiel, a dreadnought game played upon a realistic representation of the North Sea. It seems extraordinary that even after four years of war, manufacturers were still producing toys that mimicked the carnage of real-life warfare. In its shopping suggestions for Christmas 1918, *The Tatler* put forward a suggestion for a howitzer that fired a bursting shell. 'It will seem to the schoolboy almost too good to be true that for 2*s*. 11*d*., and by means of a spring the shell "explodes" immediately it strikes an object. It is marvellously realistic, nevertheless it is absolutely harmless.' This alarmingly aggressive trend in children's playthings did not go unnoticed. In a letter to *The Times* that year, a reader expressed his concern: 'Sir, it is somewhat distressing at a time when we are talking so much about permanent peace for future generations that our children should be fed mentally by means of toys associated with killing and destruction…'

Of more concern to most of the population was the provenance of their children's toys. Before the war, German imports had accounted for the majority bought in Britain, with names such as Steiff and Gebruder Bing synonymous with quality and good value. Clearly, German toys would not have been tolerated even if imports had been allowed and British manufacturers soon set to work, maintaining that their craftsmanship was more than equal to the enemy's efforts. *The Queen* magazine, pontificating on there being no place for extravagant or luxurious toys for Christmas 1915 emphasised quality over quantity and took the opportunity to criticise German products, 'for the bulk of German

Fervent patriotism was encouraged, but not at the expense of good manners and the upstanding British character. These two recruitment officers in Trafalgar Square were pictured holding the battered hat of a 'peace crank' speaker in a manner that suggested they had perhaps been involved in suppressing his views. *The Bystander* magazine commented on their ungentlemanly conduct but was forced to issue an apology a week later when the officers complained at being depicted in a defamatory manner. As officers in charge, the hat had simply been handed to them. (Illustrated London News/ME)

The Carlton Hotel at the junction of Pall Mall and Haymarket bedecked with recruiting slogans in the early weeks of the war. A 1960s office block now stands on the site. (Illustrated London News/ME)

made toys ran to cheapness, with its inevitable shoddiness of construction and lack of finish.'

In November 1915, Marshall and Snelgrove on Oxford Street held an exhibition of British-made toys with one section devoted entirely to the work of wounded soldiers and sailors. The Victoria and Albert Museum hosted the British Industries Fair in 1916, a patriotic alternative to the famous age-old trade fair held in Leipzig, Germany, where numerous examples of British workmanship were on display, including teddy bears dressed in military or Red Cross nursing uniforms. Small cottage industries, wounded soldiers and factories all went into toy manufacturing overdrive. Parkstone Toy Factory in Dorset offered dolls' houses that could be built to customers' own specifications. Lott's Bricks, a kind of forerunner of Lego designed by the architect Arnold Mitchell, ensured that its adverts clearly stated they were British made, in Watford. The Lord Roberts Memorial Workshops, dotted around the country, offered training and rehabilitation to wounded men and produced huge numbers of toys. 'These wooden toys (from Lord Roberts workshops) are always satisfactory, as the wheelbarrows, engines, etc.,

seem quite incapable of being broken', wrote *The Tatler* in 1918.

There were even toys that fed the feverish suspicion of German spies. One 'spy-scare' set included King Albert of Belgium, Sir John French, General Joffre and Admiral Jellicoe talking together around a table while a German spy hid underneath. Another featured a German Fraulein in her bed being awakened by a policeman who discovers ammunition in her trunk. They seem a clumsy attempt to assimilate children into an adult way of thinking, but anti-German feeling was rife, increasing as each new piece of evidence confirming German perfidy was revealed; the bombardment of Scarborough, the sinking of the *Lusitania*, the execution of Nurse Edith Cavell, the use of gas at Ypres, air raids over London. Spy mania was reflected by plays such as *The Man Who Stayed At Home*, starring Denis Eadie and Isobel Elsom, staged at the Royalty Theatre in December 1914, and *By Pigeon Post*, with Madge Titheradge. The seriousness with which the spy issue was taken by the War Office was demonstrated in 1918 when Sir William Orpen exhibited a painting of a mysterious young girl, at a show

The Bystander, February 10, 1915   193

"The Man of the Hour"

Everyone is talking about Mr. Horatio Bottomley, the famous Editor of "John Bull," and South Hackney's late idolised Member. He has been doing wonderful recruiting work in London and the provinces, and rumour is rife as to his early return to Parliament

Horatio Bottomley (1860–1933), journalist, financier, politician and swindler. Editor of the jingoistic *John Bull* magazine, he is pictured here in *The Bystander*, which praises him for his services to recruitment. He would later be imprisoned for embezzling subscribers' investments in war bonds. (Illustrated London News/ME)

gossip, which is, to all intents and purposes nil.' Likewise, Eve thought the ideas put forward for ridding the country of enemy aliens such as housing them close to gasworks to guard against bombs, or putting them on captured ships and launching them forth back to Germany, were 'hardly possible', even if they were 'eating up the food we ought to be keeping for ourselves'.

This was a stance adopted by *The Tatler* and similar magazines at the time. They were patriotic, they were anti-German, but hysteria or mob mentality was distinctly un-British. The sinking of the *Lusitania* in 1915 by a German torpedo, killing British and American civilians on board, sparked attacks on German shops in Liverpool and London's East End but *The Queen* magazine conveyed its disgust in a dignified tone:

There can be no wonder that the deed has been followed by an outbreak of feeling in England of a kind which hitherto has not been in evidence. The significant thing is not the attacks upon small shops kept by Germans, but the attitude towards Germans in big places of business like the Baltic Exchange and the various Stock Exchanges of the country. There is here none of the insensate hatred, which is rampant in Germany towards England; there never has been among Englishmen that stupid sort of manifestation. But there has been since the news of last Friday an overwhelming sense that the German nation has put itself utterly beyond the pale; and this country is not alone in its feeling.

at the Agnew Galleries, entitling it *The Spy*. *The Tatler* wondered, along with the rest of London, who it could be. In fact, the painting was of Yvonne Aubicq, Orpen's French lover, but Orpen elaborated his story, claiming she was a German spy executed by a French firing squad. When the truth was finally revealed, Orpen was severely reprimanded and almost lost his status as an official war artist.

For the most part, *The Tatler* treated anti-German hysteria with mild disdain. Gerald Biss, author of the magazine's motoring column 'The Bee in the Bonnet', scoffed at the notion that spies had infiltrated the RAC on Pall Mall, describing it as 'the most gorgeous piffle … spies do not go crudely to second-hand sources for such information when such admirable maps are to be bought anywhere. As for the smoking-room gossip, it is – well, other club

Soon, an inherent mistrust of any Germans began to permeate Britain. *The Sketch* reported in September 1914 how German servants and governesses could no longer be trusted, citing the example of one governess of four years whose room, when searched, yielded a secret stash of diagrams and maps detailing bridges, tunnels and barracks.

In the commercial world, any association, however slight, with Germany was quickly and vehemently refuted. Dubosch & Gillingham, specialists in hair treatments including transformations (pieces of false hair) and Guda hair powder (a type of dry shampoo), placed advertisements in *The Queen* firmly stating their entirely British credentials, despite the surname of one of its partners. 'This is NOT a German firm and we ARE British and Belgian. £100 REWARD will be paid to the QUEEN MARY FUND if any person can prove otherwise', it proclaimed, adding they were 'Employers of British labour only'. J. Lyons and Son, whose famous Corner Houses were a British institution, brought legal proceedings against rivals Liptons who had claimed the company directors were German and anyone who patronised the establishment was 'assisting the enemies of Britain'. The court granted an injunction against Liptons on 8 September 1914 restraining them from making any further suggestions.

Inevitably, German-born members of society began to find life in Britain difficult. Sir Edgar Speyer, born in America of German parents, was a financier, philanthropist, chairman of the Underground Electric Railways Company, Privy Councillor and a prominent figure in London society. But he endured much criticism and anti-German feeling in the British press, especially from the *Morning Post*. Vested interests in a German firm based in Frankfurt made his position untenable and he resigned from the Privy Council, eventually leaving England to live in America in May 1915. A more eccentric character was Madame Bertha Trost, who had moved to London from Potsdam in 1895.

A flamboyant figure with tumbling grey locks, she went about town dressed in Victorian clothes, rode in a horse-drawn carriage and, as well as owning an antiques shop in Clifford Street, ran a beauty salon next door, just the sort of business ripe for eavesdropping and indiscretions. She held bohemian parties at her house, which was said to be furnished with all kinds of exotic curiosities, not least a rosewood coffin which she had had made for her own demise. It was not entirely surprising that she was deported as 'an undesirable' in June 1915.

Perhaps Madame Trost, and certainly Edgar Speyer, were innocent victims of this necessary cull, but there was no place in Great War Britain for enemy aliens, even those who were proven Anglophiles.

As the months of war turned into years, the country found a kind of national solidarity in its singular purpose, or, as *The Queen* put it in the New Year of 1916, 'a perfect unison of opinion as to the righteousness of our own part in the war, and a oneness of desire to serve … There has been shown that wonderful unanimity of desire to sink all minor difference in the face of one common enemy…' M.E. Brooke, speaking of the influence of the war on the women left at home, described the dark streets of London and how 'Londoners have accepted the altered conditions and are regulating their lives in conformity with it', indicating that evenings spent at home and meals shared together ('champagne is seldom seen, a light wine or an aerated water taking its place') were simple pleasures to be cherished.

'There has been an awakening of the whole people from selfish ease and luxury to service of every kind and type and to a generous outpouring of money and gifts such as never before has been witnessed. All this bespeaks advance, not retrogression,' concluded *The Queen*. Total war required total effort and the country had not been found wanting.

Miss Farnar-Bringhurst, dressed as martyred Belgium, walks barefoot through Westminster, London in the Right-to-Serve procession on 17 July 1915. The demonstration was organised to demand the right for women to be allowed to share in munitions and other war work. (Illustrated London News/ME)

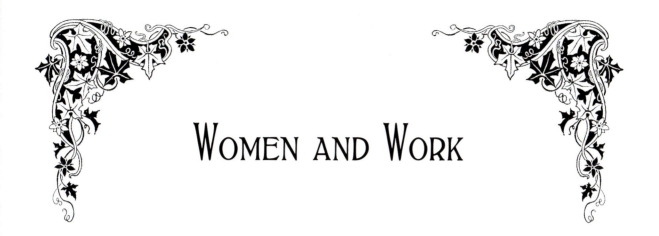

WOMEN AND WORK

On a pouring wet and windy day in July 1915, 30,000 women marched in procession through the London streets holding banners high. The messages inscribed called for immediate public acknowledgement of a growing crisis, and recognition of a solution that was plainly staring them in the face. 'The situation is serious – Women Must Help to Save It' urged one; 'We Demand Our Right to Serve' read another and, most affecting, 'Shells made by a Wife may Save her Husband's Life'. Many women came in costume; one lady, Miss Farnar-Bringhurst, representing a battle-scarred Belgium, walked the entire route in bare feet.

The 'Right to Serve' march was organised and led by Mrs Emmeline Pankhurst with the full support of David Lloyd George. It addressed the growing problem of manpower in British industry, and specifically munitions production in the light of the so-called 'Shell Scandal' in May that year, in which *The Times* and the *Daily Mail* had openly criticised the government, and specifically Lord Kitchener, for neglecting munitions production, which, claimed Lord French, dangerously hampered British efforts at the front. In blunt terms, British soldiers were dying because factories at home could not fulfil demand. Prime Minister Asquith's solution was to make the dynamic Lloyd George Minister of Munitions.

He moved quickly, taking over factories entirely concerned with war production and opening further state-owned factories, where trade union practices, traditionally opposed to 'dilution' (changing a job in order to accommodate the employment of unskilled workers or women in previously skilled roles), were suspended. Intransigent male workers were mollified with the pledge that the employment of women was temporary and that wage levels would not have been eroded by the time men returned to their jobs. Mrs Pankhurst represented British women's collective desire to work for their country, but also sought assurance from the government that they would not be exploited and would work for fair wages. Already there was concern that women working in certain industries were earning at a mere 'sweating rate'. In March of that year, *The Queen* had reported on the fact that some Yorkshire mill owners producing khaki for uniforms were paying female workers just 3*s* 4*d* for a 60-yard piece, compared to a recommended 8*s*. Elsewhere, unemployment was tackled by charities such as the Queen's Work for Women Fund, whose various schemes enabled women to remain in their jobs, by channelling contracts for army uniforms to dressmaking firms for example. At Harrods, a room was given over to Lady French, wife of the General, who turned it into a workroom for unemployed seamstresses.

The women who walked through the rain that day did not want (or in many cases, particularly need) charity. What they did want to do was something meaningful for the war effort and to be paid a living wage for doing so. The timing of the march was perfect, dovetailing with Lloyd George's shake-up and coming at a time when the pressing need for workers was becoming ever more urgent. The Minister for Munitions made a stirring speech: 'Without women, victory will tarry, and the victory which tarries means a victory whose footprints are footprints of blood', adding: 'This procession will educate public opinion.' The event received a positive response from the press, in contrast perhaps to similar suffragette demonstrations only two years earlier. The *Illustrated London News* sympathised about the weather ('deplorable') and noted that some of the crowd who had perhaps 'come to scoff' afterwards remained to encourage and admire. It predicted the demonstration would, in the future, be viewed as 'historic, and when the story of the World War comes to be written, the patriotic part played by women of the Empire, of France, of Belgium, of Italy, of Russia, will be chronicled, and this great demonstration of women craving to work for the war will find honourable place'.

The Queen magazine had no doubts about the contribution women could make in the workplaces of Great War Britain. As a new National War Register, launched in the summer of 1915, lent some structure to the process of recruitment to factories, every issue devoted column inches to sound, practical advice on training courses, to alerting women about new opportunities and, from time to time, to stirring up latent patriotism within its readers with a rousing sermon.

'The war must be won by armed men, by munitions and by money,' it wrote in October 1915. 'At this moment the due supply of these is largely in the hands of women. If the men must go we must do our utmost to fill their places. Britain is becoming a vast arsenal; for every new factory that opens – and there must be more and more – thousands of women workers are needed; women must take the places of men in all the existing munition factories wherever possible. And, besides this, women must be ready in every city, in the bank, at the desk, in the office, to take the places which will be left empty everywhere in business circles as the men rise up on the urgent call of the war bugles and leave their places empty.'

As with the rush to enlist in the early weeks of the war, the enthusiastic response from women could not be matched by the number of available places. On 10 October 1915, *The Queen* reported that out of the 59,000 women on the War Register, employment had only been found for 5,511, but it quickly pointed out that openings were being created such as the new National Ordnance Factory in Coventry, opened exclusively for women, and assured readers that 'it will probably be followed by other places during the winter.' Munition work attracted working-class women in the main, drawn by the comparatively high wages and the chance, for some, to escape from domestic service, the biggest employer of women before the war. Of the 400,000 women who left service during the war, many became 'munitionettes', where work encompassed a whole range of armament production from shell manufacture to aeroplane construction. It was generally monotonous, often back-breaking and potentially lethal work. At shell-filling factories, TNT poisoning turned women's faces yellow, earning them the nickname 'canaries'. Cases of toxic poisoning were often fatal; in 1916,

52 of the 181 reported cases resulted in death, while the risk of explosion was high. But there were advantages. Though wages were still significantly lower than male munitions workers', they were high in comparison to domestic work or employment in textile industries, and as the war progressed, crèches and nurseries enabled married women to take up employment while canteens offered workers cheap and nutritious meals. At the Vickers factory in Barrow-on-Furness there was even a specially built cinema for its workers.

Most facilities for factory workers began as charitable initiatives set up by voluntary organisations such as the Munition Workers Canteen Committee, founded by Lady Lawrence, or the Church Army's rest huts where girls could take their own food and spend their breaks in a peaceful environment and where even emotional well-being was considered. 'At each rest hut,' wrote *The Queen* in January 1917, 'there is a Lady Superintendent, who is carefully chosen for the post. She is a cheery, wide-minded Christian woman, who is willing and anxious to be a very real friend to the girls.' Eventually, the direct correlation between the welfare of the workforce and its levels of output was recognised by the government and it began to take over the running of canteens and crèches from 1917. 'The State-aided crèche during the war period is obviously not a philanthropic measure,' observed *The Queen*, 'but a reasoned national insurance of the health and vigour of the children of indispensible munition-makers.'

Despite these benefits, munitions work had little to commend it in comparison to clerical and secretarial jobs. And if an educated sec-

Ladies learn to drive

1. The Courses embrace just WHAT LADIES NEED TO LEARN.
2. The FEES ARE THE LOWEST in London.
3. You continue to learn WITHOUT ANY EXTRA CHARGE until you are proficient and satisfied.
4. The largest Motor Instruction Works in the World, and situate in the heart of London.
5. Training for ROYAL AUTOMOBILE CLUB CERTIFICATES our speciality.
6. Licensed Employment Bureau FREE FOR ALL PUPILS who require same.

at the British School of Motoring Limited

CALL OR WRITE

B.S.M., 5, Coventry Street, Piccadilly Circus, W.

Learning to drive offered some exciting employment opportunities for women during the war. The British School of Motoring, situated in Coventry Street in the heart of London, regularly targeted its advertisements at women. (Illustrated London News/ME)

tion of society was to be attracted, then clearly the industry needed its champions. *The Queen* magazine took up the baton with enthusiasm.

In November 1915, it reported proudly that the 6,000 women employed in a Glasgow factory were 'doing work which was done by expert mechanics before the war, and doing it better. The champion of the factory is a girl who is machining copper bands on shells; her "record" is 1,014 in a ten-hour shift, or say 101 per hour. And each shell has to be lifted into position and lifted out again. The weight raised in an hour can be easily calculated. This girl earns £5 per week.'

In a report on the training of munition workers in July 1917, the magazine emphasised the social mix:

drawn from every class of society, some are girls from leisured homes, previously unaccustomed to regular work, others are artists and teachers, and others, again, dressmakers or shop assistants. "It is not the rank of society from which the student is drawn that matters," remarked an experienced instructor, "it is the personality of the individual that counts." If a woman is of good physique and education, between the ages of eighteen and thirty-five years, if she has the desire to help her country in a time of need and the "will to win" in her soul, the chances are that she will prove a good munition maker.

It was not necessarily a view shared by Thekla Bowser, whose own war effort involved being a VAD in France. Writing a long piece in the same magazine two years earlier, in what to modern ears is a cringeworthy example of ingrained class snobbery, her argument lauded the superior abilities of 'cultured women' as munition makers:

The gentlewoman, surely, must bring to bear upon all such work, something more than her scantily-educated sister can do. Once having been taught the actual work, she can use her intelligence, her delicacy of handling the tools, her whole capacity, to keep those machines, not just in running condition but in the very best order … A cultured, highly-educated woman can do the work better than those of the lower classes, and can prove of inestimable use in factories because of the influence which she can exert amongst the 'hands'.

In fact, middle- and upper-class women, comprising just 9 per cent of the female munitions workforce, were mainly employed in super-

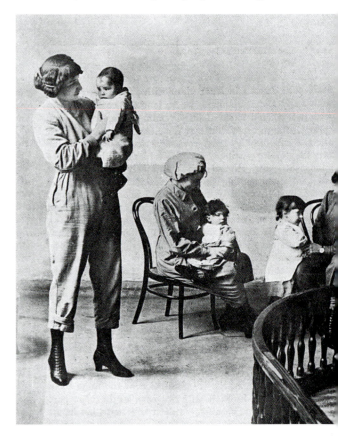

With women an essential part of the workforce, catering to their needs became increasingly necessary. Some enlightened employers introduced crèches such as this one for female munitions workers. (Hearst Magazines (UK)/ME)

visory roles. In January 1916, *The Queen* announced 'a number of openings occur for women of good education and general intelligence to act as forewomen or supervisors in factories, and to control departments where groups of girls are employed. There is likely to be a very keen demand for capable women of this type, and the influence of a good person in this work may be very considerable. The wages run from 30*s*. per week to £2 10*s*. and in some cases, higher posts are available.'

The magazine was by now reporting that girls from Girton College, Cambridge, were working in the factories; Sheila O'Neill, who had been educated at Girton and the London School of Economics, was the first woman to be appointed to be Deputy Chief Inspector of Gun Ammunition at Woolwich. 'She acquired this position by long work and experience in munition and shell filling factories, and is recognised as an expert in the detection of "duds" in T. tubes,' wrote *The Queen*. Beyond the munitions factories, there were opportunities for university-educated women to work in other specialised areas. By the end of 1917, *The Queen* was announcing that the government was willing to employ women as higher-grade clerks, but that women with science degrees were in particular demand. 'Women of the BSc rank are employed in some of the research and explosives laboratories at a beginning salary of £150. Linguists are also wanted, more particularly those who are well versed in the Scandinavian languages and in German.' Timber measurers – itinerant workers in the Forestry Corps whose duties were to measure felled trees, calculate the amount of wood in a log and mark lengths for sawing – received 37*s* 6*d* a week salary, a month's free training and a uniform. Women who had a good elementary education and 'some artistic ability' could train to be tracers under the auspices of the London Country Council at

the Shoreditch Technical Institute in Pitfield Street, Hoxton (where munitions supervisors were also trained). A tracer's job was to make exact copies in ink of technical drawings made by engineering draughtsmen, 'using compasses and other mathematical instruments'.

As for smart society, though nursing, 'canteening' and general charity work attracted most ladies, there were some who went to the munitions. In August 1915, Eve in *The Tatler* was listing some of the new workers at the Vickers' factory:

Erith is the latest craze. Here, at Messrs. Vickers', a gallant band of women are really doing it. Not just playing about, you know, but living at a hostel and taking the regular rate of pay – I think it's not quite enough to pay for two stalls at the newest revue each week. Lady Gertrude Crawford and Lady Colebrooke are among the toilers, and Lady Gatacre too ... Lady Scott, Captain Scott's widow, is also working at this particular factory, but hers is skilled electrical work. (*Kathleen Bruce, Lady Scott, spent much of 1917 manufacturing electrical coils at the factory. She also devoted time establishing an ambulance service in France, working at the Ministry of Pensions and, in 1918, put her talent as a sculptor to use helping to reconstruct the faces of wounded soldiers). Vickers are willing to take a lot more women to train during the week-ends so as to have them ready for work at the new munition factories, for there won't be enough men to go round, I'm told.

Around the same time, Viscountess Charlemont, the former Evelyn Hull, was reported to be working twelve-hour shifts at the Woolwich Arsenal, along with her husband, who had been declared unfit for military service. The actress Miss Margot Park had,

Marriage of Captain Naismith Perring of the Royal Army Medical Corps, and Miss Preston at Weybridge Church with a guard of honour formed by the bride's fellow land workers, holding pitchforks aloft as the couple leave the church. (Hearst Magazines (UK)/ME)

reported *The Sketch*, left the stage for the munitions factory and at the wedding of Stella Drummond to Lord Eustace Percy, the third son of the Duke of Northumberland in 1918, a guard of honour was formed by her former co-workers, 'who had worked side by side with the bride when she too was a munition worker'.

Cynthia Asquith, showed less commitment after a two-hour shift spent assembling respirators: 'It is such fun feeling a factory girl and it gave one some idea of how exciting it must be to do piece-work for money ... I must say I hadn't got to do a twelve-hour day. It is quite tiring.'

For those with more stamina, Lady Constance Stewart-Richardson, the aristocratic swimmer and dancer ('a star turn at the Bath Club', recalled Lady Diana Manners), recommended special exercises for munition workers. She was pictured in the garden of her dance studio in Chelsea demonstrating a variety of yoga-like stretches. 'Lady Constance is a devout believer in hard training and thinks that in view of the strenuous work that women are now undertaking everyone of her sex should follow her example and indulge in some of the simple exercises illustrated.' It is difficult to imagine working-class girls from Woolwich and East Ham bothering to take her advice after an eight-hour shift.

Familiar territory for many daughters of the landed gentry was the Forage Corps and the Army Remount Service. Though the advent of mechanised warfare increasingly marginalised the use of cavalry, horses were still badly needed at the front for transportation and haulage. The Army Remount Service, part of the Army Service Corps, played a vital role in finding and training over 340,000 horses during the war that passed through four main depots in Britain. At the depot for convalescent mounts in Berkshire, all the stable work and exercise was done by women who were 'hunting women

from every county in England', reported the *Illustrated Sporting & Dramatic News*, a magazine that, through its in-depth coverage of racing, hunting and horse-related subjects in peacetime, took a particular interest in the activities of the Army Remount Service.

A girl window cleaner, ready for business in 1915. (Illustrated London News/ME)

As an interesting aside, the District Remount Officer for the depot was Cecil Aldin, the well-known sporting and animal artist and Master of the South Berks Foxhounds, who was by that time forty-five years of age and too old to enlist. Elsewhere in the magazine, one war worker, the improbably named Miss Poppette Ginnette, used her skills as a former circus rider to help her father break in horses for the Army in a London suburb.

For others who felt the lure of the great outdoors, there was the Women's Land Army. The Women's Land Army had its roots in two organisations, the Women's Farm and Garden Association and the Women's National Land Service Corps. While the Women's National Land Service Corps had begun to recruit women for seasonal agricultural work such as fruit or hop picking, and was organising groups of women in rural areas into mini work forces to help farmers, the Women's Farm and Garden Association concentrated on the need to train women in agricultural practices, and to persuade male farmers of their suitability as workers. There were other independent organisations recruiting and training women for work on the land. In the incongruous setting of the back garden of No. 16 Carlton House Terrace, the London home of Lord and Lady Cowdray, a model dairy farm had been set up where girls were taught haymaking, milking, butter-making and horse management in a scheme organised by the National Political League Land Council. Lady Cowdray, who, according to Eve in *The Tatler*, 'is awfully keen on the fact that there's not to be any "Dresden Shepherdess" about the movement', urged other landown-

ers to give untrained women the chance to become skilled workers. The Women's Social and Political Union, which had halted all militant suffragette activity and pledged to channel their supporters' efforts into war work in 1914, also sent members to work on farms while *The Queen* magazine urged teachers to spend their summer holidays in the countryside, helping in the hayfields and orchards.

By early 1917, with an estimated three weeks' food supply left in the country, galvanised action was needed quickly. Ronald Protheroe, President of the Board of Agriculture, engaged the services of (Dame) Meriel Talbot, a leading light of the Women's

Lady Lawrence, founder of the Munition Makers' Canteen Committee in 1915, designed to maintain the good health of munitions workers with the provision of regular meals at canteens established at the factories. The work was taken over by the Government at the end of January 1917. (Illustrated London News/ME)

Lady Constance Stewart-Richardson (1883–1932), society figure, dancer and promoter of the healthy benefits of exercise. Her husband, Sir Edward Stewart-Richardson, was killed in action in 1914. Lady Constance opened a dance studio in Chelsea and she is pictured outside it demonstrating exercises designed to improve the strength and fitness of munitions workers. (Illustrated London News/ME)

MOVEMENTS FOR MUNITION WORKERS
To Enable them to Attain the Necessary Strength and Fitness.

LADY CONSTANCE STEWART-RICHARDSON—DOING HER EXERCISES
Lady Constance is a devout believer in hard training, and thinks that in view of the strenuous work that women are now undertaking everyone of her sex should follow her example and indulge in some of the simple exercises illustrated above. Nos. 1 and 4 are for the back and thighs, No. 2 for the hips and legs, and No. 3 for the waist and shoulders. In addition to being a talented classical dancer, Lady Constance is a very good game shot, a first-class swimmer, and one of the most athletic women of her day. These photographs were taken outside her studio in Chelsea

Farm and Garden Association, who became director of the first Women's Land Army. She immediately set about implementing an intensive recruitment drive, stressing that not only was it a beneficial to health but 'dwellers in some country neighbourhoods, where the yearly fruit pickers' invasion is dreaded, would be rejoiced to see educated visitors instead of the usual rough horde.'

But the WLA struggled with an image problem. Other, comparatively more glamorous women's services, such as the Women's Royal Air Force (WRAF) or the Women's Royal Naval Services (WRNS), were formed around the same time and offered not only more conducive working hours but an elegant uniform; munitions workers, of course, earned far more. Farm work meant long hours, physical toil and low wages. Furthermore, many land girls who arrived at farms full of optimism and enthusiasm found their male employers sceptical about their abilities. *The Queen*, while notifying its readers in July 1917 that 'at least 500 educated girls and women over eighteen years are required at once for the Women's Land Army with the object of training to become leaders of other women in farm work, and ultimately to take on duties of instructors', added that farmers had been assured that women were providing supplementary labour and were not to supplant male farm workers. The recruiters appealed to the patriotism of the nation's women, and peppered that with promises of a healthy, wholesome rural idyll. David Lloyd George, by this time Prime Minister, quoted in *The Landswoman* (a magazine launched in

January 1918 expressly for WLA members), added his voice to the appeal in June 1918: 'the harvest is in danger … once again therefore … I appeal to women to come forward and help. They have never failed this country yet.' A *Times* article, reporting on the 130 land girls who visited London and then Buckingham Palace for a recruitment campaign in March of that year, commented enthusiastically on 'the health and happiness, clear skins and bright eyes' of the land girls. An account by one 'tractor girl' from Wiltshire in *The Queen* painted a picture, in endearing 'jolly hockey sticks' terms, of a tough but satisfying existence: 'I do about five acres a day which is pretty good when you think that a team of horses can only plough about two acres in a day. I "live in", and get 15 s. a week as well, but it is none too much, as I wear out two pairs of gloves a week, and although I wear simply breeches and a

Burberry and a scarf round my head, even these get shabby through having to be out in all weathers. I think the worst part is having to get up at 6:30 every morning, and I am not indoors again until dark. I have lunch and tea out on the plough – generally sandwiches and tea in a Thermos flask – which is topping fun. On the whole, I thoroughly enjoy the life and my goodness, it does make one feel fit!'

The 'Lumber Jills' of the Forestry Corps were required to be particularly fit for work that involved felling and cleaning timber destined for pit props and trench poles. According to *The Queen*, 'strong, healthy girls' were needed and colonial women with experience of that kind of work were particularly encouraged (the common assumption being

that clearing forests and building log cabins were everyday tasks for Canadian women and others around the Empire). Phrynette, writing her Letter from London in *The Sketch* magazine in February 1918, noted: 'Lord Lonsdale was one of the first landowners to employ women foresters. I hear they are now doing very well, and there are some four hundred members of the Women's Forestry Corps. A member tells me it is pretty heavy work for women, and only robust folk need hope to succeed at it.' For those keen to experience the healthy, open-air existence but without the necessary muscle, re-planting was a gentler alternative.

The well-being of land workers concerned *The Queen* magazine, and in October 1917 they suggested that householders in villages should

While luncheon at the club provides opportunities for daily recurring thrills. No wonder Aunt Matilda finds him so suspiciously pleasant on his return to the domestic hearth

War changed even the most deeply entrenched of male institutions. When women replaced men as waiters in gentlemen's clubs, there was some debate about how to address them. J. M. Barrie, a member of the Reform Club, suggested 'Damsel'. By the 1920s, the club's records show that male waiters had returned the club to its status quo. (Illustrated London News/ME)

THE PRESIDENT OF THE WOMEN'S WAR SERVICE LEGION.

AND FRIEND : THE MARCHIONESS OF LONDONDERRY.

The Marchioness of Londonderry, President of the Women's War Service Legion, which has done such excellent work for the Armies by providing for them a steady supply of competent cooks, motor-drivers, and other useful aids to the prosecution of the war, is the wife of the seventh Marquess, and daughter of the first Viscount Chaplin. Like her father, she is fond of sport and of dogs, and one of her favourites, a wise and faithful-looking creature, is seen with her in this characteristic photo-graph. The Marchioness was married in 1899, and has a son, Viscount Castlereagh, and three daughters. The Marquess of Londonderry, who succeeded in 1915, has served as an A.D.C. and has been mentioned in despatches. He was made an M.V.O. in 1903, was formerly M.P. for Maidstone, and is a Major in the Household Cavalry.

Photograph by Hugh Cecil.

Lady Londonderry, formerly the Hon. Edith Chaplin (1878–1959), pictured in 1918 as President of the Women's War Services Legion (previously known as the Women's Legion) which provided thousands of military cooks and motor drivers for the War Office. A renowned political hostess, she was the first woman to be appointed DBE (Military Division) for her war work. (Illustrated London News/ME)

consider giving up a room in their homes in order for women land workers to enjoy some pleasant leisure time away from their often cramped quarters. 'If they could be given a piano, so much the better, but the great thing will be to give them a room where they will be comfortable, have some space and a feeling of ease and leisure.' At a farm in Boroughbridge, North Yorkshire, a Mrs Maynard started a nursery for children of agricultural workers, a progressive move coming some time before those opened at factories. And on Lady Cowdray's country estate, Cowdray Park in Midhurst, she employed female gardeners who wore a practical outfit she had personally designed herself.

'Chancing It' by Edmund Blampied from *The Bystander*, 1916. Working on public transport brought numerous romantic opportunities, at least in the eyes of magazine illustrators, who delighted in depicting pretty girls in roles such as this bus conductor. (Illustrated London News/ME)

Whatever the attitude to working women at a grass-roots level, both the government and the press portrayed the female war worker as a cheerful symbol of gutsy British patriotism. The beguiling sight of girls in smocks and breeches or in smart uniforms was a boon for illustrators and cartoonists who celebrated, gently poked fun and took delight in depicting the feminisation of traditionally male workplaces. In advertisements, the working woman, whether a munitionette or a land girl, became an emblematic device for selling products. Photographs of women carrying out traditionally assumed masculine tasks were featured regularly projecting a message that proclaimed no job was beyond the ability of Britain's female workforce. At times, if we are to view the coverage of female employment in the media, then it is easy to assume women were infiltrating every area of employment in their thousands. But some of the jobs featured were a novel (and therefore newsworthy) exception rather than the rule, and certain industries, without government intervention, remained resolutely male. In Liverpool for example, male dockers resisted the employment of women for the entire war. Nevertheless, magazines such as *The Tatler* and its ilk were enlightened enough to praise and publicise a burgeoning female contribution. Jobs for girls included golf caddies and lady firefighters; brewery workers, bill posters, theatre managers, women prompters, railway porters, barbers and bakers. At London Zoo, Miss Saunders became its first woman to act as a keeper while in London's Clubland, 'at the Carlton, or the Athenaeum … they've actually got women wine-butlers. Wine-butlers – think of it!' exclaimed Eve in August 1916. 'There's progress, if you like. We shall get the vote now all right, I expect, without any more trouble.' 'What title does the diner or tea-drinker hail the girl who waits on him – or who should be

From 'K' for knitters to 'S' for shepherdess, the myriad roles played by women during the war are celebrated here in a "War Workers Alphabet" by H. M. Brock from Holly Leaves in December 1918. (Illustrated London News/ME)

waiting on him?' wondered *The Sketch* magazine in its 'Small Talk' column. Waitress was deemed too ugly so it concluded it would go with J.M. Barrie's suggestion of 'Damsel'.

Mr Lloyd George and the Duchess of Marlborough were two examples of VIPs who employed women as chauffeurs. In fact, women drivers held a particular glamorous fascination, and as many upper-class ladies already drove their own cars, driving as part of the war effort was a natural progression. 'The girl hardly exists who does not hope one day to drive. There seems to be a fatal fascination about lording it at a wheel, particularly the wheel of a big car,' commented *The Bystander* in its motoring column. Early in the war, the British School of Motoring ran advertisements airily suggesting learning to drive was 'healthy, enjoyable, and if desired, a highly remunerative occupation

in which they can help their country which is in great need of women drivers owing to the scarcity of men.' By 1918, the adverts had moved to a new level of urgency declaring, 'Serious shortage of motor drivers for work of national importance. LADIES WANTED to learn in the shortest possible time.' There was, however, much opposition from tram and taxi drivers to women driving public vehicles, even though many had proved themselves perfectly capable of handling unwieldy ambulance and mobile field kitchens over the rough terrain of Northern France.

In 1915, *The Sketch* was already discussing the 'novel suggestion' that the places of skilled drivers being drawn to the front should be gradually filled by women, but dismissed their effectiveness as private chauffeurs due to their inability to repair and fine tune a car. As for

Beauty on Duty has a Duty to Beauty

ROYAL VINOLIA CREAM preserves the natural softness and bloom of the skin under all conditions.

Its antiseptic properties make it particularly useful as a healing agent in cases of burns, bruises and abrasions, and it is, therefore, the ideal Toilet Cream for Munition Workers.

In Boxes, 1/1½ & 2/-

ROYAL VINOLIA CREAM

For those who prefer a non-greasy Cream, ROYAL VINOLIA VANISHING CREAM is a delightful preparation. It imparts a dainty bloom to the skin. In Tubes, 6d. & 1/-

VINOLIA COMPANY LIMITED, LONDON—PARIS.

R V 313 14

'Beauty on duty has a duty to beauty' – manufacturers of cosmetics and creams were quick to recognise the potency of the image of the working woman. (Illustrated London News/ME)

taxi driving, the (presumably male) column-ist questioned whether women 'were equal to the racket of Metropolitan traffic … or are pre-pared to face the hardships of rough weather work'. Finally, by 1917, the ban on women driv-ing cabs was lifted, and the first official female cabbie, Miss Susan Dudley Ryder, a cousin of Lord Harrowby and a sister of Mrs Gavin, the champion lady golfer, took to the London roads. For Eve, who found the rudeness of London taxi drivers intolerable, the prospect of a feminine alternative was a relief:

For the insolence of the taxi-man reached the limit and over it ages ago, and it's my belief a polite taxi crowd would fairly rake the shekels in. We'd all be so relieved to be treated politely instead of rudely that

we'd want to over-tip. They say the Taxi-Drivers' Union officials are dead set against the idea, because women lose their heads at critical moments, and also because women can't handle heavy luggage. Well, as to the head-losing, we're prepared to take our chance; and as to the luggage-lifting, there's a war on, and there oughtn't to be any lug-gage to lift.

The year 1917 also brought with it another voluntary scheme designed to coordinate civilian recruitment. Under the overall lead-ership of Neville Chamberlain, the Women's Section of the National Service League was run by May Tennant, with a background in factory inspection, and Violet Markham, an active social reformer and anti-suffragist. The irony of Miss Markham's political views was not lost on Eve, who hooted, 'I call it funny – don't you? – that though neither fit nor worthy to handle that masculine privilege, the vote, Miss Markham should be nevertheless considered capable of fixing up how millions of women can best help to win the war.' The scheme failed, partly through a disappointing take up and partly through internal disputes leading to the resignation of Chamberlain. It is interesting to note that the Chief Controller of Women's Recruitment in 1918 was Lady Margaret Mackworth, Viscountess Rhondda, formerly a militant suffragette (and a survivor of the *Lusitania* disaster).

The failure of the National Service scheme may have been affected in part by the estab-lishment at the same time of the Women's Army Auxiliary Corps (WAAC), and later the

Lady Colebrooke, in working garb worn by her in munitions plant in Great Britain.

Alexandra, Lady Colebrooke, one of a number of upper-class women who chose munitions work during the war. She worked at the Vickers factory in Erith, one of 'a gallant band of women [who] are really doing it. Not just playing about, you know, but living at a hostel and taking the regular rate of pay', wrote Eve admiringly in her column in 1915. (March of the Women Collection/ME)

Women's Royal Naval Service (WRNS) and Women's Royal Air Force (WRAF), branches of the armed forces whose purpose was to provide backup to the combatants both at home and abroad. Tasks varied but all three of the services needed cooks, cleaners, mechanics, drivers, telephonists and clerks. These roles were freely available in other organisations, but they did not offer the glamour of a dashing uniform or the chance to serve at the very heart of the armed forces. In April 1918, *The Bystander* expressed is admiration for the fine behaviour of the WAAC girls whose duties took them close to the fighting during the German Spring Offensive. 'They refused transport to a place of safety; they stuck to their job; and when it became imperative for them to retire, they marched for fifteen miles to resume their work.'

Another organisation to attract middle- and upper-class women was the Women's Volunteer Reserve (WVR) of which the Marchioness of Londonderry, a prominent political hostess, was Colonel-in-Chief. 'Very well they look' in their uniforms, commented *The Sketch* in 1915. Such a uniform, at £2, was far too expensive for the majority of young women but the WVR were an educative force in preparing public opinion for the regular uniformed WAAC and other military units. Lady Londonderry went on to set up the Women's War Services Legion to initially recruit cooks who could specialise in mass catering in camp kitchens with the aim of reducing waste, but the organisation eventually came to supply clerical, administrative and land workers too. Fully committed to women's employment, Lady Londonderry also worked to re-employ women following demobilisation at the end of the war.

Her Women's Legion was represented at a procession of women war workers in July 1918 to mark the Silver Wedding Anniversary of the King and Queen. 3,000 workers, each wearing the uniform of the organisation to which they belonged, from VAD nurses to green-capped Foresters marched through London and were marshalled into the courtyard at Buckingham Palace where they stood in formation to hear the Royal Address. Among them were 150 workers from the Royal Arsenal in Woolwich, who had been able to change into their working uniforms in a large room at the Church Army headquarters, lent specially for the occasion. There were post office mail van drivers, tramway conductors, the nurses of Endell Street Hospital, Queen Mary's Army Auxiliary Corps, policewomen, the 'Land Workers in their smart, corduroy breeches and brown tunics' and the Wrens 'a particularly smart body who gained warm applause'. Once assembled in the quadrangle at the palace, they made 'an imposing spectacle indeed', noted *The Queen* magazine with pride. If the campaign for women to be recognised and accepted to work towards Britain's effort officially began on that rainy day in July 1915, then it could be said to have concluded in triumphant fashion on a far more clement day three years later. For many middle- and upper-class women, the war had given them their first (and often last) taste of serious work. 'It is fair to remember,' noted *The Queen* the previous year, 'that the demand for service from them is a new one. Never before has there been a war in which the nation required as a kind of right that women should harden themselves to work, not as a family necessity, or as a personal preference, but as a sheer duty.'

CHARITY AND FUNDRAISING

For most aristocratic and prominent society women of the First World War, charitable work was part of life. A relatively leisured lifestyle, good connections and an ingrained obligation inherited from their philanthropic Victorian grandmamas meant that charity work, of one kind of another, was a suitably diverting, as well as fulfilling, occupation for women who did not work, nor have much practical involvement in raising their children. The war, inevitably, was to create a new level of need. Orphanages, the poor, destitute women, animals and hospitals were soon competing for funds with convalescent homes, refugees, wounded men, widows, more hospitals (military now) and countless other war-related good causes, instigating a corresponding gear shift in charitable activity. Every strata of society from high-born ladies and members of the royal family, theatre stars and wives of military and political leaders to ordinary families keen to display their patriotism through practical means – everybody was desperate to do something.

On 12 August 1914, *The Tatler* produced what was its first war issue and wasted no time in displaying its own patriotic credentials. Inside the front cover, in a message to its readers, it vowed to dedicate as much space in the magazine as possible to appeals for help 'on behalf of the various societies which have sprung into activity on behalf of the brave men who are now fighting for us and those dependent on them'. It added, stating quite plainly the well-heeled status of most of its readers, '*The Tatler* circulates enormously among the more prosperous members of the community, and we confidently commend to their notice and generosity the appeals such as appear.'

The rush, in those first few weeks, to form societies and charities and to make a difference as quickly as possible, was often characterised by an enthusiastic lack of coordination. 'The Queen and Queen Alexandra have led the way nobly (in supporting the Red Cross and other movements),' wrote Eve on 2 September 1914, 'and everyone is doing something from duchesses to dressmakers. In fact, if anything, there's a slight danger of people doing too much, or at least doing it the wrong way – as *The Times* says, 'an "unprecedented orgy of misdirected charity".' Even two and a half years later, when Eve reported on a mass meeting of the Women's National Service League at the Albert Hall, she relayed, in her own fashion, the message of its directors, Mrs Tennant and Miss Violet Markham:

They impressed upon the surging multitude of females who'd come to immolate themselves upon the altar of the nation's needs … to stay at home till called for. And in any case not to make horrid nuisances of themselves by keeping on calling at St Ermin's where they'd already got too much to do telling those five – or was it fifty? – thousands of enthusiastic creature who wanted to go to France that for this job they only required 200 after all.

In its 7 October issue that year, *The Tatler* launched an appeal of its own, a fairly original idea which, it was probably hoped, did not have any direct competitors. The 'Tatler Games Bureau' was organised to provide recreation and amusement for the growing number of wounded soldiers convalescing in hospitals and homes around the country by providing them with a variety of games. The magazine listed 'packs of cards, jig-saw puzzles, chess sets, dominoes, patience, halma, draughts, race games', as all acceptable and suggested Harrods, Shoolbred's, Gamage's,

Hamley Bros, John Barker & Co and William Whiteley as establishments offering the widest assortment. There were regular reports and updates about the progress of the appeal and Eve was inevitably drafted in the following week to give it a plug.

Expect you've read, haven't you, of *The Tatler*'s scheme for sending games to our wounded – it's quite a good one isn't it? Convalescence for so many of our men will be a long and weary business – the common or garden Tommy's not very much of a reader, you know – and I foresee many dull hours of pain and boredom turned into quite exciting ones with the help of some of these pastimes. And it's a nice easy way too, isn't it, of doing that 'something' we're all aching to do for the men who've risked life and health for us.

Picture postcard of Trafalgar Square during a 'Feed the Guns' campaign, designed to encourage people to invest in War Bonds. The area was transformed for the occasion with tanks and guns available for investors to examine at close quarters, imitation trenches and painted scenery providing a background. (Grenville Collins Postcard Collection/ME)

On 21 October, an advertisement continuing the appeal acknowledged the kind donation of playing cards from whiskey companies, John Walker & Sons and James Buchanan and Co. By 4 November the magazine was able to publish a photograph of wounded soldiers, 'passing the weary hours with "Tatler" games', together with a long list of donors.

The Bystander ran its own appeal asking for toys to be distributed to little Belgian refugees, and *The Queen* magazine started a typically practical-minded appeal too, asking their readers to subscribe to a toilet box, containing a shaving stick, a cake of fine toilet soap, a tube of Cherry toothpaste, an ivory toothbrush and a small mirror to be sent to various regiments at the front. With remarkable efficiency, by December, crates of the toilet boxes were being shipped over to France in their thousands and letters conveying thanks were promptly posted back.

'Dear Sir, – The Officer Commanding 1st Cameron Highlanders directs me to acknowledge the receipt of twenty soldiers' Toilet Boxes, sent through your paper from Mrs Greig, and to convey his sincere thanks for your kindness in being the medium of sending these useful articles.'

In fact, a myriad of items to bring comfort, entertainment or a little luxury to lighten the hardship of life at the front were despatched overseas during the course of the war. Mouth organs were donated in the thousands after an appeal, providing much needed entertainment and morale-boosting melody on marches or while lodged in billets or in dugouts. One thousand alone were donated by Sir Francis Trippel and shipped by Harrods. Such was the ubiquity of the mouth organ on the Western Front, it was even the subject of a jokingly cynical Bruce Bairnsfather cartoon in *The Bystander* in 1917. Records were a more tuneful alternative. In 1915, Winner records donated 50,000 gramophone records to the Front, having already sent 30,000 to the fleet.

There were acts of kindness from individuals too. Mrs Buckley of Birmingham, the wife of Captain Frank Buckley of the 17th Middlesex Regiment, was photographed with her impressive pile of 420 hand-cooked Christmas puddings for Birmingham soldiers at the front in December 1915. Birmingham-born soldiers would have dined well that Christmas. *The Queen* reported that the Lord Mayor had sent a gift consisting of a half-pound plum pudding, two cheese biscuits with a slice of cheese and a Christmas card.

Everyone, even canine types, could do their bit to raise funds during wartime. (John MacLellan Collection/ME)

While soap, mouth organs and Christmas puddings were no doubt appreciated, there was one common desire among men of all ranks – 'smokes'. *The Queen* repeatedly printed requests from soldiers for more cigarettes and parcels sent in by readers (for the magazine acted as a conduit for donations from charitable readers) invariably included cigarettes or tobacco. Decades before the health implications of smoking were known, cigarettes were the fuel of the British Army. *The Bystander* quoted an officer who maintained, 'If the men can only get a "fag" or a pipe they are content. They pay no heed to discomfort in the trenches, or on the march in the worst weather. Even if they are without their rations they won't complain if "fags" don't fail. Some have been reduced to smoking their allowances of tea. Others have smoked brown paper or leaves of trees.' Smoking in hospitals was considered perfectly acceptable. A writer in *The Queen*, who had spent some time nursing the wounded, described a man who had seen all his comrades killed and wrote, 'A cigarette seemed to give new life to that man when he was desperately ill in hospital, and one could not help thinking how much more a smoke must have meant to him in the stress and strain of those awful weeks.' Tobacco rations, thought to boost morale and calm nerves, were introduced in 1916, though pipes were also in demand due to their tendency to get dropped or break while on duty in the firing line. Cigarette companies advertised their postal service to France and many sought publicity by sending large quantities overseas free of charge. Mr Bernhard Barron, for instance, owner of the Carreras Tobacco Company had, by August 1915, already sent three million 'Black Cat' cigarettes to soldiers at the front. It was no surprise that the contents of Princess Mary's Christmas Gift Box, sent to the front in 1914, was a packet of cigarettes in a distinctive yellow packet.

Tobacco companies did well out of the war but so, too, thought Mrs C.S. Peel, *The Queen*'s Household editor, did 'those who sold knitting needles and wool'. In her memoirs of life during the war, she described the civilian nation's premier wartime occupation:

> We knitted socks (some of them of unusual shape), waistcoats, helmets, comforters, mitts, body belts. We knitted at theatres, in trains and trams, in parks and parlours, in the intervals of eating in resturants, of serving in canteens. Men knitted, children knitted … It was soothing to our nerves to knit, and comforting to think that the results of our labours might save some man something of hardship and misery.

In tune with the nation's mania for knitting what were known as 'comforts', *The Queen* carried patterns on a regular basis for specially designed, practical military garb such as the trench socks, chest protectors, balaclavas or special rifle gloves (leaving the trigger finger free). There were other pieces – slippers, or hospital stockings for instance – destined for convalescent homes. The magazine reported on ladies in the Peeress' Gallery knitting during a debate in the House of Lords in January 1915, and Eve in *The Tatler*, who claimed that ladies were knitting at theatrical first nights, wondered 'are there enough sheep to provide the wool to keep the knitters knitting', likening the new vogue for clicking needles after dinner ('arriving guests carry vast brocade bags, in which are concealed interminable woollen scarves which never achieve completion') to scenes in Mrs Gaskell's *Cranford*. To ensure an uninterrupted flow, Edwards & Sons offered a 'most successful' knitting bag that could be looped over the wrist, leaving both hands free. The quality of comforts varied enormously,

A simple frock and apron traditionally worn by Belgian children that could be made by from a paper pattern purchased from the offices of *The Queen* magazine. Readers who were anxious to do their bit could make the garments and help clothe Belgian families arriving in England as refugees during the early weeks of the First World War. (Hearst Magazines (UK)/ME)

much to the bemusement of the troops – and Eve who as early as September 1914 was describing the 'piles of fearsome garments … destined for I don't quite know who.' Knitting was inevitably the subject of countless cartoons and postcards and in *The Queen*'s agony column, entitled, 'Social Problems', one lady wrote in with a particularly delicate dilemma:

Mrs A, who is collecting comforts for the soldiers, calls one afternoon on a friend Mrs B, who gives her a parcel, saying, 'I know you want more socks, so I have knitted these for you.' Mrs A thanks Mrs B and asks her to luncheon the following day, when they will look over the things and pack them, as they must be sent at once. Mrs A then opens the parcels and finds six pairs of socks all so badly knitted and so small as to be practically useless. What should Mrs A say or do?

Perhaps Mrs B should have turned her hand to needlework instead, for there were plenty of suggestions for items she could make. Sewing was a skill most women possessed and, in the early weeks of the war when the desire to do something to help had few outlets, was one they could utilise straight away. *The Queen* published patterns for clothes for Belgian refugees, special shirts for Indian troops and numerous bandages and hospital robes required for wounded men. Shoolbred's of Tottenham Court Road advertised their flannel shirts for the army and hospital pyjamas, already cut out and ready for stitching together. Lady Smith-Dorrien, wife of General Smith-Dorrien, launched an appeal asking for bags into which the personal belongings of

the wounded in hospitals and casualty clearing stations could be placed for safekeeping. The bags, which were to be strongly made of firm material, had to measure 10½ inches long by 9 inches wide when finished with a tape running string securing the top and a label of white linen stitched to one side to receive the name of the owner and his corps. The finished items were to be sent directly to Lady Smith-Dorrien herself at No. 21, Eaton Terrace. Another prominent military wife, Lady French – who, explained *The Queen*, 'is, of course, always in touch with the men actually in the trenches and also with the authorities at home' – appealed for more warm shirts, socks, cardigans and warm gloves, all to be sent to her personally at No. 39, Berkeley Square.

Many society ladies gave their time to war-related needlework. Early in the war, in September 1914, Lady Quilter of Methersgate Hall, Woodbridge in Suffolk, had organised the cottagers and householders on her estate to produce a sizeable pile of scarves, shirts and other clothing items. There were groups too such as one set up in the salubrious surroundings of Claridge's Hotel to sew woollen shirts for a Lord Tredegar's yacht, in use as a relief ship to the hospital ships on the French and Belgian coasts, or the home of Mrs R.G. Edwards at No. 22, New Cavendish Street ('one of the latest of London's beautiful homes to be devoted to the work of the British Red Cross') where a group working under the auspices of the Red Cross Central Workrooms made quantities of hospital garments and other necessities for the wounded. There were also the work-rooms of Lady Sclater in Pont Street where in a six-month period from January to June 1917, 19,813 ladies attended, making and despatching a staggering

Opposite: 'Our Superior Inferiors' by Edwin Morrow, *The Bystander*, 12 July 1916. Lady de Tomkyn (at Cabbage Charity Sale): 'How on earth are we to clean these pototoes? I DARE not ask Simpson!' A well-meaning lady hoping to help out at a charity sale cannot bear to admit her ignorance of domestic matters to her footman. (Illustrated London News/ME)

174,000 articles from life-saving waistcoats for men on minesweepers to hospital slippers. Prominent women at their sewing machines made a good photograph and set an example; Lady Gladstone, the Duchess of Westminster, Lady Curzon and Princess Helena Victoria, cousin of the King, were all pictured as seamstresses, the latter two working together at the YMCA work-rooms at Hertford Street making undergarments for soldiers. Sadly, whether many soldiers were aware their underwear had been stitched by a princess of royal blood is unrecorded.

Not all needlewomen could afford to donate their skills free of charge. The Glove and Waistcoat Fund, set up by a Miss Stokes and Miss Cox of the Ladies' Territorial Committee, recycled discarded kid clothes, as well as leather from upholstered furniture and any other of supple quality, to make lightweight but windproof waistcoats for men at the front. The difference with this initiative was that the fund employed around sixty women in making the waistcoats in their own home, meaning not only did the fund provide warm clothing for soldiers, but it also helped women with small children earn a living wage. In November 1915, a fundraising concert, 'of unusual merit', was given at Grosvenor House by permission of the Duke of Westminster and during the interval, Miss Cox gave an account of the work while a demonstration of the waistcoat making process was given in a gallery adjoining the concert room.

Combining informative exhibitions or entertainment with fundraising was a popular way to engage with the public. In 1917, Lady Drogheda, wife of the 10th Earl, a keen aviation enthusiast and an energetic worker for a number of wartime causes, embarked on a project which was to enjoy far-reaching success when she organised an Air Service Exhibition which opened at the Grosvenor Galleries in early 1917. Comprising 400 separate exhibits, including an impressive collection of balloon prints, original illustrations by artists such as George Horace Davis and Fortunino Matania (both artists for *The Sphere* magazine at the time) as well as works of art by C.R.W. Nevinson, William Russell Flint and Sir John Lavery, the piece de resistance was a captured German Fokker plane lent to her by the War Office. Such was its success that she was asked by the Army Council to arrange a provincial tour, even flying over Dublin to scatter publicity leaflets when the exhibition moved to Ireland. Eve was full of admiration for Lady Drogheda's achievements.

Sir George Robey (1869–1954), English music hall comedian and singer, known as the 'Prime Minister of Mirth', caricatured by cartoonist H. M. Bateman. The money falling through the sky into his trademark bowler hat represents the £50,000 Robey raised for war charities during the First World War. (Estate of H.M.Bateman/ILN/ME)

'We women are coming on, aren't we? She really does know a tremendous lot about a pretty big subject, you know; and the whole show, as someone says, is a "perfectly remarkable display of a woman's organizing ability." The quite wonderful catalogue ... I believe she wrote almost entirely herself. When our grandmothers (sometimes) took up their pens, it wasn't ever about such very special technical and scientific things, anyway.'

The exhibition's tour raised money for the Flying Services Fund and the Irish Hospital Supply Depots for the Red Cross while simultaneously recruiting volunteers for the Royal Flying Corps.

Lady Drogheda was again at the hub of activity, distributing leaflets from the gondola of a captured German Zeppelin during Tank Week in March 1918, when a tank from the front was exhibited to the public who were encouraged to buy war savings certificates in return for gaining access to see other exhibits inside the tank. Phrynette in *The Sketch* described the scene:

I paid an early afternoon call on 'Egbert of Cambrai' now in Trafalgar Square, somewhat battered, four men having been killed in him recently. Two charming, fur-clad ladies were sitting on ammunition cases inside, very busy stamping war certificates, and a brace of sentries guarded his hull carefully. There was a tremendous crowd in the Square and hawkers were doing a brisk business in postcards etc. The crowd was certainly half of it in khaki and there were numbers of wounded blue taking a cheerful interest in things.

Also on display was the SIA aeroplane in which the Italian airman Captain Laureati flew from Turin to Hendon, and, in front of the National Gallery, 'a mystery wagon, very

Advertisement encouraging readers of *The Queen* magazine to donate towards the building of more Church Army huts, 'the soldier's solace in frost and cold, mud and slush'. The Church Army had hundreds of huts on the home front and at the front, but employed the services of Britannia in this advert to stir British citizens into helping provide more. (Hearst Magazines (UK)/ME)

black and white with shafts for a horse' – as it turned out, a mobile pigeon-cote used for carrier pigeons at the front which had, apparently, attracted royalty when 'Queen Alexandra was one of the first to make a purchase through this novel agency'.

Many of Lady Drogheda's contemporaries followed a similarly high-profile timetable of activity in support of good causes. Society turned out in force in June 1916 for the great jumble sale at Caledonian Market, which was marred by the arrival of news of the death of Lord Kitchener, drowned at sea when HMS *Hampshire* was sunk by a German mine off

Gaby Deslys (1881–1920), celebrated French actress and dancer, playing the clown with wounded soldiers at her home in Kensington Gore, London. She was one of a number of stage stars who gave their time towards entertaining the troops. The bottom picture shows Gaby 'giving a "Hun" a turn'. (Illustrated London News/ME)

the coast of Orkney. 'It was a chance to see how the great soldier was regarded by masses and classes, which were mixed up at this wonderful jumble sale,' observed the *Illustrated Sporting & Dramatic News*, reporting that those managing stalls, Grand Duke Michael (selling blue hydrangeas), the Duchess of Sutherland and Lady Lanesborough among them, overcame their shock and disbelief to carry on the good work.

Bazaars, sales and auctions became so commonplace that Eve, by August 1916, was reporting on the lack of interest at a charity auction at the Hotel Cecil: 'Languid wasn't the word for the interest in Jellicoe's bootjack or the P.M.'s cast-off motor cap (the flappy one you know), or Sir George Alexander's old gloves, or Sir Charles Wyndham's discarded boot, or a tea gown once worn by no less a person than Clara Butt.'

At a Red Cross sale the following year she commented on how there 'seems a perfectly norful slump in Victorian relics these days of war, doesn't there?', when a waistcoat once worn by King Edward VII only fetched 6s and a glove belonging to Queen Victoria fetched no bids at all. Nevertheless, an auction of dresses by the court dressmaker Reville & Rossiter at the Savoy in aid of the Belgian Relief Fund in April 1915 attracted plenty of interest, especially as the gowns were modelled by a bevy of actresses including Viola Tree, Auriol Lee and Hilda Moore. A catwalk show was one of the features of a charity event in aid of Blinded Soldiers and Sailors at the Albert Hall in April 1917, which also included a cake stall presided over by the Duchess of Sutherland and Princess Victoria selling Liberty frocks for children. 'Topping idea to buy a frock for charity, what?', thought Eve.

At the end of the war, waning interest was revived beyond expectations in December 1918 when the sale of the Red Cross Pearls took place at Christie's. The idea had first been suggested by the King's sister, Princess Victoria, who formed a committee at the end of February to organise what was to become a seriously high-profile fundraising event. Pearls were donated by Queen Mary, Queen Alexandra, the Princess Royal, Princess Victoria herself, Princess Louise, Duchess of Argyll, as well as many society ladies and others. One pearl, heartbreakingly, was sent by an anonymous donor in memory of a soldier who had fallen in Flanders, 'in memory of a pearl beyond all price already given – my only son'. Other donations came from regiments, as well as five perfect rubies in memory of Lord Kitchener. In all, forty-three necklaces were made from the donations and with the pearls mixed up and the identity of the owners lost, the pieces took on an air of mystery and romance. Which necklace might contain the pearl given by Queen Alexandra?

The Queen magazine described King Street in St James' as 'literally besieged; people who had never been in a crowd before waited and jostled with more or less good humour, and agitated VAD's endeavoured to form the popular queue and preserve it when formed.' The sale was an outstanding success. The biggest necklace, comprising of sixty-three matching pearls clasped by a rose diamond, 'as big as a sixpence', fetched £22,000. The total made that day was £100,000 (well over £2 million today).

Well-known socialites such as Elizabeth Asquith, the youngest daughter of the Prime Minister, Vita Sackville-West and Lady Diana Manners had a particular taste for theatrical fundraisers and it felt that barely a week went by without some sort of concert, revue or matinee ('charity mats' as Eve called them) being staged in aid of causes as varied as the Concerts for the Front Fund, the Three Arts Employment Fund or the Serbian Relief Committee. Sometimes ladies took part in them, often posing in wordless tableaux which, though visually gorgeous, were a little self-indulgent and perhaps more fun for those participating than those in the audience. The Angels tableaux, staged at the Palace Theatre in November 1917, featured Violet Bonham-Carter (the ex-Prime Minister's elder daughter) and Hazel, Lady Lavery, the beautiful wife of the society painter, among others in a series of recreations of Old Master paintings – lovely to look at, but it is doubtful how exciting it was as a form of entertainment. Nevertheless, 'charity mats' were produced in their scores. In the last week of June 1915 alone Eve reported three jostling for space – 'Princess Patricia's Comforts Fund, one for her Canadian Light Infantry; Mrs Keppel's entertainment at the Ritz for the Officers' Hostel in Belgrave Square; and the In-Aid-Of at Wyndham's Theatre on Monday week for Lady Lytton's hospital in Charles Street.'

When the professionals took over at other charity shows, ladies rushed to act as programme-sellers. At a concert held at Grosvenor House in February 1916 in aid of the Star and Garter Fund, which aimed to establish a hospital in the former Star and Garter Hotel in Richmond, the lady programme sellers included Lady Mainwaring, Nancy Cunard, Bettine Stuart-Wortley and the ubiquitous Lady Diana Manners. *The Tatler* captioned them 'Some Kindly "Souls"', clearly alluding to their lineage – most of them were the children of, or in some way connected with the elite intellectual group of Edwardians known as the 'Souls'. This was the social side of charity, carried out among friends and acquaintances, all members of an exclusive club. The same crowd would be 'snapshotted' prowling the streets on Flag Days. Slightly domineering but terribly nice, these ladies would accost helpless passers-by who would be obliged to buy a flag and pin. Without doubt, there was little sacrifice or personal discomfort in helping out at a concert or taking wounded soldiers to tea. Eve, always quick with her self-deprecation, was ready to highlight the pleasant side of being charitable. Of a Wounded Soldiers' Tea Concert at the Savoy in January 1917 she wrote of it being a 'very nice easy way for people to do a little "bit". You pay your guinea and you invite ten wounded soldiers or sailors as your guests, and at the Savoy all the rest of the machinery's provided – your tea and your table and your concert. And all very nice, too.' Of a charity tennis tournament played in Surbiton

'Those &%$* Mouth-Organs' by Bruce Bairnsfather, *The Bystander*, 7 March 1917. Mouth organs were an easily transportable and relatively simple way to provide men at the Front with entertainment and in early 1915, Sir Francis Trippel presented 1,000 mouth organs to the Army Council for distribution among the troops. The novelty seems to have worn off for Bairnsfather's cynical Tommies. (Illustrated London News/ME)

No. 1172.—Vol. XCI.   WEDNESDAY, JULY 14, 1915.   SIXPENCE.

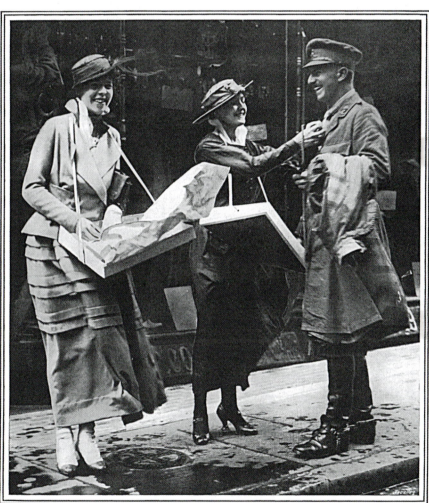

VIVENT LES ALLIÉS! FRANCE'S DAY IN LONDON.

Although the weather was unpropitious on France's Day in London—July 7—for the street collection in aid of the French Red Cross, the helpers in the cause faced the elements bravely, and the result was satisfactory. Our picture shows two French ladies selling their badges in Piccadilly. The French Flag-Day is to-day (July 14).

Ladies braving inclement weather to sell flags in aid of charity to an accosted officer on France's Day held in London on 7 July 1915. It was just one of countless days devoted to different war-related charities including Welsh Flag Day, Serbian Flag Day, YMCA Hut Day and even 'Our Day', a fundraising extravaganza spread across the capital. (Illustrated London News/ME)

in August 1916 and featuring Lady Drogheda, the Duchess of Sutherland and Countess Zia Torby (daughter of Grand Duke Michael), Eve innocently pointed out that it was a 'nice, pleasant way of working for a good cause on a summer afternoon, and not too frightfully exhausting either'.

Both on and off stage, war charities benefited enormously when stars of the entertainment industry wielded their considerable celebrity clout. Music hall comedian and singer George Robey, star of the hit musical *The Bing Boys are Here*, raised an estimated £500,000 for war charities during the period, for which he was offered a knighthood but instead modestly accepted a CBE. High-profile actors and actresses gave their time generously, whether it was selling chocolate in Selfridges for the Belgian Relief Fund, providing ad hoc entertainments for wounded soldiers or donating their fee for a performance to a chosen charity. The American actress Elsie Janis, who spent long periods of the war in London, recalled in her memoirs how 'I can't remember an idle moment during those four hectic months. Two and three benefits a week, singing for the wounded, entertaining in training camps and going to parties as if each one were the last that would ever be given.' Janis travelled to the Front to perform in 1917, as did other entertainers. In 1915, the actor-manager Seymour Hicks had taken his entertainment troupe, which included the actress Gladys Cooper, around the Front, performing to the troops in specially erected marquees.

The alluring Gaby Deslys, star of West End revues such as *5064 Gerrard* and *Suzette*, was the pin-up girl of the trenches. Eve described her appearance at the Theatrical Garden Party held in July 1915, where she was veiled in rose-pink tulle, 'which gave a sort of angelic effect – very piquant. She's a tender-hearted thing and such an impulsive child of Gaul. She saw an officer she knew coming towards her and threw out both her hands in welcome. Suddenly she saw – he had no hands to give her, only

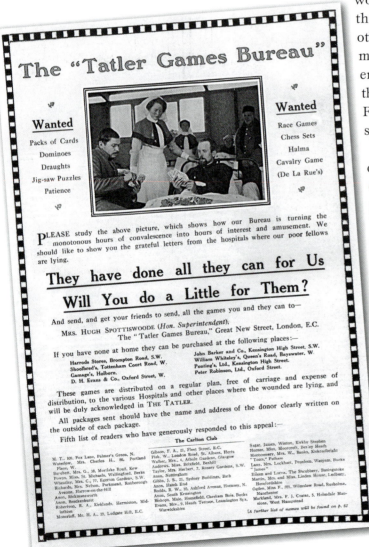

Advertisement for The Tatler *magazine's campaign to gather donations of board games, chess sets, playing cards, jigsaw puzzles, etc., for the entertainment of wounded soldiers in hospitals. Among the listed donors is the Carlton Club. (Illustrated London News/ME)*

stumps swathed in bandages. And Gaby cried out, shocked beyond words, and burst into bitter tears.' Gaby threw herself into helping the Allied cause, and photographs of her amusing a group of wounded men at her home at Kensington Gore, visiting convalescent soldiers at Brighton or, on another occasion, driving a wounded officer around in a motorcycle sidecar, began to appear in the press almost as frequently as those of her posing in her lavish stage costumes. Declared 'a nice bit of stuff' by the wounded Tommies she charmed during a visit to the London hospital in September 1914, Eve reported that she had brought them the colossal wreaths she'd been presented at the Palace Theatre the previous night (where she'd

been starring in *Rosy Rapture*) and, knowing the way to men's hearts, bought everyone cigarettes. The lovely actress Lily Elsie, best known for her role in *The Merry Widow* prior to the war, took a particular interest in St Dunstan's Hostel for blinded soldiers, a charity founded and run by the publisher Sir Arthur Pearson. Photographs of her visiting the hostel and filling the role of cox for the rowing team or lighting the cigarette of one inmate cannot have failed to tug at the heartstrings.

Nor could the pictures of the Hippodrome Ladies' 'Home' for Soldiers' Pets, where actresses of the Hippodrome had organised a 'foundling' society for dogs who had been left behind at home by their bachelor owners, offering a temporary foster home for the orphaned pets. Our Dumb Friends' League also offered to take on the pets of soldiers and sailors who had nobody else to leave them with. In April 1915, a writer from *The Queen* reported on a visit to the League's headquarters where they saw sixteen dogs, five cats and two donkeys, but also a forlorn monkey, who 'looked at his visitors with solemn eyes, and never a wink that would possibly suggest he could play tricks. It is true that at present he is missing his master very much, but it is hoped that he will be beguiled out of his woes in due course'. An RSPCA flag day for the benefit of sick and wounded horses was supported by the Duchess of Portland, who lent her house at No. 3 Grosvenor Square as a badge depot, and the popularity of Fortunino Matania's painting *Goodbye Old Man*, commissioned by the Blue

Mrs Harold Nicholson aka Vita Sackville-West pictured with Mrs Walter Rubens taking part in Lady Huntingdon's and Lady Massereene's 'Omar Khayyam' tableaux given at Mrs Marsh's house in Arlington Street in aid of war charities in June 1916. 'Charity mats' were a favourite method of fundraising among prominent members of society, though how entertaining the results of their dramatic endeavours were is questionable! (Illustrated London News/ME)

Cross Fund, raised thousands of pounds through the sale of postcards. Animals themselves, particularly dogs, obligingly dressed in uniform and carrying collection boxes on their backs, all became part of the collective, national fundraising effort.

It seemed that no stone was left unturned, no needy cause unnoticed. Collection boxes were placed on tables in restaurants, 'so that they'll catch people's eyes just when they're in a generous after-lunch or after-dinner mood', explained Eve. A National Egg Collection for the Wounded, under the patronage of Queen Alexandra, aimed to collect a million eggs in one week to ensure a plentiful supply for invalided soldiers. Eggs could be handed in to collecting depots or sent directly to the central depot at Harrod's. In July 1915, Lady Maud Wilbraham and Miss Hope-Clarke founded the Silver Thimble Fund, gathering donations of thimbles as well as other odds and ends of gold and silver that eventually transformed into funds of over £40,000, used to buy thirteen motor ambulances, five motor hospital launches, two motor dental surgery cars, one disinfector with the remainder donated to disabled sailors and soldiers and the Star and Garter Fund. Many gift books were produced, such as Princess Mary's Gift Book, with all profits going to The Queen's Work for Women Fund or Princess Marie-Jose's Children's Book published in aid of the Vestiaire Marie-Jose, a society for providing milk, food and clothing to children behind the firing line in

A woman of the Ladies' Territorial Committee busy sorting through old kid gloves. The Glove and Waistcoat Fund was an enterprising initiative devised to recycle gloves into warm winter waistcoats for men at the Front. (Hearst Magazines (UK)/ME)

The problem of what to do with the pets of men who had joined up was a real one and the Hippodrome Ladies' Home for Soldiers' Pets offered one solution. Popular stars of the stage such as Violet Loraine and Unity More became foster carers to a motley but endearing band of dogs, and pose here for photographs published in *The Sketch* magazine in February 1915. (Illustrated London News/ME)

THE HIPPODROME LADIES' "HOME" FOR SOLDIERS' PETS.

CARING FOR DOGS OUR OFFICERS AND MEN HAVE LEFT BEHIND THEM: FAIR ACTRESSES AND THEIR "WARDS."

Flanders. Articles and illustrations by well-known artists and writers were often donated for free.

The Queen magazine championed the Eau de Cologne Fund, asking for donations so the fund could provide plenty of bottles for use in hospital wards, where it was used extensively for its cleaning and refreshing qualities. They were British-made brands, of course; Erasmic, or Esprit de Liège, named to commemorate 'the magnificent self-sacrifice of Liège' and endorsed by the *British Medical Journal* and *The Lancet*.

Companies and organisations, anxious to contribute, often donated fully equipped ambulances or mobile field kitchens, emblazoned, naturally, with the name of the donors, whether they were the Ladies' Automobile Association, the Scouts, the Reform Club or Burberry.

On the opening day of the J. Lyons Corner House on Oxford Street in September 1916, half of the receipts were donated to the Star and Garter Fund. Other companies sponsored events for wounded soldiers. In November 1917, one thousand wounded men were entertained at the London Opera House at the expense of the Watford Manufacturing Company, makers of Vi-Cocoa. On arrival they were given the exotic treat of real turtle soup, Vi-Cocoa was substituted for tea (naturally), much to the men's delight and, of course, waitresses were recruited from society, the stage and the press. In June 1915, the print machine managers at the Illustrated London News & Sketch Ltd organised a river trip on the Thames from Kingston to Walton and back for wounded soldiers convalescing at the Victoria Hospital in Chelsea. The men had lunch on board and on the way back, Union Jack flags were flown from Kingston bridges and those who could stood to sing the National Anthem.

Some charitable ideas began simply but rapidly expanded. *The Queen*, well-versed in practical, domestic matters, wrote in 1915 that some sort of refreshments should be provided at railway stations for soldiers returning home on leave, and a letter in *The Times* pointed out the disgrace of men, 'cold and hungry', having no sustenance to welcome them on their arrival in the capital. By December 1915, the Sailors and Soldiers' Free Buffet at Victoria Station had been established, feeding an estimated 200,000 men at a cost of a penny a head. It was staffed entirely by volunteers, spearheaded by Mrs Kenward Matthews and with Miss Muriel Perry as quartermaster. Supported by voluntary subscription, it provided meat sandwiches, cake, tea and fruit and soon the scheme extended to other major rail terminuses, including Liverpool Street and London Bridge. The latter was organised by Lady Limerick and during Christmas 1915 Queen Alexandra herself took her turn serving up teas, much to the surprise of the men queuing. *The Queen* considered the running of the buffets of enough importance to write

an opinion of what was being served there in its leader column on 24 April 1916, insisting that quantity rather than variety was the key, as 'Soldiers and sailors are conservative creatures. They know what they like and what they want, and they do not want anything else.'

The opening of *The Queen* newspaper and Church Army Munitions Canteen at the munitions works in Hayes, Middlesex in October 1915 allowed the magazine to practice what it preached. The canteen, which could accommodate up to 1,500 people at a time, aimed to supply cheap and wholesome meals to the workers, the majority of them women. They did a roaring trade, selling out of everything in the opening few days. 'No sooner are the larder shelves filled up with pies and tarts and cakes than they empty again,' reported the magazine, beaming with satisfaction at a job well done.

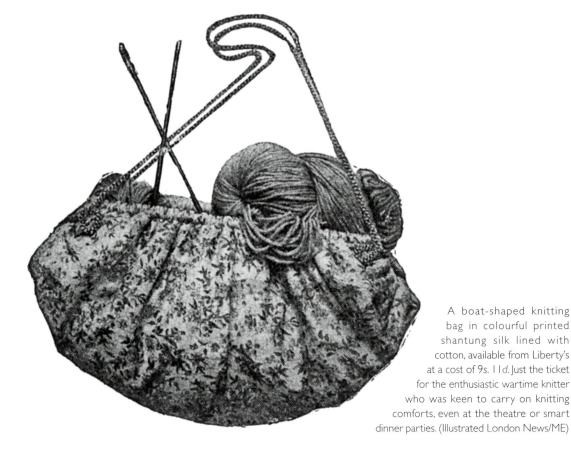

A boat-shaped knitting bag in colourful printed shantung silk lined with cotton, available from Liberty's at a cost of 9s. 11d. Just the ticket for the enthusiastic wartime knitter who was keen to carry on knitting comforts, even at the theatre or smart dinner parties. (Illustrated London News/ME)

Fundraising days were organised with such frequency that charitable largesse could sometimes wear thin. Running the gauntlet of flag sellers, one man realises that the only way he can avoid acquiring yet another badge or flag is to go out blindfolded and with headphones muffling any sounds. Illustration by F. C. Boyle in *The Bystander*, 7 June 1916. (Illustrated London News/ME)

Meat shortages and then increased taxes on tea, coffee, sugar and raisins tested the skills and culinary ingenuity of the staff, but the kindness and concern of the magazine's readers often came to the rescue. One day they received a pound note from a reader, 'to be used specially for currants and raisins for your cakes so that you need not charge more'. More and more canteens sprung up around Britain and in France, catering en masse to hungry soldiers and war workers, while 'canteening' became a popular choice of voluntary work for ladies. Miss Violet Gordon Selfridge, daughter of retail magnate Harry Gordon Selfridge, was featured in *The Tatler* in 1916 and described as 'doing a lot of hard work in the cause of

war charities, and has been also particularly employed at the army canteens, at which so many ladies are working devotedly.' There were murmurings, inevitably, that some ladies only dabbled in voluntary work for fun, or for appearances' sake. According to Eve, writing on the subject in 1917, 'Swank isn't the word for the airs a few of our most forward canteeners put on, par example, and it's my opinion that lots of this war work one hears about is just an excuse to gad.'

But that is not to diminish the efforts of the majority. Many volunteers worked surprisingly hard. Miss Natalie Courtenay was featured in *The Tatler* in December 1917, singled out for her devotion to war work at

Queen Mary's Hut in Eaton Square where her duties consisted mainly of washing up and scrubbing, which she did four days a week in eight-hour shifts. And the spirit of noblesse oblige among high-ranking society produced some quite exceptional characters. The Duchess of Marlborough, the American heiress Consuelo Vanderbilt Balsan, devoted much of her life to welfare work and was described by *The Sketch* in January 1918 as 'probably connected with more philanthropic movements than any other wearer of strawberry leaves and […] I fancy, the only one of her rank who has ever run a lodging house for women.' During the war she was also a leading member of the American Women's War Relief Fund, as was her aunt by marriage, Lady Randolph Churchill; a ward at the West Ham Hospital for wounded soldiers was named after her and she organised an auction of jewellery in aid of the Children's Fund, at which she was 'the presiding genie, seen examining the treasures sacrificed for the sake of the nation's children.' Lady Muriel Paget, frequently pictured in *The Tatler* and other magazines, was already organising soup kitchens for the poor of the East End when war broke out, and extended the concept to provide for Belgian refugees in the capital. Afterwards, she spent the remainder of the war away from her five young children for prolonged periods in Russia and Eastern Europe, where she worked ceaselessly to set up field and base hospitals as well as ambulance units.

Lady Drogheda, the flying countess whose air exhibition garnered such attention, had, in 1915, joined her friend, the actress Maxine Elliott, on board a canal barge which the latter had purchased and kitted out with the express purpose of taking food and clothing to Belgians in remote areas of the country, cut off by German invaders. When not abroad or in the air, Kathleen was a familiar face at charity functions, whether testing her forehand at a charity tennis tournament or organising a flag day for the Irish Prisoner of War Fund. At a Doll Sale at Sunderland House in 1918, in aid of the Children's Jewel Fund (which financed the founding of infant welfare centres around the country), Lady Drogheda's contribution was, characteristically, a group of 'Air Force' dolls together with scale models of aeroplanes and airships. Other contributions came from Queen Alexandra, Queen Mary and Lily Brayton (Mrs Oscar Asche), who gave a Chu Chin Chow group.

It is notable that even as the war was drawing to a close and the nation was beginning to sense victory that charitable activity did not cease. At the end of October 1918, 'Our Day', a series of events across London, received considerable press coverage. Among the fundraisers were Major George Watney's Dramatic Society, comprising munitions workers who gave a matinee performance of *Sweet Lavender* at St James's Theatre, and at the Piccadilly Hotel, Elsie Janis hosted a Lucky Zeppelin Bar where customers could come and draw the remnants of the first Zeppelin to be shot down over Cuffley. In Trafalgar Square there was a Camouflage Fair, while at midday George Robey auctioned a pig called Daisy which had been donated by the Wandsworth Allotment Holders. Over at Devonshire House a maypole had been erected in the courtyard. In November 1918, the actress Lily Elsie appeared on the front cover of *The Sketch* with news of her new crusade – to collect 10,000 gold and silver cigarette cases courtesy of 'patriotic smokers' for the Red Cross. Each donation would receive in return a letter of thanks, personally autographed by Ms Elsie.

It was a golden age of giving, but it is difficult to imagine how momentum and enthusiasm was kept at an urgent pitch during four long

No. 734, JULY 21, 1915]　　　　　　　　　　　　　　THE TATLER

AN INDEFATIGABLE WORKER
In the Cause of Our Wounded Heroes.

Hugh Cecil

MISS ELIZABETH ASQUITH

Younger daughter of the Prime Minister, who, with the Hon. Clare Tennant, arranged a special matinée at His Majesty's Theatre last week (at which Queen Alexandra was present) in aid of the British Red Cross Society. One of the distinctive features of the interesting programme was the appearance of Miss Asquith with Mr. Gerald du Maurier in Mr. Cosmo Gordon-Lennox's little duologue, "The Impertinence of the Creature." Inset is a picture of Miss Asquith and Mr. du Maurier in the play

83

Elizabeth Asquith (1897–1945), daughter of British Prime Minister Herbert Asquith, pictured in *The Tatler* who describe her as 'an indefatigable worker in the cause of our wounded heroes'. She organised and acted in a number of charity matinees throughout the war and in this case, she is pictured appearing with the actor Gerald du Maurier in a duologue called 'The Impertinence of the Creature', which was part of a matinee held at His Majesty's Theatre in the presence of Queen Alexandra in aid of the British Red Cross Society. (Illustrated London News/ME)

AN AERIAL PROPAGANDIST
Who Recently Flew Over London.

LADY DROGHEDA (OR SHOULD IT BE DROGHED-AIR)

On the last day of the "Tank Week" Lady Drogheda, whose interest in air-craft is well known, flew over London in one of our new bombing planes, which was piloted by Squadron-Commander the Master of Sempill (the Hon. William Francis Forbes-Sempill), R.N.A.S., and dropped leaflets in Trafalgar Square exhorting the public to buy war bonds. Lady Drogheda organised and managed an air-craft exhibition, by which she has raised a very considerable sum of money for war funds

Kathleen, Countess of Drogheda, pictured in *The Tatler* in a flying airsuit. Known as the Flying Countess, she arranged a major aviation exhibition at the Grosvenor Galleries, aiming to raise funds for charity and to encourage men to join the Royal Flying Corps (later RAF). It later travelled to Ireland and the United States, raising £6,000. During Tank Week in 1918, she flew over London with the Hon. William Francis Forbes-Semphill and dropped leaflets in Trafalgar Square exhorting the public to buy war bonds. (Illustrated London News/ME)

years of war. Eve, who liked to expose the chinks in the armour of do-gooders, could not quite resist a hint of sarcasm when she reported on the £150,000 wanted by Mrs Lloyd George in December 1917 for the establishment of a North Wales War Heroes Memorial and an associated college for the promotion of science in the area: 'If any of you millionaire men read this paragraph you WON'T forget to send along a cheque for a thousand or so to 10, Downing Street will you?' she wrote, mocking the optimism of the Prime Minister's wife's plans. But she concluded with a thought which was echoed by many, and by which the nation's collecting tin were kept full. There could be 'no better cause than, with mere filthy lucre, to do some small thing for the children of the men but for whom there'd BE no England to love and live for?'

Nobody forgot that, whatever sacrifices were made at home, the ones made in France and further afield were greater.

NURSING, HOSPITALS AND CONVALESCENCE

In 1914, Lady Diana Manners, the youngest daughter of Violet, Duchess of Rutland, was twenty-two years old. Though never formally educated, she was cultured, witty and one of the brightest stars in the firmament of society intellectuals known as the 'Coterie'. Her beauty, for which she was most famed, gained her the devotion and friendship of countless admirers, among them Patrick Shaw-Stewart and Raymond Asquith, both of whom would lose their lives during the First World War. Diana's celebrity was such that she appeared on the front cover of *The Tatler* magazine more frequently than any other individual.

When war broke out, she began, in her own words, 'scheming to get to the war as a nurse'. She had ambitions to go to France and petitioned several peeresses; Millicent, Duchess of Sutherland, Lady Dudley and the Duchess of Westminster, all of whom had hastened across the Channel to set up their own hospitals within weeks. But her mother refused to let her go, roping in Lady Dudley to persuade her that France would be a dangerous place for an attractive young woman such as herself and the likelihood of being ravished by sex-starved wounded soldiers was too great.

Diana abandoned her plans and instead trained as a VAD nurse at Guy's Hospital in London. Raymond Asquith's response on hearing the news was one of feigned horror. In a letter to Diana he wrote: 'Are you really contemplating Guy's Hospital? The contract is lengthy, the drudgery unbearable, and the uniform disfiguring. I don't believe even your genius could make the headwear tolerable … A hospital has all the material discomforts of a nunnery without the spiritual glamour of chastity.'

The Voluntary Aid Detachment (VAD) had formed in 1909 to offer nursing services in an auxiliary capacity to hospitals, adding much-needed manpower to the existing military nursing services, the Queen Alexandra Imperial Military Nursing Service and the Territorial Force Nursing Service. Training was expedited and was basic in comparison to fully qualified nurses. A probationary period of two weeks tested mettle – cooking, cleaning, laundry work and a range of medical procedures were all included in the VAD's job description – and volunteers were expected to serve for three months, though many stayed much longer. Initially, few VADs were sent to the Front, where their inexperience was considered a disadvantage, but as the war progressed, and the requirement for nurses increased, the role of VAD evolved towards greater responsibility. From 9,000 members in August 1914, the organisation had swelled to 23,000 nurses and 18,000 hospital orderlies by 1918, with many VADs serving in France, Gallipoli and Mesopotamia. For middle- and upper-class girls keen to contribute to the war effort, nursing was seen as a worthy and respectable calling, and joining as a VAD meant a fast track to working in a hospital without the long years of study, training and examinations. For those from a privileged background, the discipline and arduous hours were challenging, but enthusiasm was at a high ebb. Eve, writing to Betty at the end of November 1914,

talked of all those young women who were anxious to go and 'nurse the wounded, or anyway brush his hair and wash his poor dear face for him. They've got long waiting lists at Boulogne and Calais of volunteers with hospital training who're all willing to be or do anything to get over.' In the same month, she reported: 'nursing's once again the thing … such well-known young women as Lady Betty Keppel and Diana Manners and Monica Grenfell and one of the Tree girls, and not exactly the wall-flower group amongst our maidens, who're doing the Florence Nightingale touch.'

A young VAD starting for a service hospital abroad could consult *The Queen* magazine, which in early 1917 printed, in letter form, advice on the essential items to pack:

Banners requesting passers-by outside Charing Cross Hospital to keep quiet for the wounded. (Robert Hunt/ME)

Carter's Self-Propelling Chair was just one of many items to offer comfort and aid mobility for wounded soldiers. (ME)

'Whatever else you sacrifice to the necessity of cramming everything into a cabin trunk and a hold-all, find room somehow for a good supply of shoes. They wear out fearfully quickly in a camp hospital, and even if you work in a permanent building the chances are that your mess and quarters will be some distance away, so that you have a good stretch of dust or mud to traverse several times daily.' They also recommended a good macintosh, a parasol, thermometers, forceps, probe, spatula and a glass syringe.

As for Diana, Raymond Asquith's reservations were disproved and, in fact, she pulled off the role with aplomb. Naturally, a picture of her in uniform appeared in *The Tatler*, a soft-focus, beatific angel of mercy to inspire romantic notions about the glamour of nursing in any young girl. *The Sketch* talked of 'The New Diana'. 'Lady Diana Manners used to be the Botticelli of the Bath Club. Now she turns up there in nurse's dress. Incidentally, she is convincing many doubters that a uniform can be extremely becoming.' Another photograph by Rita Martin of Diana in exquisite evening clothes was published under

the heading, 'Deserter of the Drawing-Room for War: A Society Nurse'. But the reality of Diana's role at Guy's was anything but glamorous and the reality of long shifts caring for London's sick was in stark contrast to the gilded existence to which she was accustomed. From cleaning infected wounds to bathing fractious toddlers, she admitted her inexperience of basic chores in her memoirs: 'I seemed to have done nothing practical in all my twenty years.' She acquitted herself well, claiming to do everything the 'upper nurses were allowed, except dispensing', while *The Sketch* reported that 'all her hospital patients swear by her'. She even managed to squeeze in some socialising, writing in advance to friends in order to plan rendezvous, dashing out after her shift to find a taxi magically at the hospital gates waiting to whisk her off to De Keyser's restaurant or the Cheshire Cheese on Fleet Street.

Later in 1915, her mother opened the family's London home in Arlington Street to be used as a hospital and Diana left Guy's to nurse there. The Rutland Hospital housed ten patients in the golden drawing room and another twelve in the ballroom. It later

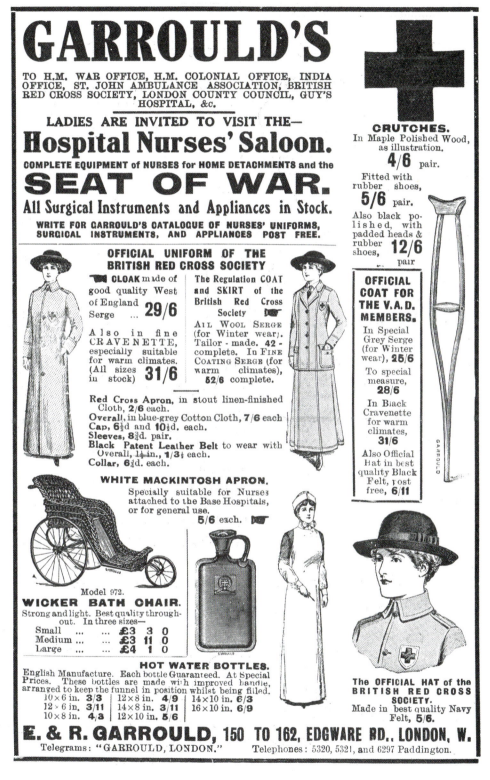

Whether embarking for the Front or working in a hospital on the home front, a trip to Garrould's on Edgware Road in London would prepare a First World War nurse for any eventuality. (Hearst Magazines (UK)/ME)

expanded to take in another twelve officers and the family's ducal seat, Belvoir Castle, also became a convalescent home. Diana found it 'soft and demoralising after Spartan Guy's', but for the patients, the well-appointed surroundings must have been most welcoming.

Arlington Street and Belvoir Castle were just two of literally hundreds of private residences given over for war purposes, both in London and around the country. The rush to offer houses for use as hospitals, charity headquarters and convalescent homes was so overwhelming in early months that the War Office was forced to announce in May 1915 that 'no further offers of private houses need to be made' (*The Queen*, 1915).

It did seem as if literally every stately home in the country had become a hospital of some kind or another. Lady Katherine Thynne, daughter of the 4th Marquess of Bath, was pictured with wounded soldiers in the magnificent baronial hall at Longleat in 1917, while up in Cheshire, Eaton Hall, the vast pile of the Duke of Westminster, was used to accommodate wounded soldiers too. The tennis courts at Cliveden in Buckinghamshire were converted into wards for the Duchess of Connaught's Red Cross Hospital and at Highclere in Berkshire (more familiar in recent years to television viewers as the setting of *Downton Abbey*), Almina, the Countess of Carnarvon was photographed reading at the bedside of a wounded soldier. Highbury, the Birmingham home of the late Sir Joseph Chamberlain MP, provided convivial amusements for recovering soldiers who entertained themselves with the help of the house's fine billiard tables. Across Britain, halls, drawing rooms and ballrooms that had once hosted dances and country house parties were now filled with beds, patients, nurses and wheelchairs; unsurprisingly, the illustrated magazines delighted in such an incongruous contrast.

Eve ticked off a number of offered properties in *The Tatler*'s 19 August 1914 issue, listing Taplow Court, the home of Lord and Lady Desborough (who would lost their two elder sons, Julian and Billy Grenfell in the war), Lady Sackville was fitting up the great hall at Knole, and Lord Londonderry was lending Seaham Hall. By mid-November, she noted a large number were already up and running:

> Eaton Hall's now a hospital, so's Highclere Castle, where at this time of the year Lady Carnarvon's usually giving shooting parties, and Lord Rosebery at Dalmeny and Lord Ellesmere at his Lancashire place have a lot of wounded in charge … Mr John Walter – he's the son of the man who owned 'The Times' before Lord Northcliffe's day, you know – has several wounded at Bear Wood, and Lord Gerard, Lord Stradbroke, Lord Newton, Lord Derby, Lord Normanton and Lord Onslow are just a few more among the many hosts of our valiant wounded.

The aforementioned Lord Stradbroke was the owner of Henham Hall in Suffolk, where his wife, Lady Stradbroke, took control as matron, efficiently superintending the hospital which, due to its location, received convoys of wounded directly from France. After being treated at Henham, they would then be passed on to the Red Cross once sufficiently well. In April 1915 she was pictured in *The Tatler*, dressed in her uniform, holding bombs dropped near the hall. If Henham Hall escaped German bombs, it did not fare so well with the wrecking ball. It was demolished in 1953.

In London there was barely a Mayfair square or street that did not have a hospital: 'In Park Lane half of the houses seem to be hospitals,' observed Eve. There was the famous King Edward VII Hospital for officers in Grosvenor Gardens, founded during the Boer War and

The Coulter Hospital in Grosvenor Square was opened in September 1915 in a house lent for the purpose by Sir Walter Greenwell. The hospital, which was overseen by Lady Juliet Duff and had space for 100 beds for officers, had unusual origins, being founded by an American psychic, Charlotte Herbine, who had been advised by the spirit of her family doctor to go to London. Many society women nursed at the Coulter Hospital and here a group pose on the balcony for a photograph. Miss Teale is pictured holding a copy of *The Tatler*. (Illustrated London News/ME)

do you think it may have an opposite effect? I mean, why hurry out of such luxurious surroundings,' she wondered mischievously.

But there were buildings other than private residences put to good use as well. Several Oxford colleges, the Guildhall, Hampton Court Palace, the Crystal Palace and Alexandra Palace were all used as hospital accommodation and at the Tate Gallery at Millbank, convalescents could enjoy a little culture with their recuperation as they read or played games under the old Masters still hanging on the walls. The Royal Academy at Burlington House, gave over seven of its galleries for the Red Cross Central Workrooms, where hospital supplies were made and collected for distribution to hospitals. Over the course of the war, over 1,200 voluntary workers, none giving less than four half days a week, worked and made to a standard pattern no less than 73,216 garments and 700,102 bandages. When wool became scarce, the workrooms enterprisingly experimented with dog hair, spinning it into yarn on site!

Lord Tredegar, himself a soldier and nephew of a Crimean veteran, even fitted out his yacht as a hospital ship. Some wealthy and particularly altruistic people gave, rather than simply loaned houses. John Leigh, a member of the great Oldham cotton firm, presented two houses to the Red Cross; one of them, Woodbourne near Manchester, became the John Leigh Memorial Hospital for shell-shocked soldiers.

run by its namesake's former mistress, Agnes Keyser. During the First World War, the hospital expanded to take up four houses, where, according to Eve, 'officers pay only 5s. a year for the right of treatment there, and it's real first-class treatment, needless to say.' Equally prestigious was the American Hospital for Officers at Lancaster Gate, which could boast the cream of London society in attendance: 'Lady Harcourt as matron, Mrs John Astor as head pantry-maid, Lady Randolph Churchill as chairman and the Duchess of Marlborough and a few more millionairesses and things as "workers". White panelled walls and blue silk hangings ought to help our woundeds get well very quick – or

In 1915, a new hospital opened in a former workhouse in Covent Garden, where all the staff, from radiographers and pharmacists to orderlies and transport officers, were women. The Endell Street Military Hospital was founded by two prominent suffragettes, Dr Flora Murray and Dr Louisa Garrett Anderson, daughter of the pioneering female doctor, Elizabeth Garrett Anderson and niece of the suffragist, Millicent Fawcett. After successfully running two hospitals in Wimereaux and Paris for the French Red Cross they were invited to do the same in England under the Royal Army Medical Corps, and the 573-bed hospital received more than 24,000 casualties direct from Charing Cross Station during the course of the war. Another London hospital, this time located in exclusive Mayfair, had equally interesting, but perhaps more unusual origins. The Coulter Hospital at No. 5 Grosvenor Square accommodated 100 officers and had Lady Juliet Duff as its Commandant. It was founded in September 1915 by Mrs Charlotte Herbine, an American psychic from Indianapolis, and was named after Dr Coulter, the spirit of a family physician with whom Mrs Herbine had communicated with since she was a child. A number of society women nursed there, including Miss Marjorie Lowther – niece of the Earl of Lonsdale, who, in September 1917, married George Guest, 8th Baron Rodney – and the Hon. Mrs Michael Scott, formerly Cecilia Bruton, wife of the youngest son of the Earl of Eldon.

The press had a particular fascination with British women who had crossed over to France and Belgium to set up hospitals or provide nursing services closer to the seat of war, though it took time for female medical units to be accepted by the British Army. Dr Elsie Inglis, an Edinburgh doctor, was famously told, 'My good lady, go home and sit still – no petticoats here', when she explained her desire to set up the Scottish Women's Hospitals unit to provide aid on the Western Front to an official at Whitehall. Good connections helped and some of the first women to cross over to France were a small troop of members of the First Aid Nursing Yeomanry who worked instead on behalf of the Belgian Army, which was happy to accept their services. Many FANYs came from privileged backgrounds but were renowned for their

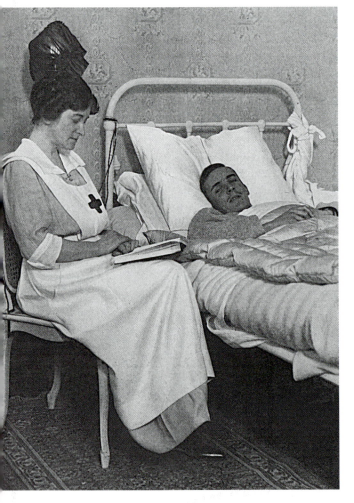

Almina Herbert, Countess of Carnarvon (1876–1969), wife of the 5th Earl, pictured reading at the bedside of a wounded officer at Highclere Castle in Berkshire, where a large portion of the house had been turned into hospital for the wounded. (Illustrated London News/ME)

One-legged and one-armed men playing billiards at Queen Mary's Hospital in Roehampton. Known as the human repair factory, the hospital specialised in fitting amputee soldiers with artificial limbs. Men were not released from the hospital until they had undergone a process of rehabilitation and were fully satisfied with their new arms or legs. (Illustrated London News/ME)

gutsy and daring exploits at the Front where they gamely drove ambulances, carried stretchers and took on the running of first-aid posts, hospitals, soup kitchens and canteens. Though only numbering 120 by the end of the war, the corps could nevertheless boast seventeen Military medals, a Légion d'honneur and twenty-seven Croix de Guerre awarded to its members. It was, perhaps, more than appropriate that Grace McDougall, Commandant of the corps, entitled her memoirs of this period *Nursing Adventures.*

The Duchess of Westminster – formerly Shelagh Cornwallis-West – whom Diana Manners had hoped to join in France, was one of the most high-profile nurses of the war, not least because her Red Cross hospital was housed in the Casino of the fashionable Le Touquet, 'where in peace time the play runs very high, and there are sometimes a score of tables surrounded by eager crowds'. With initially room for 160 beds for patients, and the opulent chandeliers still hanging from the high ceilings, it is little wonder *The Sketch* described it as 'quite the perfection of a ward',

and in war, as in peacetime, Le Touquet was a wonderful tonic: '… the surgeons say that it is astonishing how quickly wounds heal and bones set in the quietude and the splendid atmosphere of the forest by the sea.'

Shelagh, whose sister, Daisy, Princess of Pless had married a German prince and was consequently nursing German soldiers in Berlin, took her role seriously. She was pictured at her sewing machine, busy making supplies for the hospital, and according to *The Tatler* gave £1,000 and guaranteed £400 a month to keep it running. The *Illustrated War News* described her as 'quite one of the most energetic of these voluntary helpers … an average of something like 350 wounded are cared for in this hospital which is officially recognised as one of the best in France, and the Duchess herself, assisted by Mrs Whitburn, gives particular care to the linen-room'. The X-ray and electro-therapeutics department carried out pioneering work, and the accompanying description of the Duchess and her staff in *The Sketch* in March 1918 noted that 'all the ladies are expert masseuses'.

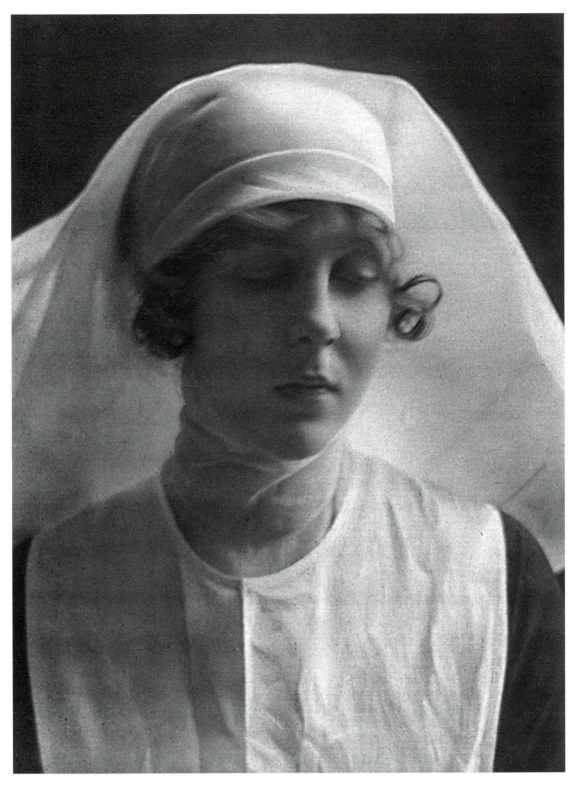

Lady Diana Manners (1891–1981) was a ubiquitous figure on the smart, social scene but 'abandoned the drawing room' for nursing at Guy's Hospital during the war. She later moved to the Rutland Hospital at her family's London home. (Illustrated London News/ME)

Mrs Whitburn of linen cupboard fame (Clarissa Sofer Whitburn) had, in fact, an inauspicious start to her nursing career in France when she contracted chickenpox on the way over. She spent several weeks in Paris recovering before being able to join the Duchess!

The presence of such prominent females close to the Front naturally concerned the authorities, who must have feared for their safety: 'they have to be watched over and protected from possible mishap with a care which it isn't considered necessary to take about nurses and other women workers less in the public eye. The Duchess of Westminster of course, has taken her faithful wolfhound with her, and a copy of Longfellow's poems, and Sir Thomas Lipton was her pilot across the Channel', reported Eve in October 1914. Whether Shelagh did indeed take strength from Longfellow's poetry is unrecorded but she was frequently photographed with her dog. She also emerged from the war with a new husband. Her marriage to the difficult and overbearing Bendor had been foundering for some time, with only the war delaying the inevitable. In June 1919, the pair divorced and in January the following year she married, in a brief ceremony, Captain James Lewis, a 30-year-old RAF Captain who she first met when he was stationed close to her hospital.

Shelagh's hospital garnered much publicity and her work received public recognition when she was awarded the CBE, but she was by no means the only peeress abroad. Millicent, Duchess of Sutherland had been one of the great society beauties of the late Victorian and Edwardian age, but she also had a passion for social reform, earning her the nicknames the 'Democratic Duchess' and 'Meddlesome Millie'. While Shelagh was still at her sewing machine in England, Millicent had travelled over to Belgium a few days after war had been declared, taking her ambulance

unit to Namur, where they nursed and cared for wounded Belgians in a convent as the town bore heavy bombardment and was eventually captured by advancing German troops. She escaped and later became director of No. 9 British Red Cross Hospital at Calais. For her outstanding efforts, she was awarded the Croix de Guerre, the Belgian Royal Red Cross and the British Red Cross medal.

Lady Helen Vincent, Viscountess D'Abernon, another celebrated socialite of the Edwardian era, exchanged her ballgowns for theatre scrubs when she trained as a nurse

Shelagh, Duchess of Westminster, pictured (centre) with her hospital staff in France where she ran her own hospital in the Casino at Le Touquet (known as No. 1 Red Cross, Duchess of Westminster's Hospital). The hospital pioneered many new methods of healing for wounded soldiers and had an electro-therapeutic department and X-ray department. All the nurses were expert masseuses. Others in the photograph are Captain Stone, the X-ray expert, with his orderlies, Miss Molesworth, the Duchess and Miss Richmond, VAD nurse. (Illustrated London News/ME)

Enough to make a modern-day medical professional reel in horror, smoking was positively encouraged, even in hospital. (Illustrated London News/ME)

anaesthetist. She served with the Red Cross in Europe, often in makeshift hospitals close to the Front, where she acquired a reputation as an undaunted professional in the operating room, helping to treat thousands of patients. There was Lady Dorothie Feilding, second of the seven daughters of the Earl and Countess of Denbigh, who served with the Munro British Red Cross Ambulance Corps, founded by Dr Hector Munro. Dorothie worked fearlessly to bring men from the firing line to casualty clearing stations, the details of which she recounted in her chatty letters home. Her cheerfulness and courage, not to mention her fluent French, were an asset to the team, and by January 1915 *The Sketch* was already commenting on 'Lady Dorothie's splendid record in France … characteristic of the keenness with which they (women) have all thrown themselves into the distractions of the field.' Lady Dorothie was joined at Dr Munro's

Ambulance by two extraordinary women, Elsie Knocker and Mairi Chisholm. The pair had met through a shared love of motorcycling, and broke away from Monro's team to independently set up their own first-aid dressing station in the cellar of a bombed house just 100 yards from the trenches at Pervyse, north of Ypres. Elsie concentrated on providing medical attention while Mairi transported injured soldiers to the base hospital 15 miles away, often in highly dangerous conditions. The bravery of the 'Madonnas of Pervyse' attracted journalists and photographers who sought them out for pictures, stories and quotes. They would periodically return to Britain to accept awards and raise funds for the establishment of more – and better – casualty clearing stations, which were so badly needed. No longer supported by the Belgian Red Cross, their own building was reinforced, complete with a new steel door from Harrods, with the help of these donations. During a brief spell in England in February 1918 they appeared on stage at the Alhambra Theatre in Leicester Square as part of a fundraising show organised by their friend, the actress Eva Moore.

But back in Flanders, their proximity to the Front meant they were vulnerable. On 17 March 1918, both women suffered badly in a gas attack (Elsie's beloved terrier did not survive). Now patients themselves, they had to be nursed back to health in England. Mairi attempted to return to carry on the work but was gassed again and the clearing station was closed. The pair's courageous and selfless activity on behalf of others earned them the military medal and the Order of Leopold II, personally awarded by King Albert of Belgium. In many ways, they had been lucky to survive. Other nurses abroad were not so lucky. Madge Neil Fraser, a distinguished lady golfer and International captain, died of fever while nursing in Serbia in 1915. Mrs Katherine Harley, sister of Lord French, was killed by an enemy shell in Monastir while working for the Red Cross. She had recently been decorated by General Sarrail in Salonika, in recognition of her work done with the Scottish Women's Hospital in Serbia. The danger of death was ever present for women working at the Front, though in comparison to men, fatalities were low. But nursing was physically taxing. Hours were long and sleep was often only snatched in short bursts; feet perpetually ached. It was not unusual for portraits to be featured in magazines such as *The Tatler* with an explanation that the sitter was 'taking a rest from strenuous war-work'. In Brighton, Eve observed it was 'the thing there now, you know, for worn-out women war-workers to take the air (with Pekes) in those very comfy, nicely-swung bath chairs that are really a great refuge from that seething crowd which adorns the Brighton front.'

Overall, women showed themselves more than up to the physical challenges of nursing. *The Queen* magazine, writing in 1915, recognised the benefits of female participation in sport in more recent years. 'It is fair to remind ourselves that what we have to be grateful for is not only the patriotism of our women, but the fact that for a good many years now they have played hockey and lawn tennis and golf so much that we have been able to draw upon a really vast supply of women in the best condition, hard enough to stand campaigning.' The pressing need to preserve the health and mental strength of the country's nurses soon came to be recognised and various clubs and hostels, where nurses could go to rest and recharge, began to appear to cater for this. In Ebury Street, Victoria, the Imperial Nurses' Club comprised a dining room 'with small tables with pretty delicately coloured tablecloths' (*The Queen*, 1917), a lounge with comfortable chairs, and a drawing room where informal concerts were held. Eve reported in 1918 that Devonshire House, where once upon a time only society's elite would have enjoyed the privilege of being inside to see its interior, had become the latest war-workers' club for VADs. 'They are to use, without entrance fee or subscription, the great shady garden AND the three tennis courts, and three of the big ground-floor rooms are given up to them for dining, drawing and writing rooms. It'll be a godsend, but – dear me! – ISN'T it enough to make its late chatelaine turn in her grave and ask what the world is coming to?' The repurposing of Devonshire House was just one of the many shifts in the accepted order of things brought about by the war.

The nation's medical workers showed themselves to be invaluable at every stage of a soldier's recovery, while the quantity and variety of injuries necessitated some pioneering work. In London, at No. 17 Mulberry

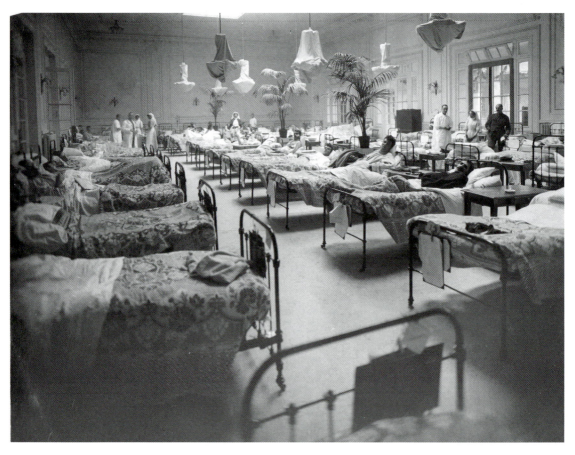

Once the playground of smart society, the chandeliers are temporarily covered up at the casino at Le Touquet, which became No. 1 British Red Cross Hospital run by the Duchess of Westminster for the duration of the war. Among the patients who were cared for here was the author J. R. R. Tolkien, who was suffering from trench fever. (David Cohen Fine Art/ME)

Walk in Chelsea, under the auspices of the Surgical Requisites Association, a group of women led by two sculptresses, Anne Acheson and Elinor Halle, worked voluntarily to invent anatomically accurate splints – 'to help Tommies' limbs heal better,' wrote *The Queen* in a long article about their association. In an excellent example of wartime recycling, the best material for making the papier mâché from which the splints were formed as old paper sugar bags, collected via the boy scouts and public appeals.

The very modern idea of colour therapy was introduced at Miss McCaul's hospital for wounded soldiers in Welbeck Street in 1917, with the opening of a special ward decorated

and furnished in a colour scheme specially planned by 'a well-known artist in decoration, Mr Kemp-Prossor, with a view to having a soothing, cheering effect on the nerves of the patients and so helping in their cure'. Walls were of lemon yellow, the ceiling a firmament blue and the floors and paintwork a soft, spring green. At the Duchess of Connaught's Hospital at Cliveden, Sister de Merrall, a Danish lady married to an English officer, practised a form of physiotherapy called Swedish treatment on wounded Canadian soldiers, who went through a variety of exercises to strengthen the muscles.

Mary Eleanor Gwynne Holford was so profoundly moved by her visit to a military

AN UNTIRING WORKER
On Behalf of Our Brave Wounded.

Yevonde, Victoria Street

MILLICENT DUCHESS OF SUTHERLAND

Who has been nursing in France since the very outbreak of war. The duchess established and runs a large hospital in France, to which she devotes unremitting energy and attention

Millicent, Duchess of Sutherland (1867–1955), society hostess and social reformer, who travelled to Belgium within days of the war's outbreak. She nursed and cared for the wounded in a convent in Naumur before setting up No. 9 Red Cross Hospital at Calais. (Illustrated London News/ME)

hospital that, she resolved afterwards, 'I will work for one object, and that is to start a hospital whereby all those who had the misfortune to lose a limb in this terrible war could be fitted with the most perfect artificial limbs human science could devise.' The 200-bed hospital she set up in Roehampton House became Queen Mary's Military Auxiliary Hospital and admitted its first twenty-five patients on 20 June 1915. It expanded rapidly and by the end of the war, the 'human repair factory' had 900 beds and a waiting list of 4,321. It began to develop a worldwide reputation as the leading limb fitting and rehabilitation centre for amputees. Not only were men enabled with the help of false limbs, the hospital was also committed to helping limbless men adapt and learn new skills such as carpentry and motor mechanics for life beyond the war. The same principle applied at St Dunstan's Hostel for blinded soldiers and sailors in Regent's Park, where again, men who had given their sight for their country learnt basket weaving, tray or mat making, and at the Lord Roberts Memorial Workshops, with eleven centres around the country, where self-sufficiency for disabled soldiers was encouraged and the inmates produced a vast range of products all of which could claim to be British-made.

The comfort, amusement and eventual rehabilitation of the most badly wounded remained one of the primary objectives of the war. Signs and banners outside city hospitals reminded passers-by to be quiet for the sake of the patients inside, and in Parliament, in January 1916, the Home Secretary was asked if he could do anything to curb noise in the capital, particularly the whistling for taxis, because of the disturbance to wounded men. 'Not that the wounded, the Tommies, anyway, mind noise quite so much as people think', commented *The Bystander*. 'The convalescents sit out in front of their London hospitals, in the middle of the roar and crash of traffic, and seem quite to enjoy it, and I've met some in country hospitals so bored stiff with the peace and quiet (or dullness) that they'd have given their heads for the sights and smells of any old city.' Whether in town or country, hospitals did their best to provide amusements for their patients. Visits from well-known stars of the stage or army entertainment troupes were arranged, sports days, sing-songs, donated board games and books, visitors and film screenings all helped to break up the monotony. In August 1918, the *Illustrated London News* carried an illustration on its front cover showing staff at an American base hospital in France projecting a Charlie Chaplin film onto the ceiling for the benefit of bedridden patients. At Christmas time, special efforts were made to ensure the wards were festive. *The Queen*, writing in November 1915, reminded readers that Christmas trees (being German) were out of favour, but pyramids of drums decorated with Allied flags were an alternative, while at Lady Juliet Duff's Coulter Hospital in Grosvenor Square, 'the big wards seemed transformed into fairy scenes, with glistening snowflakes filling the air, fluttering down from the ceiling and wreathing the pillars with snow-tipped garlands that might have been wrought by fairy fingers.' At another London hospital, a visit by Queen Alexandra on Christmas Day inspired patients to each wear a rose in their buttonhole. Fresh air was considered key to recovery and at the Royal Victoria Hospital, one of the largest dedicated military hospitals close to Southampton, patients were wheeled outside on their beds to greet the King during a royal visit. At many other country houses with extensive grounds, convalescents could while away the hours sitting out on the lawns, though as *The Bystander* implied, it could be a tedious if scenic way to spend a convalescence.

For some whose injuries were not life changing, a spell in hospital must have been a welcome respite from the horrors of war and a chance to mentally, as well as physically, recover; something which the War Office, against commonly held assumptions, did in fact recognise. By November 1914, Eve was reporting that Lord Kitchener had 'decided to put a curb on the ambition of some of our men to get back to front at the earliest possible moment. Quite a lot who have returned broke down within a week. They hadn't reckoned with their nerves, which this war strains as no war ever did before. So the order's now gone forth that three or four month's leave's to be taken, whatever happens, and a good many I'm told, are to stay here altogether to train the new army'.

With these extended periods of leave, 'our dear woundeds', as Eve often described them, were a familiar sight in their uniform of blue flannel and red tie – at the theatre, in motor cars being taken for a drive or being pushed in wheelchairs through London's parks or at seaside resorts. Magazine advertisements suggested a wide variety of convalescent aids, from Dryad Cane Furniture and Carter's Self-Propelling Chairs to Allwin's Folding Wheelchairs or the Carbrek Utility and Bed Table, all to ease mobility and make rest more bearable.

It was one of the greatest tragedies of the war that many of the lives that had been saved by careful and tender nursing were then snuffed out by the influenza epidemic which swept ferociously round the world just as the war was ending. Lady Diana Manners, soon to leave her duties as a nurse behind her, wrote to her husband-to-be, Duff Cooper, that 'this pneumonia plague is ferocious. Lovely Pamela Greer, nee Fitzgerald, dead in three days...' By December 1918, *The Tatler* was reporting on a number of people in society who had been affected by the epidemic. Some of them had been nurses themselves, such as Mrs Dubosc Taylor, who had turned her house in Portland Square into a hospital and had fatally caught influenza while nursing in France. Miss Lavender Sloane-Stanley, 'who had been doing excellent work as a VAD', was laid up after a serious attack while war-working in Winchester. Lady Victoria Brady, the only daughter of the Earl and Countess of Limerick, was another victim, as was the millionaire Sir Richard Sutton, one of the richest men in England, who owned sizeable chunks of Mayfair real estate. He served as a Captain in the 1st Life Guards, was wounded twice, served as ADC to General Sir Henry Rawlinson and was awarded the Military Cross in January 1917. Having safely come through the perils of the campaign in France, he succumbed to influenza and died of pneumonia, aged twenty-seven, just when peace was in sight.

Food

The year of 1917 was a good year for marrows: weeks of rain through late summer, the same rain that had turned the battlefields at Ypres into a quagmire, resulted in a vegetable glut back at home. *The Queen* magazine was optimistic that the abundance could be transformed into jam; a tasty treat to brighten the austere culinary landscape of wartime Britain. 'It is to be hoped that the Food Production Department may see its way to rescind the decision which has apparently been made that jam-making sugar allowances may not be used for making preserves of vegetable marrows… With the addition of ginger and lemon, marrow jam is quite good, and nothing that can add to the store of more or less sweet foods, especially, should be under a ban.'

For Great War Britain, food shortages, and the measures put in place to remedy the problem, would increasingly impact on people's daily lives. Sugar was one of a number of foods in short supply and was the first to come under compulsory rationing on 31 December 1917, followed later by meat, fats and bacon. Marrow jam, according to a recipe published in *The Bystander* two years earlier, required a pound of sugar per five pounds of vegetable. Cooks would have to instead transform them into chips or soups, or stuff them with mushrooms or minced meat.

Early in the war, prices had inflated dramatically; bread, for example, the staple food of the working classes, increased by a halfpenny on a 4*d* loaf in just a couple of days in 1914, and by June 1917 had risen to an all-time high of 11½*d*. The fundamental problem lay with the fact that many basic foods had been imported before the war. In the case of sugar, the entire supply came from abroad, with almost two-thirds from Germany and Austria. Reliance on foreign imports for around 60 per cent of its food was Britain's Achilles heel, a fact ruthlessly exploited by the Germans who, as the war progressed, operated a relentless strategy of U-boat attacks on merchant ships, hoping to eventually starve Britain into submission. The problem was a very real one; the 'submarine menace' succeeded in sinking an average 300,000 tonnes of Britain-bound shipping every month and a poor North American wheat harvest in 1916 exacerbated the situation. Those who could afford to hoarded food, despite exhortations from the government not to do so, and newly solvent war workers were frustrated that there was very little to actually spend their wages on. As demand rose and supplies decreased, shopkeepers were accused of unpatriotic profiteering and queues soon became a daily irritation. A Cabinet Committee on Food Supplies was formed on

7 August 1914 to fix maximum prices for key commodities but despite fervent criticism of hoarders and profiteers in the press, it was not until December 1916 that the Ministry of Food was formed, with Lord Devonport (succeeded by Lord Rhondda) appointed as Food Controller. Devonport launched an economy campaign to encourage frugal housekeeping and issued an appeal for voluntary rationing, where citizens were asked to restrict their consumption to a weekly maximum of 4lb of bread, 2½lb of meat and ½lb of sugar.

The 'Eat Less Bread' campaign was even supported by the King, who issued an official proclamation declaring that members of the royal household would, where possible, reduce the consumption of bread and the use of flour in pastry. The Palace's commitment to the cause also extended to giving up alcohol and turning the royal flowerbeds into vegetable plots. In December 1917, *The Queen* reproduced the following pledge, part of a campaign devised by Sir Arthur Yapp, the Director of Food Economy: 'I realise that economy in the use of all Food and the checking of all waste helps my Country to complete Victory, and I promise to do all in my power to assist this Campaign for National Safety.' Householders who took this pledge could apply directly to Sir Arthur Yapp directly for a membership card, certificate and badge embossed with the words 'I Eat Less Bread'. The latter was fashioned out of card and ribbon

after a metal design was rejected due to the Ministry of Munitions being unable to guarantee sufficient supplies to manufacture them.

It was almost impossible, though, to discourage the labouring man to cut down on his daily bread and the campaign's success was limited, despite royal endorsement. The Ministry's measures ranged from banning the throwing of rice at weddings to restricting the size of cake portions in tea-shops to measly 1½oz slices. Meals in restaurants were restricted to two courses at lunchtime and three courses in the evening, though people who could afford to could still eat well in London restaurants. Phrynette of *The Sketch* reported in March 1918 of how she had:

The body-building power of Bovril was tested out for real by one male munitions worker who drank the beef extract drink over a year and emerged 'the very picture of splendid health and energy.' Published in the *Illustrated London News* in 1916, this advertisement also reminds readers that despite the rising cost of beef, the price of their product had not increased since the beginning of the war. (Illustrated London News/ME)

BRITAIN'S FOOD IN THE LAST WAR: RATIONED AND UNRATIONED ITEMS.

Sugar is RATIONED
½ lb Weekly for an Adult or Child.

Tea.
Use Tea with care.
Use Coffee and Cocoa more freely than Tea.

Butter and Margarine are RATIONED.
← Weekly Ration.
4 ozs. for an Adult or Child.

Bread for Men on ordinary industrial or other manual work 7 lbs. per head per week.
1 lb. Daily Ration

Use Potatoes freely.

Bread for Women on ordinary industrial work or in domestic service 4 lbs. per head per week.
9 ozs. Daily Ration.

Milk.
Use with care.

Jam
Use moderately.

Eggs.
No limit.

Oatmeal Rice &c
TAPIOCA SAGO
Use with care.

Fruit Use freely
Bottled Fruit with care.

Cheese
Use with care.

Use Vegetables freely.

Fish. No restrictions.

A DIAGRAMMATIC DRAWING OF BRITAIN'S RATIONED AND UNRATIONED FORMS OF FOOD DURING THE WAR OF 1914-18—THE UNRATIONED ITEMS SHOWN BEING ON A VOLUNTARY BASIS, AND INCLUDING FISH, VEGETABLES, FRESH FRUIT AND EGGS.

Continued.]
England has not, as we write, announced details of food rationing. Food control committees, however, are being set up by each local authority. Each committee is to consist of fifteen members, to include five members representative of the local retail trades. The remaining ten, of whom at least two are to be women, are to be representative of all classes of persons in the area. The powers and duties of the committee are to be assigned to them by the Board of Trade. As regards the comparisons of England and Germany in 1918, it will be observed that, except for sugar, where the rations were about the same, the British quantities were far superior. An interesting point of the British ration schemes in force in the last war was the voluntary basis for many of the items.

A diagram from the *Illustrated London News* in 1939, shortly after the outbreak of the Second World War, looking back at the foods that were rationed and those that remained freely available during the Great War. Rationing and 'digging for victory' had already seen the nation through one conflict and it would do so during another. (Illustrated London News/ME)

Dined last night at Treiglie's, the little Italian restaurant in Church Street where Caruso always had a table when he was singing in London. Time changes, but the quality of the food here never. Lord Rhondda may decide the weight of what we have (and every rule is observed), but I don't think the threat of being shot in the Tower would persuade the proprietor to serve hot food on cold plates, or place badly prepared dishs before his guests. Surely it's a national economy to have plate so carefully prepared that you never waste a crumb and actually long to lick your plate (oh hush!).

The feeding of stray dogs was forbidden and there was some criticism about the keeping of pet dogs. Eve, who like any society lady had her own canine best friend, Tou-tou, was indignant on behalf of her dog-keeping sorority in May 1918, regarding 'all this fuss about no dog food' when, according to her, the food consumed by the 'swarms' of enemy alien women and children in Britain 'would keep in luxury all the British dogs in the country for years!'

In February 1918, the threat of perilously severe shortages hastened a move towards compulsory rationing, first in London and the Home Counties, which had a concentrated population of 10 million, and then to other areas of the country. Each individual was issued with ration cards for meat, fats and sugar and were allocated to a particular grocer or butcher, to ensure equal distribution. The *Illustrated London News* issued helpful pictorial diagrams illustrating what foods were and were not rationed ('vegetables are plentiful')

and also printed others to demonstrate how in comparison to starving Germany, British rations were positively luxurious.

The main spokesperson for *The Queen* magazine on food matters was Constance Peel who, since 1913, had been engaged as their Editor of the Household Department, writing under the name Mrs C.S. Peel. She held the post for seventeen years and through her food column, entitled 'Le Ménage', as well as her own memoirs, gives a detailed insight into what Britain ate during the four years of war. 'I spent considerable time in experimenting in the use of cocoa-butter, beans, war-margarine, and war-flour, and, because fuel was now strictly rationed and costly, in such dishes as did not need long cooking', she recalled, and indeed, week after week, 'Le Ménage' was filled with resourceful suggestions for economical meals

Parcels from home were eagerly anticipated and the contents often eased the monotony of rations. In this illustration by Fortunino Matania from *The Sphere*, January 1918, a group of British soldiers share the contents of a hamper that has been delivered to them at the Front. (Illustrated London News/ME)

and menus as well as fuel saving ideas. In 1917, her experience led her to be appointed a Co-Director of the Women's Service at the Ministry of Food along with Maud Pember-Reeves (wife of the Minister of Labour and Education in New Zealand and author of the book *Round About a Pound a Day*), a position which she held while continuing to write for *The Queen*. Their objective was to 'assist the people to understand, first, why there was a food shortage, and secondly, the best means of meeting it' during this period of voluntary rationing between March 1917 and March 1918. 'The task,' she explained, 'was to increase production and to reduce consumption and waste, and not only waste occasioned by the throwing away of food fit for human consumption, but also that occasioned by bad or improper cooking.' During these twelve months, Constance, not in the greatest of health (she would later be diagnosed with diabetes), travelled the length and breadth of the country as best she could on the seriously taxed railway network, to make an impressive 176 public addresses. She was, by all accounts, a moving, powerful and intuitive speaker, sensitive to the audiences she was speaking to and mindful not to patronise working-class audiences. As well as this and her work for *The Queen*, she and Mrs Pember-Reeves organised cookery demonstrations, exhibitions on war economy and produced leaflets which were distributed in their millions. It was an impressive achievement and one that prompted Lord Northcliffe to invite her to take up the post of Women's Editor at the *Daily Mail* in 1918.

This patriotic Christmas cake, adorned with the Union and French flags, featured in *The Queen* magazine in November 1914. The abundant icing would be a short-lived luxury as sugar became increasingly scarce, becoming the first food item to be subject to compulsory rationing in 1918. (Hearst Magazines (UK)/ME)

A witty and topical fancy dress outfit for 1918, themed around the prevalent issue of food control. (Grenville Collins Postcard Collection/ME)

Her advice in *The Queen* was prescriptive but always inventive, tackling different ingredients each week, suggesting novel and economical methods of cooking and planning out menus for parties or Christmas dinners. Some recipes sound rather delicious; others unpalatable. There were cakes without eggs, cakes bulked out with potato and cakes cooked by steaming or frying, or made during cake-making parties in order to save fuel. Jam without sugar, an oxymoron if ever there was one, was another suggestion and in among various methods of preserving vegetables was one that involved burying them in sand. Readers were encouraged to experiment with fuel saving haybox cookery, an idea first proposed by Mrs Beeton in the nineteenth century, and recipes for soups, the eating of which was enthusiastically encouraged, included turnip, French soufflé and the bewilderingly odd-sounding semolina. Her

opinions were forceful, but sensible. When writing about the great British breakfast she confessed she found it an unnecessary extravagance, 'therefore in reply to several correspondents who deplore the cost of bacon, eggs and fish I ask, "must you continue to eat hot dishes at breakfast?"' She suggested coffee or cocoa, wholemeal bread and butter or porridge with jam or stewed fruit, 'as nourishing a meal as anyone can really require.' Her sound advice still holds good a century on.

The Queen magazine took up the 'Eat Less Bread' campaign with gusto. Subliminal messages, such as 'One Slice Less', appeared at random in the magazine each week and on 28 July 1917, 'Le Ménage' published a seventeen-point guide to saving bread taken from 'Food Economy' by J. Grant Ramsaym, Principal of the Institute of Hygiene. Number six stated bluntly that 'Waste of Food is a sin' and worse than stealing; point ten suggested

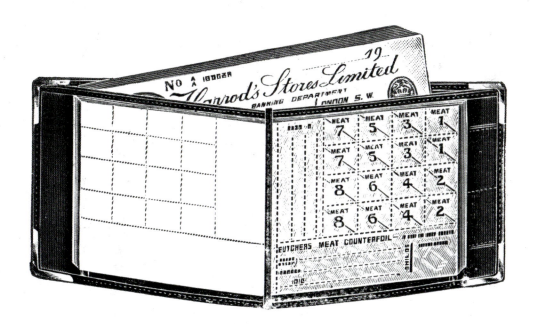

A ration book holder from Harrods department store, available in a number of variations. The simplest form provided a back pocket for a chequebook and a pocket for notes, registration cards and visiting cards. They were available in pigskin, morocco leather or khaki cloth. (Hearst Magazines (UK)/ME)

that most people wasted bread simply by eating it too quickly, 'without thorough mastication'. More obvious still was the plain fact that 'white bread is not economical' and that turning the loaf down on its cut side prevented drying out.

The magazine was keen to encourage its readers to experiment with freely available produce. In October 1917, it published a number of recipes, including Stewed Chub, Carp en Casserole and Dace à L'Ecossaise,

using coarse fish which had fallen out of favour due to the belief that those fish caught in 'sluggish streams' tasted awful. In August the same year, Mrs Peel highlighted the abundance of venison due to the absence of gamekeepers, deer stalkers and ghillies who had left their jobs to fight for the country. Deer were posing a threat to crops and farmers had been granted permission to shoot them, resulting in a commission, set up under the guidance of the Marquis of Breadalbane, Lord-Lieutenant of the County of Argyll, to arrange for the fair and systematic distribution of supplies of venison meat around the country at half the cost of beef. In anticipation of the forthcoming feast, there were recipes for jugged venison, pies, patties and, in homage to the Lord-Lieutenant, Venison à la Breadalbane, a hearty casserole of venison and pearl barley. There was also a surplus of game birds, particularly as the outbreak of war in 1914 coincided with the start of the shooting season, but grouse and partridge were not to everyone's taste. Eve relayed reports she had heard that in hospitals, 'The patients don't like eating it and the cooks don't like cooking it … and poor people don't care for game of any kind.' With tongue firmly in cheek, she concluded, 'I suppose the people who shoot it will have to eat it, and nothing else. How bored we shall all get with our grouse and our partridges. But even this sacrifice, I suppose we shall cheerfully undertake.'

It was one of the ironies of war that normally luxurious foods such as venison became relatively more affordable while basic foodstuffs became increasingly scarce. Foods such as chicken, ducklings, peaches and hothouse melons all fell in price, due in part to the lack of

Dorothy Constance Peel (1868–1934) aka Mrs C.S. Peel, who wrote the weekly column, Le Ménage, on cooking and food economy during the war. She was appointed a co-director of the women's service in the Ministry of Food along with Maud Pember Reeves (1865–1953) in 1917. (ME)

SPECIAL OFFER
for Troops at the Front.

Your soldier friends will appreciate the gift of a few bottles of Lea & Perrins' Sauce to use with their War Rations. It makes Bully Beef appetizing, and when mixed with jam is an excellent substitute for chutnee.

Messrs. Lea & Perrins will send

one dozen special bottles
(half ordinary size)

LEA & PERRINS' SAUCE

The original and genuine "Worcestershire"

securely packed direct to any member of the Expeditionary Force on the Western Front,

carriage paid for 5/-

The case will be forwarded immediately on receipt of Postal order with full name and regimental address of intended recipient.

LEA & PERRINS,
11, Midland Rd., WORCESTER.

Advertisement for Lea & Perrins Worcestershire sauce, suggested as a perfect gift for soldiers at the front to use with their war rations – 'makes bully beef appetizing and when mixed with jam makes an excellent substitute for chutnee [chutney].' The advert has a special offer for troops at the front – a box of one dozen special bottles at a half size for five shillings, carriage paid for. (Illustrated London News/ME)

entertaining. In an address that Mrs Peel gave at St James's Theatre in March 1917, she spoke convincingly that if expensive foods were within the reach of larger incomes, then there was no objection to richer members of the population taking this course, particularly as it stopped them 'competing for the food of the poor'. By eating foods like oysters, eggs, game birds and poultry, it meant, with a logic that unavoidably emphasised rigid class distinctions of the time, greater quantities of plainer fare were left for the masses. 'The more the rich can avoid the consumption of flour in all its forms, the larger will be the balance left for the working classes of the country.' These types of luxury foods suggested as sustenance for the rich were just the kind of delicacies included in food hampers advertised by Fortnum & Mason for delivery to fighting men. For 15s customers could send a lucky recipient at the Front delights such as Herrings in Tomatoes, Camp Pie, Tongue and Gooseberry Pudding. For

The famous Maconochie's stew of beef and vegetables was a favourite source of sustenance in the trenches but was eaten at home too, one of the numerous time-saving and economical 'ready meals' gaining popularity during the war. (Hearst Magazines (UK)/ME)

Christmas that year, 30s could buy a Christmas box containing real turtle soup, roast turkey, Christmas pudding and brandy sauce. In her memoirs, Lady Diana Cooper (then Manners) described the food she gathered together for a Sunday picnic with her future husband, Duff, on a day off from her nursing work. Comprising eggs in jelly, chicken breasts, rationed butter, fresh bread, strawberries and cream from her family's Belvoir estate and a big bottle of hock cup, she wept when the bottom of the box in which she was carrying this feast gave way and her picnic ended up on the pavement of a St James's street. In comparison to a menu suggested at a cookery demonstration at a working women's club in South East London reported by *The Queen* in December 1915 – potato soup, savoury lentils and currant pudding – it seems that war did little to change the stark disparity of eating habits between the classes.

Eve in *The Tatler* found the whole notion of well-heeled aristocrats practising war economy faintly ridiculous. Commenting on the same meeting Mrs Peel had spoken at and the concept of voluntary rationing, she admitted:

I just COULDN'T see the Duchess of Rutland, f'rinstance, or her Grace of Abercorn, or even Lady Lansdowne, who all "supported" on the platform, taking that intimate an interest in their stockpots which, 'cording to the PM's wife (Mrs Lloyd George) is the Frenchwoman's secret. And I'm making a tour of Mayfair first fine morning just to see, in how many Mayfair windows they've stuck up the Food Controller's card.

This card, on which was printed a pledge of 'In honour bound we adopt the national scale of voluntary rations', was designed to be displayed prominently as a show of economical solidarity. Of society's commitment to such a cause, Eve was clearly sceptical. At the National Economy Exhibition held in July 1917, she was unimpressed by Lady Rhondda's 'latest suggestion in the way of self-strafing – a whole foodless day for all non-war-workers. Enuff to drive the laziest to war work, isn't it?'

But she, like many, echoed the growing preoccupation with food and its procurement as the war carried onto into its fourth year. A *Sketch* reader wrote into Phrynette with a poem that summed up the mood of the nation:

My Tuesdays are meatless
My Wednesdays are eatlesss
I am getting more eatless each day
My home it is heatless
My bed it is sheetless
All sent to the YMCA.

The bar-rooms are treatless
My coffee is sweetless
Each day I get poorer and wiser
My stockings are feetless
My trousers are seatless
My God, how I do hate the Kaiser!

In 1918, Eve wrote to Betty about dinner parties:

Quite one of THE signs of the times, isn't it, the way we all talk about food these days? At dinner-parties, 'stead of pretendin' as we used to that it was the company of your hosts you came for, no one cares who knows that it's your rations we want.

And as course succeeds course, louder and louder grow our shrieks of joy and welcome. 'What: caviare!' we yell, and no one mentions hoardin'. Salmon and cucumbers suggests profiteering and with greatest diff. do guests restrain themselves from fallin' on the necks of the princelily generous hosts. When we leave it's 'Thanks for the simply toppin' feed, old bean!' or 'It really was too sweet of you, dear; such a duck of a dinner.

MANY NUTRITIOUS DISHES CAN BE PREPARED WITH POTATOES, ONIONS AND OTHER VEGETABLES AND

OXO

A handbill containing recipes for OXO and vegetable dishes, etc., will be sent free on receipt of a postcard addressed to—
OXO Limited, Thames House, London, E.C.4.

According to Phrynette in *The Sketch*, by January 1918 the leading dressmakers were noticing the impact of food shortages too. 'Some people puzzled by the food problems are dressmakers. In pre-war days it was quite usual for every well-dressed woman of the world to have wooden mannequins made to her size in the ateliers of her favourite couturier in Paris, so that clothes could be made to fit her perfectly from afar. The war has changed this somewhat. I hear from Paris that most mannequins no longer stand for the correct replicas of the clients – who keep on becoming slimmer and slimmer as the war goes on!'

Eve was intrigued about the opening in April 1918 of 'the very first of the "West-end" National Kitchens at Chelsea Town Hall, where the food, I am told, is to be not at all of the rather ladled-out-from-a-copper kind that is, rightly or wrongly, associated with the Communal Kitchen. It is even intended that customers shall be able to order food in advance. All you have to do is to fetch it all hot and ready – which really does sound, doesn't it, a great solution of the awful servant question?'

The first National Kitchen was opened by Queen Mary in Westminster Bridge Road on 21 May 1917, after which she lingered to serve some of the meals herself. Not only did they aim to provide affordable and nutritious meals for the poor, and for busy workers, but catering en masse was cheaper. Ensuring that war workers received regular, nutritious meals was another concern, answered by the establishment of canteens at factories – but there were other experimental food outlets. In Edgware Road in London, the Fortune of War Café was run by Lady Moore and a Mrs Hunter, where they practised a number of economical wartime recipes. When Phrynette visited in February 1918 they were busy experimenting with potato cakes: 'The potato is to be used to lessen the cost of your rock-cake and if you patronise the café – 1d. instead of 1½d., it is hoped will be the price of a cake that will melt in your mouth. I am told the great thing is to boil potatoes, rub them through a sieve when soft – minus the peel, of course – and replace a quantity of the flour by potato snow. Result – a delicious cake, a feeling of virtue and a heavier pocket-book. "Eat potatoes and save your Bradbury's" (£1 notes) is Lord Rhondda's slogan.'

Keeping up the strength of land workers was important too, a fact not forgotten by Mrs Peel in 'Le Ménage' who offered some ideas for 'pocket lunches' in August 1918. Cornish pasties and chocolate cakes (made with optional dried egg) was Monday's suggestion, bacon and potato sausages with rock cakes on Wednesday and pâté of liver sandwiches with plain Madeira cake on Thursday. In the absence of butter or margarine, grated cocoa butter was used for fat.

Established food brands were quick to publicise the nutritional and time-saving benefits of their products. Bird's custard offered a solution to sugar rationing, claiming that 'a distinguished scientist testifies that this enjoyable dish adds 25% to the calorific and nutritive value of plain milk'. Nestlé suggested their condensed milk as another replacement for sugar, adding that not only did it lend itself to far more methods of cookery than it was as a rule generally used for, but, equally important, there had been no alteration in price. Advertisements carried requests from soldiers for tins of Nestlé milk to add to their tea – 'Save us from milkless tea!' – and advised readers

Opposite: Oxo gave endless advice on how to create nutritious meals out of vegetables in order to economise and cope with meat rationing. Despite shortages, the lady in this advertisement appears to have retained her servant or cook! (Illustrated London News/ME)

This cartoon by Will Owen, published in the *Illustrated Sporting & Dramatic News* in December 1918, comments on the public feeling towards the communal, or 'National' kitchens introduced during the war. Their aim was to provide cheap and nutritious meals by catering on a mass scale to the poorer classes and war workers. Besides the National Kitchens, munitions and other industrial workers began to benefit from the introduction of canteens in the work place, a move instigated by charitable organisations. (Illustrated London News/ME)

to write to Nestlé with the name of their grocer to receive a subscription card for tins. Gong Soups, offered in twelve different varieties including mulligatawny, kidney and hare, were time-saving and versatile, equally useful for feeding a family of hungry children as for heating up in a jerry can in the trenches, and Maconochie's, a tinned beef and vegetable stew manufactured in Aberdeen, advertised itself as a warming and satisfying meal the whole family could enjoy. It was also used alongside bully beef in the trenches and in reality was considered only just palatable. *The Bystander*, which was widely read by officers at the front (and no doubt passed on to soldiers), thoughtfully published some recipes using bully beef in March 1916,

including beef fried in batter ('serve with mashed turnips') and a shredded beef casserole enhanced by the addition of Ju-Vis or a little Bovril. Condiments such as Pan-Yan pickle traded on their popularity with men at the front, who used them to disguise the monotony and sometimes downright inedible nature of their daily rations. In 1915, Lea & Perrins advertised a special offer for their Worcester sauce ('makes bully beef appetizing and when mixed with jam is an excellent substitute for "chutnee"'), where for 5s they would send a securely packed box of twelve bottles to the front.

Oxo's advertising campaign during the war was particularly comprehensive. A cup of Oxo could help win the war, quite literally, by

Eve attending a rather sorry looking society dinner party, with guests wrapped in furs against the cold and feasting on a single plate of hot potatoes — a humorous comment on the food and coal shortages affecting Britain — even in the most comfortable homes. (Illustrated London News/ME)

Eve lecturing Lord Rhondda on his food economy campaign. She argues that he 'had made no allowances for the perversity of human nature', and that telling people to save or eat less will only make them think more about food! David Alfred Thomas, 1st Viscount Rhondda (1856–1918) was a Welsh industrialist and Liberal politician who served at Food Controller at the Ministry of Food towards the end of the First World War, implementing a successful system of rationing. He died in July 1918. (Illustrated London News/ME)

meeting the needs of hungry munition workers who, revived by the beefy drink, sped up their output. Its rival, Bovril, ran an advertorial in the *Illustrated London News* in 1916, showing how a munitions worker, inspired by the image of a muscular war worker in a previous Bovril poster, had undergone a year-long body-building programme fuelled by the drink. The results were impressive. Another advert included the testimonial of one soldier who claimed to have survived a week in no-man's-land existing solely on biscuit and a trusty tin of Oxo. Others carried recipes that could be enhanced by the addition of Oxo such as potato pears, cabbage and chestnuts or, in a recipe devised by 'a celebrated chef', War-Time Pudding comprising suet, flour, carrots, celery, tomatoes, potato and pearl barley.

Ovaltine and Horlick's promoted their restful and restorative properties, featuring convalescent soldiers or hard-working nurses in their advertisements. 'Guard against nervous breakdown, which results from strain of overwork, worry and concentrated mental effort', advised one advert for Ovaltine.

Christmas time brought many challenges to the wartime nation, but finding food that could be considered in some way celebratory was particularly difficult. Phrynette, writing in the New Year of 1918, mourned the fact that 'there was no sugar on the mince pies this year, no raisins, almonds or oranges (fivepence each my dears!) and I missed the Christmas cake at tea-time, with its familiar almond-icing, sugar-coated, and pink and white frill.' Even holly and mistletoe were in short supply, its import into London being strictly limited.

Mrs Peel, as ever, had suggestions for a variety of budgets. In a menu costing *4s 5d*, a family could dine on:

Potage Parmentier
Stuffed Shoulder of Mutton
Braised Celery, Baked Potatoes
Fruit Pie & Custard

And for a shilling more:

Celery Cream Soup
Braised Beef à la Bourgeoise
Brussels Sprouts, Duchess Potatoes
Orange Pudding

There were also recipes for Patriotic Plum Pudding and Mincemeat for Patriotic People, so-called because of their strictly economical use of dried fruits.

Thanks to a combination of campaigning, education, increased production at home and a judicious rationing system, Britain was nourished during the Great War, if not exactly satisfied. Meat shortages saw a protein intake drop by 9 per cent in the average Briton but overall, calorific intake dropped by only 3 per cent. Away from restaurants and the plentiful supplies of country estates, food could be plain and unappetising but with committed and clever housekeeping, some enjoyment could still be derived from mealtimes.

'To feast is now a sin against the nation,' wrote Mrs Peel, the nation's wartime food guru; 'let us eat, and eat well, for this we can do without extravagance, without waste, depending on the excellence of the cooking, to make our fare attractive.'

FASHION

Dressing in wartime presented some awkward moral quandaries for the fashion-conscious. It was usual, before the war, for well-heeled ladies to refresh their wardrobe each season with the latest modes from Paris and the salons of Mayfair, and to spend every day undergoing several costume changes dependent on the time and the social occasion. The exigencies of war, however, did not smile favourably on such habits.

From the outset, the government advised the nation to curb extravagance in all areas, including clothing. Conspicuous consumption was officially frowned upon and nothing, perhaps, was more conspicuous than a frothy new dance frock or to be seen in three outfits in the same day.

Reginald McKenna, Chancellor of the Exchequer in Asquith's government from 1915 to 1916, explained the advice in simple terms during an interview: 'All classes of society should realise that in exercising any possible thrift they are directly helping to shorten the war.' His revenue-raising measures during the war extended to a heavy duty on imported luxury goods, including, to the dismay of many stylish ladies, hats. *The Bystander* published a cartoon by Mabel Lucie Attwell on its cover in September 1915 showing a tearful fashionista bemoaning McKenna's

ruthlessness, and *The Tatler*'s Eve delighted in casting the Chancellor as fashion's bête noire; a sartorial spoilsport. In January 1916, in her general chatter about cutbacks, she imagined 'Mr McKenna' as someone 'whom somehow one can't quite see as an authority on what a woman really wants', going on to declare that, 'I don't mind a bit doing without rice pudding and porridge and dull things like that, but I simply couldn't live without bath-salts or shoe ribbons or real silk stockings, or flowers, or Tou-tou, or taxis, now could I?'

In fact, despite the official line, the advent of war, and its impact on women's roles, took fashion in a fresh and transforming direction. Lavish spending may have been curtailed but it seemed that clothing simply adapted to the circumstances and presented followers of fashion with novel avenues to explore. For magazines whose advertising revenue relied heavily on London's clothing emporiums, the argument for continuing to spend on fashion found numerous legitimate reasons. On 9 September 1914, just a month into the war, *The Tatler* in an article about 'The War & Fashion', lectured that there were:

> ... two kinds of economy practised today – the wise and the foolish. It is wise, for instance, to be saving of sugar since sugar

is undoubtedly scarce; it is foolish on the other hand to do without new clothes or the like this autumn, since the materials to make these are fairly plentiful, and the factories must be kept going. Once factories shut down a host of evil results will follow until the national credit totters. All means should be taken, therefore, to keep trade as normal as possible and to keep England's mass of workpeople fully employed. Indeed, it is more charitable both to oneself and to the nation at large to spend normally, buying pretty well as one would buy in ordinary circumstances, than to give large donations to relief funds.

This business-as-usual approach and the determination to keep workers employed (thus avoiding the associated social problems caused by unemployment) was a repetitive theme and one echoed by shops themselves, whose advertisements sent out a very clear message. Dickins and Jones, a stalwart of London's Regent Street since the 1830s, placed an advertisement in *The Tatler* in November 1914 announcing their rich, brocaded crêpe shirts, which they were selling at 'special war prices in order to keep workers and staff employed with profits sacrificed altogether, or with the lowest possible margin.'

Nor was the French dressmaking industry forgotten. On 26 August 1914, *The Tatler* published a spread featuring four fur ensembles from Parisian fashion houses with the advice that, though the 'thought of new and expensive clothes may seem at first sight grotesque … the plea for steady trade must not be ignored by those whose purses are long, and the plight of the thousands of dressmakers and designers who will be earning very little wages during these next few months must not be forgotten.' Later, in 1917, with the advent of paper restrictions, *The Queen*

magazine announced that it would be devoting fewer column inches to fashion reporting (especially as 'the lady writer who has been responsible for "Fashion's Forecast" for some time has herself resigned this duty in order to take up national work'), but it would continue to follow Paris fashions as 'it is a plain duty to support the French so far as we can in maintaining their industries.'

Supporting British (and French) industry was one reason to maintain a sensible clothes shopping regime. Health and practical budgeting was another. M.E. Brooke, writing in *The Tatler*'s 'Highway of Fashion' column in November that year, advised prudent spending: '… it is to be hoped that wardrobes will be replenished as opportunity arises, not lavishly, but with discretion, else in the course of a few months they will become denuded and the inroads made at one fell swoop on the dress allowance will be appalling. Warm garments are a sine qua non now that the cold weather has arrived, otherwise influenza and other troublesome winter ills will have an easy victory, and will add their toll to that levelled by the war,' adding at the end, 'shopping with discretion at the present moment, helps everyone.' And there was a somewhat desperate justification for buying evening dresses given by *The Queen* in February 1917, claiming, 'Simple evening dresses still have their uses; indeed, they often play an economical part in saving day frocks, as well as one of considerable psychological importance where rest of nerves and stimulation of spirits are concerned.'

In the logic of many, dressing well fulfilled a patriotic duty. It embodied the time-honoured British tradition of keeping up appearances. After all, 'it would be regrettable were we to be regarded as a nation of frumps when the women of France are ever to be seen well dressed', wrote M.E. Brooke in March 1916.

BARKERS *of* KENSINGTON

ROYAL WORCESTER CORSETS

The New Military Curve

TO-DAY Fashion presents a delightful surprise—the new Military vogue. Already it is becoming the rage. Its freshness, its vivacity, its freedom, are captivating the entire world of dress. The new Royal Worcester Kidfitting Corsets, which we are now featuring in our Corset Department, have caught the elusive spirit of this bewitching new mode with striking fidelity. Every model has the new Military Curve, upon which the present vogue entirely depends for its perfect expression. As these Corsets are designed by the foremost Parisian Corsetry artists in collaboration with the recognised Ateliers of creative fashion, their authenticity is beyond question.

The British lady is fast beginning to realise what her Parisian sister has always known by instinct—the economy of paying a fair price for her corsets and getting the best. The small saving one might possibly make by buying a lower-priced corset than the "Royal Worcester" would be worse than wasted; it might mean the ruination of your gowns, because no dressmaker could give you Fashion if your corsets were unfashionable.

To buy corsets without investigating the merits of the "Royal Worcester" is to set at nought the experienced judgment of the world's greatest authorities on Fashion, who practically without exception pronounce for Royal Worcester Kidfitting Corsets. We cordially invite you to call and have a pair fitted, or to send for a selection on approval, for nothing so quickly and completely establishes the superiority of these Corsets as an actual comparison.

A large Showroom is now devoted exclusively to Corsets

MODEL 977. WITH THE NEW MILITARY CURVE.
Very chic new style. Silk elastic gore below hip. In white fancy broché. Average Figure. Sizes 20-30. Price **52/6**

The NEW MILITARY CURVE HAS TAKEN THE TOWN BY STORM

All the best & latest shapes can be found at **BARKERS** who have been appointed sole agents for a very large part of London, W. Prices from— **4/11 to 4 Gns.**

Ladies who cannot favour us with a visit, should write for the beautiful **Illustrated Catalogue** which shows styles suitable for every type of figure.

MODEL 507
Petite Figure.
Height of bust from waist, 4 ins.
Height of back from waist, 5 ins.
Length of back below waist, 10½ ins.
Chic new model designed especially for the little lady. In white coutil.
Sizes 19-26 Price **8/11**

MODEL 5820
Average Figure.
Height of bust from waist, 5 ins.
Height of back from waist, 6½ ins.
Length of back below waist, 11 ins.
Free hip, straight skirt, good shoulder support. In white broché.
Sizes 19-28 Price **12/11**

MODEL 9038
Average Figure.
Height of bust from waist, 4½ ins.
Height of back from waist, 5½ ins.
Length of back below waist, 13 ins.
Gives the very straight, flat appearance so much desired for back and hip. 6 hose supporters. In white coutil.
Sizes 20-30 Price **25/9**

MODEL 843
Full Figure.
Height of bust from waist, 5½ ins.
Height of back from waist, 5½ ins.
Length of back below waist, 12½ in.
Gives fulness over diaphragm. 6 hose supporters. In white.
Sizes 22-30 **16/11**
Price
(*Sizes 31-36, 2/- extra.*)

JOHN BARKER & CO. LTD., KENSINGTON HIGH ST., LONDON, W.

e **✱✱**

The military vogue in fashion during the war even extended to undergarments. The Royal Worcester military curve corset ensured a fashionable silhouette underneath gowns. (Illustrated London News/ME)

'Furthermore, the men when on leave are brightened and cheered by seeing their womankind prettily dressed. The new fashions are perfectly delightful, and as the brave French dressmakers have designed them for us, it would be base ingratitude not to show our appreciation of their efforts by wearing them.'

An advertisement for Redfern in *The Tatler* in May 1916 – one of the leading couture houses of the day, holding a royal warrant from Queen Alexandra – used the same reasoning, advising ladies that 'it is patriotic to treat our soldiers well, and to look your best when they are home on leave. To provide yourself with a smart and pretty gown for Whitsuntide is a compliment that should please them.' The feminine ensemble suggested would have pleased Ella Hepworth Dixon, who, writing her column 'Woman's Ways' in *The Sketch* in January 1915, was sharply critical of the emerging trend for military fashions:

If there is one thing we ought to impress upon our youthful female contemporaries at the present juncture, it is the extreme undesirability of dressing in the military fashions. Reginald, when he comes back from the front for a few days, does not want to see you in a busby, or a khaki overcoat, but in something nice and fluffy. Imagine the attractions of velvet and chiffon, of ermine and chinchilla, after the trenches

The recent Zeppelin raid has suggested to our artist that smart pyjamas are a necessity. Black crêpe de chine trimmed with black-and-white ribbon has been employed for those depicted above

Though probably not an entirely serious suggestion, these pyjamas in black crêpe de chine would make the wearer presentable should they be seen in public during a night time Zeppelin raid. Pyjamas were one of the increasingly modern and practical garments becoming available to women during the war, though they would still only be worn by the most adventurous. (Illustrated London News/ME)

ELIZABETH, Ltd.
45, South Molton Street, Bond Street, W. 1

Sale Commences
Monday, July 1

All Models
Greatly Reduced.

SPECIALISTS
in
CHILDREN'S
SCHOOL
OUTFITS
and
LADIES'
PRACTICAL
OVERALLS
and
FROCKS.

Sole Makers of the Olva Outfit for Women Workers on the Land.

Haymaking Frock in Old English Print or Flowered Cretonne   ...   .   **3½ Gns.**

Old English Sunbonnets from **10/6 to 21/6.**

The romantic notion of working in the open air led to fashion houses such as Elizabeth producing picturesque, old English style smocks for lady land workers, though the gruelling nature of land work must have rendered such garments impractical in all but the most clement harvest time weather. (Illustrated London News/ME)

or a shakedown in a devastated barn? How mysterious and alluring a very femininely dressed woman must be, seen in her own delicately lighted and exquisitely furnished drawing-room, after scenes of horror in hospital and camp. And by adopting military fashions – frogs, gilt buttons, aigrettes, and plumes – a woman does not look like a soldier, but like a ludicrous travesty of one in some trivial spectacular play.

But Ms Hepworth Dixon's views, along with her vision of women as winsome, decorative accessories, were quickly becoming outdated. Military inspired fashion was everywhere, borrowing patterns, embellishments and tailoring from the regiments of the Allied armies fast becoming a familiar sight in London and Paris. As early as 5 August 1914, Annie Fish's drawings in Eve illustrated the growing influence of militarism on fashion with helmet-style hats, while Eve mused presciently that 'probably owing to rampant militarianism on the Continent and Ulsteritis at home, the modes are getting very soldiery.'

Paris, charmed by the arrival in France of the kilted Highland regiments, produced a rash of checked and tartan outfits in 1915. The Russian influence too was marked, manifested by an enthusiasm for astrakhan and fur trimming of all kinds, even on lingerie. Muted colours became de rigeur, notably khaki, but also blue – fashion's homage to the Poilou's uniform of bleu d'horizon. Elsewhere, details such as frogging, Napoleonic collars, epaulettes and braiding were used with dashing effect. As foreseen by Eve, hats too took on a military tone. A December 1914 issue featured a trio of designs under the heading, 'The Effect of Mars upon Venus – how the war is affecting the fashion of ladies' headgear' and described the feminine translation of a kepi (the cap worn by French troops), a hussar

style and 'a picturesque variation of a Russian headdress'. The following year, Mrs Benedict Birkbeck (Jacqueline Alexander, whose second husband, after the war, was Bror, Baron von Blixen, the big-game hunter) had her photograph published in the magazine wearing a jaunty Bersaglieri hat, as worn by the Italian allies.

Even undergarments stuck to the theme. The Royal Worcester military curve corset, advertised in the autumn of 1915, ensured a fashionable silhouette under gowns claiming that without it even the new season's gowns would look passé. With both whalebone and steel in short supply, corsets or stays often used compressed paper and rubber as a substitute. Underwear had certainly become more comfortable and facilitated physical activity for war workers, but their makeshift skeletons easily rotted and sagged.

It was the new silhouette that was in fact the most significant and lasting change in women's fashion during the war years. In the summer of 1914, fashionable ladies wore the hobble skirt; long, tubular and narrow at the ankles, together with a long-line tunic over the top, which tended to flare out slightly from the hips. Soon, the physical requirements of war work necessitated a more practical shape and while the hobble skirt had measured just one and a quarter yards in circumference, a wider, flared or bell-shaped skirt began to emerge, measuring closer to five yards. By the middle of 1915, the double layer of underskirt and tunic became less prevalent and a simpler shape, rather like a longer skater dress, became de rigeur. Bodices and basques mined various historic periods from the fichus of revolutionary France to the high, ruffed collars of the Tudor era, and the skirts themselves often featured frills, flounces or a fur trim. Eve, always with her finger on the pulse of fashion, talked of the new shape as early as December 1914:

Don't let a Zeppelin
catch you in Curlers

Have Natural Wavy Hair and look your best under any circumstances.

MARCEL'S is unlike any other.	**PERSONAL SERVICE CHARGES.**	Successful results Guaranteed.
	Permanently Waving the front of hair from £1 1 0	
	Permanently Waving the entire head from £3 3 0	

Straight hair abuses your face, it is the plague of many a woman's life, no other thing is such a nuisance.

A grateful lady writes:

"Come, listen, straight‐haire l
 sisters,
A secret I would tell;
About a firm in London,
By name—Messrs Marcel.

Would'st know how once my hair
 looked—
Greasy, and straight as well?
So tried Syntonic Hair‐wave,
Permanent—by Marcel.

'Ten years younger!' said my
 spouse;
So haste! the numbers swell
Of those who've gain'd true beauty
By visiting Marcel."

BY ONE OF THE BEAUTIES.

If you cannot visit Marcel's you should not hesitate to use Marcel's new invention for making your hair naturally wavy at home. Your requirements can be supplied at a very small cost.

Super Systaltic Family Outfit
Wave lasts about
 12 months **45/-**
Systaltic Home Outfit.
Wave lasts about
 7 months **35/-**
Perm. Outfit.
Wave lasts about
 3 months **25/-**
Sansperm. Outfit.
Wave lasts about
 3 weeks **12/6**

You are safe when Marcel's supply you with their service. *There is no other Syntonic Permanent wave than Marcel's patented process and appliances* No fees accepted unless the wave produced resists shampooing. Marcel's **guarantee** that their Syntonic process is the most satisfactory and beneficial treatment for all straight, greasy, or thin hair.

MARCEL'S PERMANENT HAIRWAVING INSTITUTE
534, OXFORD ST., MARBLE ARCH, LONDON, W.

Marcel permanent waving avoided the embarrassing scenario of being caught in curlers during a Zeppelin raid! The popular technique was still in use to curl hair two decades on. (Hearst Magazines (UK)/ME)

The advantages of practical garments that freed women to carry out important war work is demonstrated in this advertisement for Zambrene waterproofs, illustrated by Claude Shepperson. (Illustrated London News/ME)

And so our tight skirts are dead aren't they? No wonder they've been sale-ing at Lucile's and Hayward's and places, for frocks made yesterday are as different from the ones made to-day as chalk from cheese. My newest came home this morning, and Tou-tou, dear sweet duch, quite thought it was a new game. The hem's so wide, and there's nearly a mile of fur on it.

The Sketch magazine, reporting on the trend in February the following year, hailed the new style as the sartorial homage to the pluck and energy demonstrated by wartime womanhood:

Our pre-war finicking way of slipping along with very narrow skirts will now give way to the erect, alert, military gait, which will be much better for us, and much more characteristic of the women of Britain now that they have come into their own again, and recovered the true British spirit. With the new, side skirts and short coats, the military walk will be almost a necessity, to carry the fashion properly, and to wear these clothes with the requisite air.

More conservative members of the press struggled to conceal their outrage at rising hemlines. It was a fashion that 'should be regarded with suspicion by women of good taste', fumed the *Daily Mail*, discussing the trend in the middle of 1915. But soon women of all tastes and persuasions were adopting the new style and by 1916, skirt hemlines were an unprecedented six inches above the ground. Evening wear echoed the skirt shape, flaring out with the aid of a number of petticoats, while the upper bodice usually had a low, horizontal décolletage held in place by shoulder straps, fashionably revealing a lady's back to the point where Eve wondered if 'people'd think sometimes some of us were just going to

take a bath instead of only really going to see the latest revue'.

The sudden appearance of calves and ankles gave rise to another popular trend – silk stockings, which, though usually black for daywear, were available in a number of flamboyant colours and patterns for the more daring. Jay's offered stockings in stripes and checks, while *The Tatler* in May 1915 featured two novel designs from Peter Robinson, one pair inexplicably decorated with squirrels at the ankle, the other 'a pair of silken hose with the Allies flags embroidered on them, complete with shamrocks and ribbon garters in Allied colours' for the 'patriotic debutante'. Even more patriotic were the garters featured in *The Sketch* a few months earlier bearing miniature portraits of Admiral Jellicoe and Lord Kitchener, though quite what the two men may have thought of this compliment remains unrecorded. Stockings (artificial silk stockings were first introduced in 1912), previously the preserve of the rich, soon became a trophy purchase for newly solvent war workers who for the first time in their lives could enjoy a little everyday luxury. Mrs C.S. Peel, *The Queen* magazine's food columnist, wrote in her memoir of the war years how munition workers, particularly, 'spent lavishly on their clothes, and very well dressed many of them were, in smartly-cut tailormades of carefully chosen colour, with hat and blouse, gloves and stockings all to match, and particularly neat boots or shoes'. She recalled one male fitter at a factory describing the munitionettes as 'smart as monkeys'.

This sudden imbalance in appearance amongst the classes was much parodied in magazines, *Punch* in particular delighting in depicting the aristocracy in ragged versions of current fashions. But, though simplicity was preached and extravagance frowned upon, fashion's wealthiest patrons could still afford to dress well when the occasion demanded, even if eyebrows were raised. The fabulously rich heiress Consuelo, Duchess of Marlborough, patron or founder of a number of philanthropic ventures during the war, rarely dressed in anything less than the height of chic. Eve, writing in March 1916, noted ironically the appearance of the Duchess at a war economy exhibition:

Talking of female pioneers, suppose you know that the leader of 'em, the Duchess of Marlborough, has now joined that latest of causes, the war-time economy one. And they had a big meeting at Sunderland House the other day, with Dean Inge and Lady Ferrers and other no doubt very economical people on the platform. They say her grace is really frightfully keen on saving, though she does dress so frightfully well, and of course it is rather funny economy talk coming from Sunderland House, isn't it?

Margot Asquith, wife of the ex-premier, was known for her flamboyant and often eccentric mode of dress – 'one of the bravest women in London about clothes,' confided Eve. 'Sometimes they're so new they're positively the word AFTER the last word', and yet, Mrs Asquith put everyone to shame at a Private View in December 1917 when she arrived 'sans furs, feathers, gloves, jewels, embroideries, everything [...] the ex-PM's wife put the dis-

tinctly dressy rest of us if not to shame at any rate obviously right out of the Economy-for-Ever stakes.'

A proposed luxury tax on further goods, introduced towards the end of the war, sought to raise additional income from a whole range of items from motor cars to musical instruments, but included furs, osprey feathers, perfumes and jewellery as well as clothing retailing over certain set amounts (£1 15s for trimmed hats, or a dress costing more than £5 5s). 'Just now every prudent husband is betraying an unaccustomed interest in the chapeaux and the chiffons of his wife and daughters,' wrote Phrynette in *The Sketch*, 'for the prosaic reason that he knows that he must foot the bills anyway, and that he wants the inevitable purchases completed before the imposition of the luxury tax increases the cost.'

Even *The Queen*, despite its self-imposed cutbacks on fashion reporting and its vociferous support of war economies, continued to intermittently run its colour plates detailing Paris fashions throughout the war, and it satisfied any paucity in this area by instead reporting in exquisite and laboured detail on the outfits worn by royalty and society at numerous charitable events, right down to the beaded embellishments on

'War strain' played havoc with the complexion and while many women increasingly invested in creams and cosmetics to improve their looks, some visited beauty salons to counteract the effects of wartime living. Here, a woman undergoes light treatment to eradicate wrinkles at the salon of Helena Rubinstein. (Illustrated London News/ME)

Lady Newborough, formerly Grace Carr of Kentucky, USA, pictured in elaborate mourning garb following the death of her husband, William Charles Wynn, 4th Baron Newborough, as a result of active service in 1916. (Illustrated London News/ME)

Queen Mary's dress or the particular shade of eau-de-nil worn by a pretty, young Viscountess.

But while the upper classes wavered over displays of conspicuous wealth (many were photographed in nurse's uniforms, which solved the dilemma neatly), there was one place where the public thoroughly expected to see lavish and flamboyant fashion.

Theatre thrived during the war years. Light-hearted revues filled with songs, comedy and spectacle was the order of the day – no soldier on leave wanted to sit through anything serious or, worse, tragic – and the leading ladies of the stage assumed the role of leaders of fashion, their magnificent stage costumes a justifiable expense in order to bring a little light and joy into the lives of their audiences. Queen of all style queens was Gaby Deslys, 'the one and only Gaby', as she was dubbed. The French actress was an all-round entertainer, charming audiences in Britain, France and America with her singing, graceful dancing and memorable gowns in which she posed for hundreds of publicity photographs. Her celebrity was given an exotic piquancy by a mysterious past (some claimed she was of Moravian rather than French birth) and a romantic liaison with the exiled King Manuel of Portugal. When Gaby appeared in *Rosy Rapture*, a show penned by J.M. Barrie, at the Duke of York's Theatre in London in 1915, an advertisement appeared in *The Sketch* from the fashion house providing her clothes for the production: 'Everyone knows the perfect taste which the French artist deploys in choosing her dresses. The Maison Callot Soeurs of Paris, an authority in Gowns, has made the models of good taste and elegance which charm the eyes of the public every evening…'

Callot Soeurs, a Parisian fashion house founded by four sisters in 1895, specialised in exotic details, exquisite lace embellishments and pioneered the use of gold and silver lamé – a perfect choice for Gaby's shimmering stage presence. Clearly, fashion designers had recognised the potentially lucrative synergy between style and celebrity. Eve in 1916 underlined theatre's influence by writing, 'No one misses a revue nowadays as from the toilettes there seen, many valuable hints may be gleaned, although the dresses in their entirety are too elaborate for general wear.' In 1917, when Gaby was starring in *Suzette*, Eve admitted that, 'You go to see Gaby, or rather Gaby in her frocks. These, as

Tunickers for land workers, devised by Messrs Thomas and Sons of Brook Street, London, were a practical, serviceable and sensible garment for women occupied in strenuous war work. Combining tunic and knickers in one, they were fastened with buttons or clips at the waist. The tunic could be detached and worn as a cape when occasion demanded. (Hearst Magazines (UK)/ME)

a man critic puts it, are, "so many, so extraordinary, so overpowering, that it must need the verve and personality of a Gaby Deslys to prevent the wearer of them seeing to be no more than a dressmaker's dummy or a mannequin'", adding in reference to Gaby's extravagant headdresses and dresses: 'in these days of economy, even in the theatres there's a pleasant air of lavishness and hang-the-expense about the whole thing.' She also admired the 'wildly expensive' simplicity of the frocks by Lucile worn by Lily Elsie in the same year, as well as the orchid-mauve dress of ninon on Shirley Kellogg in *Joyland* at the Hippodrome.

In 1916, Eve herself became a fashion icon when she was translated to the stage in the revue *Tina,* which ran at the Adelphi theatre in spring that year. She was played by Phyllis Dare, who wore a succession of the inimitable, stylised 'Eve' outfits based on those originally dreamed up by Annie Fish, illustrator of *The Tatler* column. The sight of Ms Dare and her co-stars in the characterful, cartoonish designs – doll-like, A-line shapes, high collars, jaunty hats and striking monochrome patterns – inspired dressmakers to copy the look and both *The Tatler* and *The Sketch* ran spreads of designs mimicking Eve's style until what was fictional and what was real in fashion terms became somewhat blurred. The following year, pendant lucky charms and brooches in the shape of Eve could be purchased from the Goldsmiths & Silversmiths Company.

Another favourite, and very much human, clothes horse was the American dancer Irene Castle. Born Irene Foote, her partnership with her husband Vernon earned them the name 'America's Sweethearts'. Commanding high fees for their performances, they danced all the way to the bank, making a fortune not only from stage and film work, but also from a number of fashion branding initiatives. In May 1916, a portrait of Irene appeared in *The Tatler*

wearing a dress of 'Vernon Castle' lace manufactured to her own design, and she lent her name to a variety of hats, dresses and toiletries. Described as an 'almost absolute arbiter of fashion in New York, and what she wears to-day America wears to-morrow', she combined grace and elegance with an unconventional flair. She featured on the front cover of *The Sketch* in February 1917 in an unusual headdress she had designed herself to wear in the film *Patria*, and even after Vernon was killed in a flying accident in 1918, she was described by Eve as 'a smart thing in war widows, what?' At a matinee organised by the Marchioness of Carisbrooke she appeared dressed in black and white with a mauve orchid and, later that day, danced with the Prince of Wales.

Even in bereavement, Irene Castle cut an elegant figure, and many of the society ladies who experienced widowhood sought to present a smart but sombre appearance. There were plenty of specialists in mourning clothes and fashion pages regularly featured suggestions for becoming ensembles for widows to wear. *The Queen* advised a visit to Madame Emma Gulley of Regent Street in London, who bore 'the high-water-mark of irreproachable taste', offering as she did all types of mourning attire, including parasols trimmed with crêpe and a variety of black blouses with detachable collars and cuffs of delicate widow's lace. A state of mourning did not necessarily preclude a trip to the photographers. Death and its consequences had become a part of everyday life; the Victorian habit of displaying grief and respect through clothes continued, with well-heeled society figures often photographed in outfits similar to those sketched in magazines. Lady Newborough, the American wife of the 4th Baron, was widowed in 1917 and appeared in *The Tatler* dressed in black but for her pearls, wearing a high-crowned hat with a sumptuous veil of crêpe, almost theatrical in its drama. In reality, the majority of grieving widows could not afford such elaborate creations. Many sewed their own – Courtauld's advertised their 'waterproof crape, for fashionable mourning', and department stores up and down the country offered services to the recently bereaved, often visiting them in their homes to put together a proper but affordable mourning wardrobe.

Mourning clothes were needed in abundance but so too were the type of practical, purposeful garments needed by the growing army of female war workers, and for upper-class women who might help out at canteens, as drivers or on the land, there was the novelty of kitting oneself out in something rather dashing. Firms such as Burberry's, Aquascutum and Dunhill's all began to recognise this new lucrative market and soon, practical jacket and skirt sets in warm wool, tweed or drill with masculine details such as useful patch pockets and buckled belts were proliferating. In 1915, *The Queen* magazine described the 'irreproachable motor attire at Dunhill's' as of 'an even greater importance than ever, since so many women are now driving their own cars in consequence of the fact that chauffeurs are among the most valuable of our recruits.' Dunhill's also offered a lady chauffeur costume – a tailored suit of velvet Persian skin with a hat to match. In *The Tatler*'s fashion column, M.E. Brooke described the trench coats for canteen workers available from Aquascutum, which were built on exactly the same principles as the officer's trench coat: 'Really useful, and oh so warm … they are made of Aquascutum khaki drill interlined with oil silk, with a detachable fleece lining.' The coat cost £7 7s and could be bought with a matching skirt for £3 3s to complete a smart and durable outfit. Patrons of Burberry could be satisfied that their shopping also combined an element of altruism when, towards the end of the war, the company began to advertise its 'Blighty Tweed', manufactured by wounded soldiers and sailors, with each piece marked inside with its maker's name.

Clothes for land workers rather captured the imagination of fashion editors, who revelled in the image of bucolic romance and wholesomeness. In October 1915, *The Queen*, in a piece about women's work and their clothing, waxed lyrical about 'girls who had wandered far afield to milk the farmer's cows (who) wore a brown smock with a band around the waist, high brown boots, putties (sic) and straw hats turning up at the side, just such as Kate Greenaway's shepherdesses wore in the long ago before the war had come upon us.' It printed illustrations of yokel-like smocks, calling them 'a faithful copy of many old-world fancies', and Elizabeth Ltd of South Molton Street advertised floral-sprigged old English smocks and sun bonnets, conjuring up a Hardyesque world where pretty damsels brought in the harvest in sun-dappled fields. The redoubtable and ubiquitous Lady Drogheda, a veritable war-working whirlwind, was pictured in *The Bystander* in the spring of 1918 ploughing a field in a picturesque dress.

The reality, of course, was far different. Agricultural work was often cold, wet, muddy and generally filthy. Fortunately, there were practical solutions to complement the rustic idyll. The wearing of breeches and trousers became widespread for the first time, though mainly for the sake of safety and practicality (they were also worn by many female munitions workers). Various versions appeared including a patented idea – 'tunickers' – from Thomas & Son's, 'Ladies' Sporting Tailors' of Brook Street. Tunickers, which the firm suggested were ideal for remount, ambulance, farm and garden work, consisted of a pair of knickerbocker breeches covered over with a skirt which, during inclement weather, could be removed and worn as a cape, thus negating

"HARNESS" FOR THE LADIES: A WAR-TIME DRESS IDEA.

WITH "HARNESS" MADE BY SHELL-SHOCK PATIENTS: THE HAWKEY NATIONAL DRESS, WITH VARIATIONS.

Standard suits for civilians have already received royal approval. The same can be said of the Hawkey national dress, several of which have been ordered by the Queen of Spain. Except the last (in the right-hand lower corner) all the above photographs show Mrs. Hawkey, the inventor of the costume, wearing the same foundation dress (as seen in the first photograph), varied by the addition of different "harness" in the shape of collars, with long ends containing pockets, and belts. This "harness" is made by shell-shock patients at Lady Neville's shops for the disabled.

Photographs specially taken for " The Sketch " by Topical.

Mrs Allan Hawkey, inventor of the national standard dress, modelling its versatility exclusively for *The Sketch* magazine in 1918, and showing off a number of harnesses (combined collars and pockets) made by shell-shocked soldiers at Lady Neville's workshops for the disabled. The national standard dress was an attempt to introduce a low-cost, economical and simple form of dress, easily sewn and adaptable. (Illustrated London News/ME)

the need for a coat. In July 1917, *The Queen* spoke glowingly of Mr Harry Hall of Oxford Street, who devised a divided skirt 'specially designed for motorcycling, and for such purposes it is certainly unique.'

Society magazines in general applauded the advent of this innovation in women's costume. To *The Queen* magazine, whose *raison d'être* during the war was to find sensible and practical ways for women to help, masculine dress made perfect sense, while for *The Tatler* and *The Sketch* anything new and outré appealed to their urbane, modern tastes. Illustrations of female war workers – including those in breeches – appeared with increasing frequency, and although the girls were always pretty, and the jokes sometimes a little chauvinistic, there was an underlying note of admiration. In April 1917, *The Tatler*'s front cover featured a photograph of a young woman in Hyde Park's fashionable Rotten Row wearing riding breeches, with its caption – 'What WOULD Grandmama have said?' – exuding an air of mischievous, faux shock.

In 1918, another innovation was introduced; the National Dress, though *The Sketch* reassured its readers that 'the Government have not, at present any intention of putting in a Dress Controller, so that the wearing or ignoring of the new garment is a matter upon which women are left complete freedom of choice.' This 'standard' dress was designed by Mrs Allan Hawkey, who claimed a single frock could be sewn in around three hours ('but I can see a fractious Phrynette making it days,' wrote *The Sketch* columnist) and was based on a simple, fastening free pattern, which could be decorated and personalised in a number of different ways. Mrs Hawkey gave lectures on its economic advantages and in June 1918 was

LORD KITCHENER AS ORNAMENT FOR A LADY'S GARTER! PATRIOTIC FERVOUR IN ITS LATEST FORM.

ADMIRAL JELLICOE AS ORNAMENT FOR A LADY'S GARTER! PATRIOTIC FERVOUR IN ITS LATEST FORM.

Garters featuring miniature portraits of Lord Kitchener and Admiral Jellicoe. Shortening hemlines meant that for the first time, legs were on display and unusual, patterned stockings became all the rage. A number included designs that reflected a fervent patriotism. (Illustrated London News/ME)

photographed for *The Sketch* wearing the dress with a variety of 'harnesses' in the form of collars elongated to form pockets down the front, sewn by shell-shock patients at Lady Neville's workshops for the disabled. Even Princess Mary was reported to have experimented with one. But coming as it did at a late stage in the war, when despite taxes and cutbacks, society's elite wished for a little glamour in their lives, the idea never quite took off. Another curiosity was the 'Belle Alliance' dress, introduced in early 1915. It was modelled by the novelist Marjorie Bowen and was designed by, according to *The Sketch*, 'a little band of women-artists who have started a dress-designing studio where they employ their artistic talent and deft fingers in creating and making beautiful dresses.' The dress, simply cut but in an artistic print, was reminiscent of the rational dress worn by pioneering, bohemian types in the nineteenth century, but whatever happened to the little collective is unknown as no more was written about it, and that appears to have been the Belle Alliance dress's one and only moment in the spotlight.

There were other novelties that had more longevity. Week after week, throughout the war, numerous magazines carried advertisements from jewellers such as Charles Packer & Co. of Regent Street, offering a wide array of regimental brooches, enabling ladies to pick the insignia of whichever

regiment their husband, sweetheart, father or son was serving with. Eve was delighted particularly with the brooch of the Royal Flying Corps, writing excitedly in 1917: 'It's very fortunate for us, isn't it, that those topping R.F.C. wings make such a perfectly sweet brooch in diamonds and enamel and platinum? – which isn't platinum now, I believe, but "palladium". And colourable imitations of the coveted wings, I notice, too, make sufficient decoration on the best morning hats these days.'

The magnificent Gaby Deslys was renowned for her flamboyant stage costumes, and particularly her vertiginous headdresses and hats. This caricature by John Kettlewell on the front cover of *The Sketch* epitomises Gaby's glamorous Gallic style. (Illustrated London News/ME)

A rather more drastic and permanent way of expressing allegiance was with a tattoo, though Eve outlined the potential disadvantages of such commitment:

By the way, talking of fashions, I can't help thinking it's really quite dangerous the way some of us have been having army badges tattooed on our arms. In the new hardly-any frock it shows rather too much, and I do think it must be a bit annoying for, say, a Coldstreamer to spend an evening next to a nice girl with an Inniskilling badge on her arm. Really the only safe place is on one's leg, and there it's not much good 'cos you do want to show it sometimes.

Though it is unlikely tattoos were adopted by any but the most adventurous upper-class woman, beauty and adornment took on a new aspect of importance. Companies purveying lotions and elixirs to beautify emphasised how essential it was to care for one's appearance and to attempt to reverse the damage done by the hardship of war. 'Anxiety for loved ones at the Front, grief for those who have "gone west" and the strain of voluntary war work, all act injuriously on the skin. Every care is needed in these trying times to preserve beauty of the complexion', went the copy in an advertisement for Ven-Yusa Oxygen Face cream. Other face cream companies, such as Royal Vinolia and Pomeroy, employed images of industrious yet glowing munition workers in their advertisements. Vinolia's vanishing cream ensured 'clear, cool, supple skin and a complexion of dainty bloom, even if the worker's days are spent in the dusty atmosphere of the workroom'. The Valaze Hand Cream of Helena Rubinstein, who had moved to London in 1908 and by wartime was already well on her way to establishing her global cosmetics empire, was recommended for war workers' hands. At her salon, ladies could undergo treatments such as a skin clearing facial or Rubinstein's Blue Light treatment to counteract the ageing effects on the face of strenuous times, for it really was, lectured *The Tatler*, 'the duty of women to do everything to retain and preserve the beauty that Nature has given them'.

Face creams, hair treatments and fragrances were advertised widely, but cosmetics were not. 'There was a time, not so very long ago, when making-up was socially both a crime and a blunder,' wrote Efemera in *The Bystander* in 1916; 'it was an offence even more heinous than to be smartly dressed, or fanciful in the matter of under-linen. It was looked upon as "French" – therefore foreign and reprehensible.' But, she went on to say, 'We have lost all sense of false shame in the matter (as the young woman) now takes out her vanity-bag and touches up her face where she may happen to find herself.' Her advice was that you could 'improve' cheeks, lips, eyebrows, and hair, 'but once you touch your eyes you are finished'. Powder was used but lipstick and rouge were slower to be accepted and the fact that the predominantly working-class munition workers adopted lipstick with enthusiasm was probably enough to discourage ladies of gentler birth – at least until after the war, when cosmetics increasingly become part of the new woman's arsenal.

What of men's clothing during the war? Did they ever get a look in? Undoubtedly they did, but there was only one course to follow and that was khaki, widely termed in the press at the time as 'the only-wear'. Men who were seen in civilian clothes in public often faced awkward questions from fervent amateur recruiters and those who had been declared unfit, or who had attested and were waiting to be called up, wore armbands to clarify they were anything but 'shirkers'. Dressing in a dandyish manner was particularly frowned upon and young men who did so were nicknamed, 'k'nuts', a term further popularised by the actor Basil Hallam, who parodied such a type in his role as Gilbert the Filbert, Colonel of the Nuts, in the 1915 revue *The Passing Show*. Men's outfitters, if they conspicuously offered an alternative to uniform, were as good as endorsing a civilian life in opposition to a military duty. And so Burberry advertised endless variations on the trench coat, service overcoat and Army, Navy and Royal Flying Corps uniform. Advertisements for quality boots from Manfield, Cuirass waistcoats from Harrods, ready-rolled puttees for officers from Turnbull and Asser, cardigans from Frederick Gorringe, anti-barbed wire gloves, name tape from Cash's and even bullet-proof jackets from Wilkinson Sword filled pages every week. Occasionally, an advertisement for Aertex underwear or a practical dressing gown for convalescent soldiers might appear, but still their purpose was war-related. Every emphasis was put upon equipping the fighting man with clothing that was as practical, comfortable and warm as possible. And as with women's clothing, the constant recommendation was to invest in quality. A long text-only advert by H. Dennis Bradley, of Pope & Bradley, implored officers going to the front to invest in a quality uniform, stressing that 'the Government allowance of £50 for kit is not granted out of philanthropy, but to enable the newly gazetted officer to procure his uniforms from first class military tailors, and those who are induced to save a few pounds by purchasing a cheap kit will find they have practiced a suicidal economy.'

Economic pressures, the changing roles of women and a spirited 'live for the day' attitude were all factors in the evolving style of the Great War period. M.E. Brooke, in her Highway of Fashion column in *The Tatler* published two days after the signing of the Armistice, mused on the transition of fashion and predicted optimistic post-war styles: 'Now that peace is within measurable distance, a strong desire makes itself felt to get out of uniform as soon as possible. There is a monotony and lack of individuality about it that in the times of peace would have a deleterious effect on the mentality ... Notable dressmakers are showing the loveliest materials in the gayest colours. The Directoire period was delightful from a dress point of view. As it harmonises with the spirit of happier times it is believed it will prevail with the next evolution of the wheel of fashion.' By November 1918, the clothes worn by women had moved, in a period of four years, from the constricted, full-length costumes of the Edwardian era to simpler styles bearing all the hallmarks of the 1920s. Whether fashion would have undergone quite such a transformation without the war is debatable. It would undoubtedly not have happened quite so rapidly.

HOTEL CECIL, LONDON.
FROM RIVER THAMES.

The magnificent Hotel Cecil, sprawling from the Strand down to the Embankment, was completed in 1896 and one of London's most fashionable hotels. Like many buildings, it was requisitioned during the war; first as the temporary base for the Sportsman's Battalion and then in 1918 as the headquarters of the newly formed RAF. (Jazz Age Club/ME)

To the Women of Britain.

Some of your men folk are holding back on your account

Wont you prove your love for your Country by persuading them to go?

PUBLISHED BY THE PARLIAMENTARY RECRUITING COMMITTEE, LONDON. POSTER NO. 55.   THE ROWNELL PRESS, STRAND, LONDON.

Many recruitment posters, such as this one, appealed to the women of Britain and asked them to demonstrate their patriotism by encouraging their husband or sons to join up. To obey such exhortations cannot have been easy. (National Army Museum/ME)

Recruitment poster for the Sportsman's Battalions designed by Norman Keene. The motorcycle despatch rider with bandaged head and Douglas motorbike epitomised the sort of pluck and determined character the battalion sought to recruit. (National Army Museum/ME)

Above: A hand-coloured fashion plate by Georges Barbier for the celebrated French fashion journal, *Gazette du Bon Ton*, depicting fashions for the summer of 1915 by such lauded names as Paquin and Doucet. Designer fashion such as this was beyond the purse of all but the wealthiest. Nevertheless, the flared, full skirts and jaunty hats were typical of the period and Parisian fashions were often copied by London department stores. (ME)

Opposite: In 1916, Eve of *The Tatler* came to life on stage and was played by actress Phyllis Dare as part of a revue, *Tina*, at the Adelphi Theatre. The costumes – cartoonish accentuations of the new wartime silhouette – inspired dressmakers and milliners to create 'Eve' hats and gowns. (Illustrated London News/ME)

PHYLLIS DARE AS EVE, AND TWO CHARMING SUPPORTERS IN THE "EVE" DRESSES WHICH PROVIDE "THE NOTE" FOR THE COMING FASHIONS

The original Eve, for aught that is known to the contrary, may have controlled the fashions in the somewhat exclusive society in which she moved; but her lineal descendant, the lady who so greatly adorns the leading pages in "The Tatler" and who has been materialised by Miss Phyllis Dare and her attendant nymphs in "Tina," is undoubtedly going to do so during the coming season. Unless our dress and fashion vedette is greatly deceived, "Eve" clothes—modified, of course—are to be worn by all those who aspire to be really well-turned-out and in the movement. Dressmakers and milliners are busy creating "Eve" hats and "Eve" gowns which the many feminine admirers of that little lady are demanding

MILITARY BADGE JEWELLERY
FROM A COLLECTION AT
THE GOLDSMITHS & SILVERSMITHS COMPANY, Ltd., 112, REGENT STREET, W.

THE ROYAL IRISH REGIMENT
£17·0·0

IRISH GUARDS
£23·10·0

THE BLACK WATCH
£23·0·0

THE ROYAL ARTILLERY
£9·5·0

AUSTRALIA
£2·2·0

CANADA
£1·17·6

XXXVITH SIKHS
£5·10·0

GRENADIER GUARDS
£4·17·6

NEW ZEALAND
£2·15·0

THE WILTSHIRE REGIMENT
£4·0·0

5TH ROYAL IRISH LANCERS
£9·0·0

SOUTH AFRICAN HEAVY ARTILLERY
£2·15·0

The Regimental Badge of almost every unit of the Empire's Armies is represented in the Goldsmiths & Silversmiths Company's collection of Military Jewellery. These Regimental Badges, which may be had in Gold or Palladium or set with Diamonds and other precious stones, are reproduced with the utmost fidelity to the original and represent the finest quality in this class of work.

Above: Regimental badge jewellery, such as this selection by the Goldsmiths and Silversmiths Company, allowed those women who could afford it to express their allegiance to a particular regiment. The brooches were made of gold or palladium set with diamonds and precious stones. (ME)

Opposite: Fashion plate by the illustrator 'Zyp' from *The Queen* magazine, 1 April 1916, showing three outfits for spring with the wider and shorter skirts which had become *de rigeur*. (Hearst Magazines (UK)/ME)

Above: Known as 'the only-wear', khaki uniform soon became the only acceptable clothing for men of military age. Around the country, gentlemen's outfitters and military tailors advertised the importance of investing in good quality kit. (National Army Museum/ME)

Opposite: Lectures and lessons on war cookery aimed to help women economise while providing nourishing meals to keep the nation healthy. *The Queen* magazine regularly reported on available courses, though this young girl seems rather reluctant to attend a lecture on how to 'make two courses out of a nut and a banana'. (ME)

CROCK'S RESTAURANT

" 'Till the Boys Come Home "

Above: Restaurants continued to do business during the war and it was possible to eat well, despite food restrictions. Phrynette in *The Sketch*, writing of a recent meal enjoyed at Treiglie's Italian restaurant, asked, 'Surely it's a national economy to have plates so carefully prepared that you never waste a crumb and actually long to lick your plate?' (Illustrated London News/ME)

Opposite: Public information posters emphasised how, collectively, small changes at home could lead to victory. This poster recommended cutting bread more thinly in order to help defeat the U-boats that were targeting merchant ships bringing wheat imports from abroad. Other posters reminded civilians that for every 100,000 tons of wheat saved through economy, 28,000 troops could be transported from America. (Onslows Auctioneers/ME)

DON'T WASTE BREAD!

SAVE TWO THICK SLICES
EVERY DAY, and
Defeat the 'U' Boat

MINISTRY OF FOOD . F.C. No. 18   CLARKE & SHERWELL, LTD., PRINTERS, LONDON

Above: If those fighting at the Front were prepared to make the ultimate sacrifice, then those at home could afford to make small sacrifices — one of many posters exhorting the nation to save food. (Onslows Auctioneers/ME)

Opposite: "E's a good sort 'e is' was the conclusion of one Tommy who observed the King during one of his several visits to the Front. The King insisted on seeing the trenches of the front line for himself and is pictured here being shown a captured German dug-out. (Grenville Collins Postcard Collection/ME)

The Sefton Fabrics

Above: A souvenir commemorating the visit of the Kaiser and his wife to London in November 1907. Though a cause of celebration at the time, such trips to England by Wilhelm and other members of the German royal family were viewed with retrospective suspicion. (David Cohen Fine Art/ME)

Opposite: As the wife of the owner of Sefton Fabrics, Annie Fisher contributed designs for a new range of dress fabrics in June 1918. An Eve-like character starred in their advertisements. Note the delicately patterned stockings. (Illustrated London News/ME)

'The Patriots' by Annie Fish. Prolific childbearing was positively encouraged. This cartoon from December 1915 shows an officer returning home on leave to find that his wife has dutifully given birth to triplets. (Illustrated London News/ME)

"A DUCK'S EGG."

The titillating fantasy of Raphael Kirchner's illustrations was a hit with readers of *The Sketch* when the magazine published them during 1915. Even more popular with the troops, the Kirchner girls decorated the walls of dug-outs and were the forerunner of the pin-up popularised in subsequent decades. (Illustrated London News/ME)

Above: A poster advertising the benefits of Harrogate spa in North Yorkshire. With the German spas previously frequented by smart society now crossed off the map, Harrogate enjoyed a newfound popularity during the war years. (The National Archives/ME)

Opposite: 'Beauty on duty has a duty to beauty' – manufacturers of cosmetics and creams were quick to recognise the potency of the image of the working woman. (Illustrated London News/ME)

We're all doing our little bit!   Nous faisons toutes ce que nous pouvons.

Above: A line-up of five female war workers – a land girl, policewoman, nurse, munitionette and postwoman. Such images were popular subjects for postcards of the period. (March of the Women Collection/ME)

Opposite: Recruiting poster for Queen Mary's Army Auxiliary Corps, 'the girl behind the man behind the gun'. 57,000 women served as WAACs during the war as cooks, cleaners, gardeners and waitresses all in support of the Army. (National Army Museum/ME)

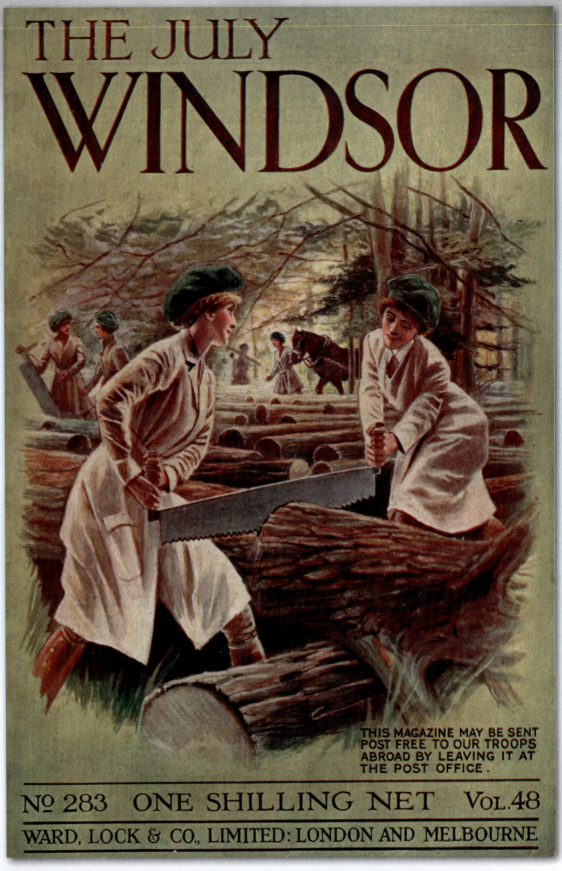

THE JULY

WINDSOR

THIS MAGAZINE MAY BE SENT POST FREE TO OUR TROOPS ABROAD BY LEAVING IT AT THE POST OFFICE.

Nº 283   ONE SHILLING NET   Vol.48

WARD, LOCK & CO., LIMITED: LONDON AND MELBOURNE

Women of the Timber Corps, a division of the Women's Land Army, were known as 'Lumber Jills'. According to *The Queen*, 'strong, healthy girls' were needed and colonial women with experience of that kind of work were particularly encouraged. (March of the Women Collection/ME)

Are we Downhearted? No! not at
Brighton

A postcard with an optimistic message from Brighton. The seaside town played host to thousands of wounded soldiers throughout the war. (Grenville Collins Postcard Collection/ME)

Above: Sulhamstead House in Berkshire converted into a military hospital and painted by the artist Frank Dadd. Convalescent soldiers still wore a uniform – of a loose-fitting blue suit and red tie – ensuring they were identified as having done their duty. (David Cohen Fine Art/ME)

Opposite: Poster advertising British toys made by wounded soldiers at the Lord Roberts Memorial Workshop in Fulham. The workshops aimed to rehabilitate wounded men and employed soldiers and sailors in eleven workshops around the country where they were trained to be self-sufficient and to learn new skills. (ME)

WOODEN·TOYS

LORD · ROBERTS
MEMORIAL·WORKSHOPS
FOR
DISABLED·SOLDIERS·&·SAILORS
HEAD·OFFICE·FULHAM·LONDON

BLINDED FOR YOU

Founded in 1915 by Arthur Pearson, St Dunstan's Hostel aided the recovery and rehabilitation of servicemen blinded during the First World War. This charity postcard produced for the hostel shows a blinded serviceman being led by a young girl and bears the poignant line 'Blinded For You'. (Grenville Collins Postcard Collection/ME)

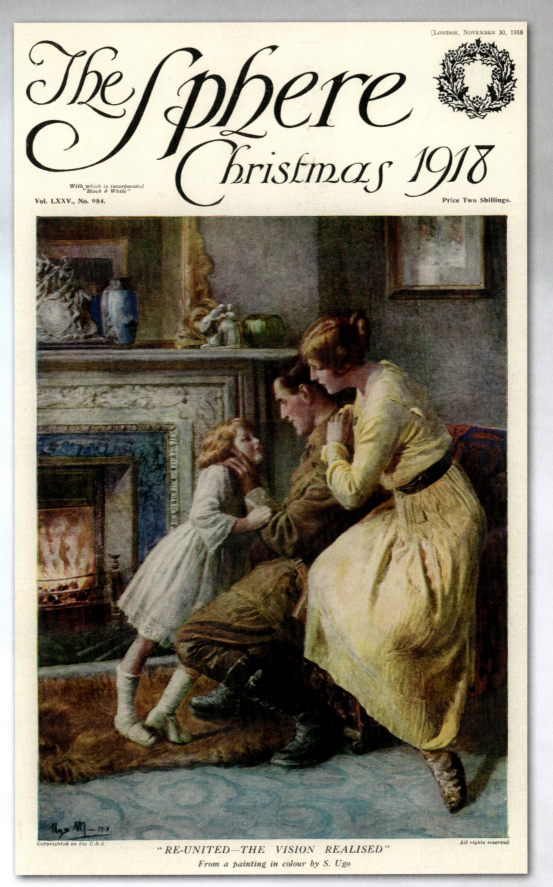

[LONDON, NOVEMBER 30, 1918

The Sphere

Christmas 1918

With which is incorporated
"Black & White"

Vol. LXXV., No. 984.

Price Two Shillings.

"RE-UNITED—THE VISION REALISED"
From a painting in colour by S. Ugo

The *Illustrated London News* and *The Sphere* often opted for heartwarming scenes of family reunion for their wartime Christmas number covers. Christmas 1918 still drew on the same theme, but this time, this soldier's homecoming is permanent. (Illustrated London News/ME)

Eve pictured on the cover of *The Tatler*'s Peace Number, discarding khaki in favour of something altogether more frivolous. She seems fully prepared to step effortlessly into the 1920s. Eve would depart from *The Tatler* later that year and re-emerge in the short-lived magazine 'Pan.' Annie Fish continued to have a successful career as an illustrator, but Eve's original creator, the journalist Olivia Maitland-Davidson, died prematurely following an operation in 1920. (Illustrated London News/ME)

A joyful *Bystander* cover from 7 May 1919, painted by the artist Herbert Pizer, celebrating peace in Europe (though the Treaty of Versailles would not be signed until the following month). Female representatives of Britain, Belgium, Italy, France and the USA, raise their glasses in a toast to peace. The absence of Russia is notable. (Illustrated London News/ME)

Your King and Country Thank You.

HOME WORDS NO. 168

Christmas Greetings from .... to ....

Above: A patriotic postcard depicting King George V thanking representatives of the Army and Navy for their contribution during the War. Despite nationwide celebrations following the signing of the Armistice, the King and other members of the Royal family continued their round of visits and duties. (Grenville Collins Postcard Collection/ME)

Opposite: Annie Fish's illustration on the cover of *The Tatler*'s Christmas number in 1915 shows the magazine in a blaze of stylish patriotism. Even Tou-tou holds a flag in his mouth. (Illustrated London News/ME)

Prince Louis Alexander of Battenberg (1854–1921), First Sea Lord of the Admiralty. Louis married Princess Victoria of Hesse, Princess Alice's eldest daughter, in 1884 and is the grandfather of the current Duke of Edinburgh. Having entered the Royal Navy in 1868 as a cadet, he was a naturalised British subject and instrumental in ensuring the readiness of the Fleet when war broke out in August 1914. But his Germanic roots – and the view of the populist newspapers on the subject – made his position untenable. He resigned in October that year. (ME)

ROYALTY

'I suppose there never was a war more full of the ironies of fate,' mused Eve, *Tatler*'s columnist in September 1914. 'Three first cousins of King George, all closely connected with England, hold commissions in the German Army and have to fight against this country and their royal relatives, such as Prince Arthur of Connaught and the Queen's brothers, the Tecks.'

It was indeed ironic. As king, what George V may have lacked in panache and personal charisma, he more than made up for during wartime with his strong sense of duty and patriotism. That this should be compromised by the shadow of relatives fighting for the other side must have been both irritating and distressing, and it took a combination of measured diplomacy, judicious name-changing and official disassociation of blood connections to retain the British royal family's unblemished reputation throughout the conflict.

The inherent Germanic character of Britain's royal family was difficult to deny. For more than a century, marriage alliances between the British and German royal families had been forged, beginning, naturally, with the Hanoverian monarchy and continuing in 1838, when Queen Victoria married her Coburg cousin, Prince Albert. Having found marital nirvana with her own German princeling, she continued to scour the duchies and courts of Germany for eligible spouses to suit her own brood. Of Victoria's nine children, four of her daughters were matched with German husbands, while two of her four sons found German wives. The result was a seemingly inextricable intermingling and cross-fertilisation of Anglo-German royalty, which in peacetime provoked little more objection than grumbling about the cost of maintaining these imported foreign royalties, but in wartime met with more audible disapproval. The zealous matchmaking of Queen Victoria and the web of marriage bonds she had woven so carefully between her children and her children's children in Great Britain and Germany quite suddenly became, in 1914, a cause for embarrassment, and within the family a source of sadness and torn loyalties.

The first of the three cousins in question, the Duke of Brunswick, was the nephew of Queen Alexandra through his mother, Princess Thyra of Denmark. But he also enjoyed the distinction of being the Kaiser's son-in-law, having married the German Emperor's only daughter, Princess Viktoria Luise in May 1913, swearing loyalty to the Kaiser and receiving a commission as first a cavalry captain and company commander in the Zieten-Hussars, a Prussian regiment. The wedding, held in

Berlin, and attended by Tsar Nicholas II and King George V, had been the last great gathering of European royalty before war unravelled the close-knit family ties binding them. On a visit by the Kaiser and Kaiserin to London in 1911 for the unveiling of the Queen Victoria Memorial Statue in front of Buckingham Palace, Viktoria Luise, known as 'Sissy', had forged a friendship with Princess Mary, also an only daughter. Just three years later, the two young women's countries were at war.

Another cousin to find himself on the opposing side to that of the country of his birth was the Duke of Saxe-Coburg-Gotha, formerly Prince Charles Edward of Albany, posthumous son of Queen Victoria's youngest son, Prince Leopold. Charlie had had the misfortune to succeed to the German Duchy in 1899 at the age of thirteen when the heir-apparent, Prince Alfred of Edinburgh, had died in mysterious circumstances. Legend has it that his cousin and contemporary at Eton, Prince Arthur of Connaught, who by order of precedence should have been first choice to fill the role, threatened to beat him if he did not accept the dukedom. Charlie's strong sense of duty and destiny, instilled in him by his mother, meant he accepted his fate, leaving friends and family to learn the ropes and the language at Lichterfeld military academy at Potsdam (suggested by the Kaiser), until he came of age three years later. When war broke out, Charlie was in England with his mother and sister, and was forced to resign his colonelcy in the Seaforth Highlanders before heading to his adopted country. Had Prince Arthur of Connaught become Duke of Saxe-Coburg instead of his younger cousin, then each may very well have found themselves serving on the opposite side.

In the event, it was unlikely that either of them would experience close-hand fighting. Prince Arthur, who had fought in the Boer War, acted as Aide-de-Campe to Generals French and Haig, and then to his cousin, the King. Charles Edward was made a General but was never given command. And despite *The Tatler*'s prediction of kinsmen divided by the sword, the third cousin, Prince Albert of Schleswig-Holstein, son of Queen Victoria's third daughter, Princess Christian (Helena), did not see action either. Albert, possibly more at home on the golf links at Sunningdale, was created heir to his uncle's duchy of Schleswig-Holstein, on the proviso that he took German nationality. Sensitive of his British roots, the German Army did not ask him to bear arms against his mother country and he spent the war on the Staff of the Governor of Berlin. In October 1917, when his father, Prince Christian, died at his London home, Schomberg House, the war prevented him travelling to Britain to act as chief mourner.

Other Teutonic family members, who had once visited England frequently to see friends and relatives, were suddenly persona non grata. Kaiser Wilhelm was of course enemy number one. The man who had posed and preened in his uniforms for countless photographs published in English magazines was now lampooned and caricatured repeatedly, pictured variously as monstrous, bloodthirsty, posturing or cowardly. His eldest son, the Crown Prince, was portrayed as a chinless sneak. It was only in May the previous year that England's bête noire, as he soon became, had appeared on the cover of the *Illustrated London News* with his cousin George V. The latter was wearing the German uniform of 1st Dragoon Guards while the Kaiser repaid the compliment in the uniform of a British admiral. By August 1914, he was dubbed 'Wilhelm Iscariot' in *The Bystander* as it printed photographs of him feigning friendship with various European heads of state though all the while plotting his ruthless 'crucifixion of Europe'.

PHOTO
CENTRAL NEWS.

H.R.H. PRINCESS MARY.
PHOTOGRAPHED AT BUCKINGHAM PALACE.

107.L.
BEAGLES' POSTCARDS.

Britain's own pin-up princess: Princess Mary accompanied her parents on their relentless programme of visits and tours, was patron or involved in several charities and trained as a nurse at Great Ormond Street Children's Hospital. (ME)

Sophie of Greece, another granddaughter of the Queen and aunt of George V, had the misfortune to be the Kaiser's sister as well as wife of the vascillating King Constantine. The press, viewing her unequivocally as 'pro-Hun' but with little evidence to support their claims, made mincemeat of her. *The Tatler*, usually a laconic critic, was particularly vociferous in 1917 when Constantine was deposed in favour of their son, Alexander, jeering, 'GOOD BYE-EEE, We're so glad to see your back, dear lady' in a caption over a photograph of the Queen. 'The Queen has unquestionably been the power behind the throne which has in no small measure, been responsible for the unsatisfactory and highly explosive condition of affairs in Greece for the last two years or more. The deposition of King Constantine and the elimination of the German influence are the most

satisfactory incidents of the whole campaign.' It was a far cry from the same magazine's attitude to the Queen in July 1914. Commenting on a visit of the Queen to Eastbourne in July that year, it spoke of her 'purely private and particular affection for the country to which her mother was so supremely devoted.'

One of the injustices of anti-German hysteria in the early months of the war was the resignation of the First Sea Lord, Prince Louis of Battenberg, husband of Queen Victoria's granddaughter, Princess Victoria of Hesse. Having entered the Royal Navy in 1868 as a cadet, he was a naturalised British subject and instrumental in ensuring the readiness of the Fleet when war broke out in August 1914. But his Germanic roots – and the view of the populist newspapers on the subject – made his position untenable. He resigned in October that year, much to the regret of the King, numerous members of the Cabinet and much of the press. 'It is hoped,' commented *The Bystander*, 'that, having drawn the official blood of Prince Louis, our papers will now leave the men at the helm alone … If he is of Germanic descent, so, Englishmen should be reminded, is the British Royal family itself.'

Pre-war visits to England by members of German royalty, such as Queen Sophie's and more public events like the unveiling of the Queen Victoria Memorial in front of Buckingham Palace in 1911, were suddenly, with the benefit of hindsight, seen in a different light. *The Bystander* devoted a double-page spread to printing pictures of the Kaiser's visit to Highcliffe Castle in the New Forest

Prince Charles Edward, 2nd Duke of Albany, Duke of Saxe-Coburg-Gotha (1884–1954) in German military uniform. When the Duke of Saxe-Coburg-Gotha's son Alfred died in 1899, Charles Edward became the heir and was uprooted from his life in England, much against his wishes. He ended up a General in the German Army during the First World War, exemplifying how the war divided European royalty. (Charlotte Zeepvat/ILN/ME)

THE ILLUSTRATED LONDON NEWS

REGISTERED AS A NEWSPAPER FOR TRANSMISSION IN THE UNITED KINGDOM, AND TO CANADA AND NEWFOUNDLAND BY MAGAZINE POST.

No. 3867.—VOL. CXLII.   SATURDAY, MAY 31, 1913.   SIXPENCE.

The Copyright of all the Editorial Matter, both Engravings and Letterpress, is Strictly Reserved in Great Britain, the Colonies, Europe, and the United States of America.

THE KING AS A GERMAN OFFICER: HIS MAJESTY AT THE INSPECTION OF HIS REGIMENT, THE 1st DRAGOONS
OF THE GUARDS, IN BERLIN.

On the wedding-day of Princess Victoria Louise, King George inspected his German | across the field to where the regiment was drawn up. Later, the force was divided
regiment, the 1st Dragoons of the Guards, upon the Tempelhofer Feld. His Majesty | into attackers and defenders, and there was a skirmish lasting some forty minutes.
drove to this Parade Ground of the Berlin Garrison, on which, there is a boast, all | A march past the King followed. He is here seen with the Kaiser, looking at some
the armies of Europe could find standing-room, and there mounted a charger, to canter | photographs of previous festivities in connection with the wedding.

PHOTOGRAPH BY NEWSPAPER ILLUSTRATIONS.

King George V pictured on the front cover of the *Illustrated London News* during a visit to Berlin for the marriage of the Kaiser's only daughter, wearing the uniform of the 1st Dragoons, a German regiment of which he was honorary colonel. Less than eighteen months later, the two cousins' countries would be at war and the British monarchy would start the process of dissolving these once most publicly displayed familial bonds. (Illustrated London News/ME)

some years previously. Alongside photographs of him entertaining village children, planting trees and walking to church, the magazine asked, 'Was Espionage the Motive of his Memorable Visit of 1907?' Eve, in a fit of retrospective indignation, wrote of what 'a spying crowd the whole Hohenzollern lot are, aren't they? In the days before the war every single petty German royalty somehow used to find reasons for making summer trips to England. Prince Henry of Prussia, we all know, was here for anything but friendly purposes. And on the last "private" visit of the German Crown Prince and Princess, they spent most of their time looking at empty houses in the country round London – for what purpose we can only guess, but certainly not with any idea of living in 'em.' After the bombardment of Scarborough, *The Bystander* recalled with sarcasm that 'quite recently Prince Henry of Prussia (also a cousin of the King) was the guest of Lord Londesborough at Londesborough Lodge, Scarborough. The Prince knows well enough how much of a "fortified town" is Scarborough. It will, I hope, be many moons before any English coast resorts will welcome to their peaceful precincts any more Princely spies.'

These comments were made in 1917, the year that the Titles Deprivation Act was introduced, depriving German princes such as Charlie of Albany, now Karl Eduard of Saxe-Coburg, of their English royal titles, and removing any ambiguity over the royal family's

'One of the most sterling and representative of sovereigns …' King George V visiting the wounded in France. (Pump Park Photography/ME)

Englishness in the process. This was carried further when the royal family's own German surname was replaced by the unimpeachably English Windsor, a suggestion made by the King's private secretary, Lord Stamfordham. Princess Beatrice, who since her marriage to her late husband had been known as Princesss Henry of Battenberg, had dropped the Battenberg some years previously; her eldest son, Prince Alexander ('Drino') of Battenberg, became the Marquess of Carisbrooke and Prince Albert of Schleswig-Holstein's sisters, Princess Helena Victoria and Princess Marie Louise, both of whom worked indefatigably for good causes during the war, simply used their first names, no other introduction being required. The Tecks, brothers to Queen Mary, were demoted too. Prince Alexander of Teck (married to Charlie's sister, Princess Alice) became Alexander Cambridge, 1st Earl of Athlone, and his elder brother, Adolphus, relinquished the Duke of Teck title inherited from his father to become the Marquess of Cambridge. Prince Louis of Battenberg took the name Mountbatten and became Marquess of Milford Haven, wryly alluding to his transformation in the guestbook at his son George's house, 'Arrived Prince Hyde, departed Lord Jekyll.'

Eve, in a mischievous mood, commented on this 'regular summer sale of royalties', wondering aloud about how this would affect order of precedence. 'People who've been 'bobbed' to since their cradles'll find it a shock to find themselves treated almost like any mortals. And there's the other rather ticklish point of where they'll be put in the British peerage and whether they'll come top or bottom of their new ranks. Top, I suppose – be a bit awkward wouldn't it, if the coroneted daughter of a plutocratic pork-packer from Chicago, Ill., went into dinner before any ex-princess and H.H.?'

To King George V, the furore over German titles was trivial in comparison to the more pressing duties of a wartime sovereign. Nor did he agree with the overt anti-German feelings expressed by papers like the *Daily Mail* or the jingoistic *John Bull*. But if his patriotism was ever in doubt, he let his actions speak for themselves. Over four years of war, the King paid seven visits to British naval bases, held 450 inspections, personally conferred an estimated 50,000 decorations, visited 300 hospitals and went to the Front five times to visit the armies in France. During a visit to the Front in 1915, the King fell from his horse as it reared up, frightened by cheers of the troops. He was badly injured with a broken pelvis, an injury that was to aggravate the King for the rest of his life. But even from his sick bed, he carried on, awarding the Victoria Cross to Lance-Sergeant Oliver Brooks while in a hospital train. In addition to this, he toured factories and industrial regions, training grounds and bombed areas. Anyone critical of the British King's German heritage would be hard-pressed to find a more hard-working, committed and dutiful monarch. In September 1914, Eve reported on the regal timetable and revealed a tolerant view of the Germans that was to be eroded as the war progressed:

The King and Queen are visiting the wounded from the front at various hospitals and houses practically every day. At Netley, their graciousness to the German wounded was much remarked (by the way, Betty, there's such a nice one – wounded German officer, I mean – in King Edward VII's Hospital), and they're sending grouse and venison and white heather from Deeside to the hospitals.

As well as visits and inspections, the palace ensured that almost every facet of the royal timetable was bent to help the war effort.

The King loaned vehicles from the Royal Mews to the Volunteer Motor Mobilisation Corps so that convalescents could be taken for a daily drive to aid their recovery. In March 1916, Buckingham Palace hosted a tea party for wounded soldiers in a marquee at the Riding School – 'with lots of the Court people doing the most unaccustomed things in the way of entertaining,' wrote Eve about helpers like Mrs Keppel, Mrs Asquith and Princess Arthur of Connaught acting as waitresses for the occasion. The *Illustrated Sporting & Dramatic News*, inspired by the success of the event, gave a particularly grateful summary of the King and Queen's contribution to the war effort:

There has been a wonderful certainty in their Majesties' touch with the people ever since the nation's time of trial began. Never have they failed to do just what was wanted, and always they have thought of and done yet more and more. This last evidence of their appreciation of our glorious men brings them deeper down to our heart's love and loyalty.

Eve quoted another magazine, *Nineteenth Century*, who wrote of the King in 1918, describing him as 'sincere, direct, simple, in intimate congruity with the social sentiments of the British people … the nation is learning

Prince Henry, later Duke of Gloucester, third son of King George V and Queen Mary, pictured second from left marching in the ranks at the Eton College Officers' Training Corps. (Illustrated London News/ME)

A ROYAL EXAMPLE

To the Young Unmarried Men of the Empire.

Buckingham Palace.

All must realise that the present time of deep anxiety will be followed by one of considerable distress among the people of this country least able to bear it.

We most earnestly pray that their sufferings may be neither long nor bitter, but we cannot wait until the need presses heavily upon us.

The means of relief must be ready in our hands. To allay anxiety will go some way to stay distress.

A National Fund has been founded, and I am proud to act as its Treasurer.

My first duty is to ask for generous and ready support, and I know that I shall not ask in vain.

At such a moment we all stand by one another, and it is to the heart of the British people that I confidently make this most earnest appeal.

EDWARD P.

THE PRINCE OF WALES JOINS THE GRENADIER GUARDS ON THE OUTBREAK OF HOSTILITIES

Inset we print the stirring appeal which the Prince of Wales has issued to the nation. The Prince has done his duty. Now readers who can spare something, it is up to you to do yours

'A Royal Example' – a nervous-looking Prince of Wales in training with the Grenadier Guards within days of the war's outbreak. In the event, the Prince was not to take part in any military action. Much to his frustration, he was given a staff position and prevented from being anywhere near danger. (Illustrated London News/ME)

to appreciate one of the most sterling and representative of British Sovereigns.'

Or to put it in plainer terms, ''E's a sport, 'e is!' was, Eve heard, one Tommy's verdict on the King after a visit to the front in 1916 where he had walked around 'dangerous places', went 'over the top' of one of the older first-line trenches to see how it felt for the thousands who had to do it and stood to attention and saluted when he came suddenly to a grave with the inscription: 'To an Unknown British Soldier.'

Leading by example even extended to rationing in the royal household. 'No one can accuse the present royalties of fiddling while Rome's burning so to speak, can they? Picture to yourself – not a drink for the Duration, not a dinner-party, not a lunch, except to family and such like … If we'd only all gone on those lines, what thousands and thousands we'd have had to put in War Loans, wouldn't we?' said Eve in January 1917. Even by then, the tea parties for the wounded had lost their shine and the 'piercing cold stables' were no longer a novelty.

The King felt duped by Lloyd George about his decision to give up drink for the duration of the war. 'I hate doing it, but hope it will do good,' he confided to his diary. But despite royal abstinence, pubs, clubs and restaurants continued to do a booming trade in 'the cup that cheers', albeit within the confines of licensing restrictions. Ministers and visiting dignitaries to royal residences were disappointed that their host was sticking so rigidly to his teetotal pledge and General Joffre, in particular, was

The dashing Prince Maurice of Battenberg (1890–1914), youngest son of Princess Beatrice and Prince Henry of Battenberg, pictured in top hat and tails at a society event in the summer of 1914. Maurice joined the 60th regiment of the King's Royal Rifle Corps and held the rank of lieutenant. He was hit by a shell while leading his company at Ypres in October 1914, and died of wounds on the way to the dressing station. (Illustrated London News/ME)

said to have been rendered speechless when served barley water during a meeting with the King at GHQ. In June 1918, Eve reported on a sale of royal wines in aid of the Red Cross admitting that she was keeping her eye on some of the buyers so that she might enjoy a nip of the royal sherry (bought at 16 guineas a dozen) or a 'a glass or two of King Edward's "private port" (50 guineas a dozen).' It says something for the King's commitment to the cause that he was able to auction off some of the finest vintages from the royal cellars and watch those less abstemious enjoy the pleasures thereof.

The eldest of the King's five sons, Edward, Prince of Wales, was twenty years old when war broke out, and was keen to enlist despite the reservations of the establishment. 'What does it matter if I am killed?' he argued with Lord Kitchener, 'I have four brothers.' Kitchener replied that it would be more problematic if he were captured by the enemy, but eventually relented with a caveat that the Prince would not be allowed anywhere near the firing line. He joined the staff of General French, tasked mainly with paperwork and carrying despatches, a role that often frustrated and embarrassed him, but the press were delighted to see the heir to the throne in uniform, and glossed over the non-combative details of his actual role. In its first issue relating to the war, fired up with patriotism and recruiting zeal, *The Tatler* published a photograph of the Prince in training as an infantry officer with the Grenadier Guards. Looking nervous, a little puny and considerably younger than his actual age, the picture was entitled 'A ROYAL EXAMPLE – To the young, unmarried men of the Empire. The Prince has done his duty. Now readers who can spare something, it is up to you to do yours.' Eve reported a couple of months later on the Prince's enthusiasm for soldiering:

Yes, they did say the Prince of Wales wasn't to go to the front at first, but I believe there was no holding him ... and now they haven't got the excuse that he doesn't know enough soldiering yet, for he's so keen he's simply been slaving away at it every day ever since the war started; and he's to be on staff anyway, which isn't, of course, quite so risky as the firing line. But here's luck to the dear boy!

On one occasion, while visiting the battlefront during the Battle of Loos, he returned to his car to find his chauffeur killed by shrapnel. It was probably the closest he ever got to personal danger and when awarded the Military Cross and French Legion d'Honneur he argued strongly that he did not deserve them.

Nevertheless, the reports on his conduct that filtered back to England were favourable. *The Sketch* spoke of his 'extraordinary fitness', covering a great deal of ground either on foot, on horseback or by motor car, which he often drove himself – 'Even if not under orders to "go and be quick", he works out an active day's programme; motoring till lunch, and a walk of a dozen miles or so before three!' This ability to walk great distances is borne out by his letters from the time. *The Bystander* described the men calling him 'our little bit of luck' and related that 'his pluck, his keenness and sense of honest duty have vastly increased the anxieties of HQ but by our millions of fighting men it will never be forgotten. This recognition will be a bulwark to the throne.' During his short leave home to England, the magazine remarked on the fact that 'the Prince of Wales has seized the opportunity to put in some more hard and useful work in his country's service', as he was pictured arriving at a meeting of the Royal Patriotic Fund Corporation. The Prince was also founder and poster boy of the National Relief Fund, set up within the first few weeks of the war to provide aid to those suffering hardship due to the war. The fund raised millions, much of which was generated by the sale of a postcard featuring his image.

The Queen magazine, perhaps a little naively, credited the Prince with liking the simple life while on duty at the front – 'a cold bath helps to keep the young Prince fit; he is most sparing in his diet, eating very little and drinking less, and likes plenty of exercise by way of keeping fit. At present the Prince of Wales shows no signs of caring about society as such … his physical appearance has much improved since he went out to France, as he has filled out wonderfully, though still not tall.'

The Queen magazine was not, of course, privy to the Prince's inner thoughts. As the most eligible bachelor in the Empire, speculation over who he would marry began in earnest, especially since the fracturing of relations between England and Germany struck a number of potential candidates off the list.

In December 1914, Eve was already convinced that he would marry a Russian:

I can't swear it's the gospel truth, but they do say the Prince has found one silver lining to this cloud of war. 'Shan't have to marry a German now anyway!' was the way he put it – in the story. It'll be a Russian alliance he'll make now, of course, when the moment comes for the marriage question to pop up again, and that'll be a good thing from the point of view of what everybody thinks so much more important now than they used to – beauty, I mean. German women are the limit in plainness, don't go in for brains, and can't put their clothes on either – not that they're worth putting on – and get fat as surely as a cat gets kittens. Russian women are not such models of virtue p'r'aps in the way of 'Kinder-Kuche-Kirche'. But they've got brains and they've

got chic, and the Russian Imperial princesses in particular have beauty.

In 1918, Princess Yolande of Italy was another princess rumoured to be a contender, while Eve gossiped that a 'daughter of the ducal house of Buccleuch is now in the running for the Queen of England stakes' – though out of the five of them, she did not specify which. In fact, the third daughter, Alice Montagu-Douglas-Scott, would marry the Prince of Wales' brother Henry in 1935. By the time of the Armistice, when there were no longer any Russian Imperial princesses to marry, Eve was squeaking excitedly: 'On it, the next thing is to cement the royal position still more firmly in these rocking days of European revolution is the heir apparent's marriage. And as it'll really almost have to be a mere British commoner now – our own brand of princesses being so very small and the foreign ones so very much washed out – a 'citing prospect isn't it?'

It's highly likely that many readers of *The Tatler* were well aware that the Prince had been first in love with Rosemary Leveson-Gower, daughter of the Duke and Duchess of Sutherland, and, by 1918, had already embarked upon a liaison with the married Freda Dudley-Ward. But for a gossip magazine, *The Tatler* was remarkably discreet. In any case, it could not possibly have guessed at the cataclysmic consequences arising from the type of wife the Prince would eventually choose almost two decades later.

Edward's younger brother, Albert ('Bertie'), was serving as a midshipman on HMS *Collingwood*, where he remained and took part in the Battle of Jutland as a sub-lieutenant in 1916. He suffered dreadfully during this time with stomach problems and was diagnosed with a duodenal ulcer, for which he underwent an operation in 1917. Eve sympathised with the prince during one

The TATLER

Vol. LX. No. 783.
London, June 28, 1916

REGISTERED AT THE GENERAL POST OFFICE AS A NEWSPAPER

Sixpence.

Photograph by H. D. Girdwood, B.A., F.R.G.S.; Crown Copyright

"OUR PRINCE" AT THE FRONT

The Prince of Wales has probably seen as much of this war as anyone, as he has not only served on the Western front with his regiment, the Grenadier Guards, but has also visited the Italian front on the Isonzo sector, and has had an opportunity of inspecting the magnificent army of our allies. His Royal Highness is extremely popular wherever he goes, and in Paris he is adored by our warm-hearted neighbours. For his good service in the field the Prince of Wales has been awarded the Military Cross, which distinction has, we believe, pleased His Royal Highness more than any other decoration which he bears

'Our Prince at the Front' – the British press made much of the Prince's service in France, but in reality he was kept out of the firing line and, in his opinion, his role was not worthy of mention. (Illustrated London News/ME)

BIG WILLIE'S FAVOURITE SISTER
A Recent Photograph of "Tino's" Consort.

S.M. SOPHIA QUEEN OF GREECE

The Consort of King Constantine, and who is the third daughter of the late Kaiser Frederick of Germany and the sister of the present Kaiser, whose health it was reported was considered sufficiently bad for the family to be summoned to Potsdam. The Berlin reports assure us that it is "nothing," and that the Kaiser is returning to the front. Queen Sophia was married to Constantine of Greece in Athens in 1889, and he succeeded his father, George I. of Greece, in 1913. The Queen is forty-six years of age, having been born at Potsdam in 1870. She is a Prussian of the Prussians and a keen politician—hence, perhaps, a good deal of the present complications in South-Eastern Europe

Youngest daughter of Princess Victoria, the Princess Royal, Queen Sophie of Greece retained a great fondness for her mother's country of birth, holidaying frequently at Eastbourne with her children. However, as sister of Kaiser Wilhelm II, she was portrayed negatively by the British press, which claimed her sympathies lay with Germany. (Illustrated London News/ME)

spell spent convalescing: 'awful hard luck on Prince Albert, isn't it, getting ill again, and in such a very trying sort of way? But his "mention" ought to help to keep his spirits up, and if he feels like it, of course, there are plenty of opportunities for a prince on sick leave to have a topping time of it, 'specially just now when men are so dreadfully in the minority. Think of the myriads of maidens of all sorts, sizes and colours who'd love to take up l'education de Prince in the way of teaching him, say, a foxtrot or "the saunter"!'

The King's three other sons were too young to serve. Prince Henry was at Eton, and later at Sandhurst where, according to the King's strict instructions, he was to have no privileges whatsoever and was to go through the same course as all other cadets. Prince George was at school in Broadstairs, and Prince John, the youngest, was epileptic and rarely appeared in public.

Princess Mary, the only girl, was in the public eye far more than her brothers during the war and was adopted as a sort of unofficial national emblem in the same way that Belgium had the cute, frizzy-haired Princess Marie-Jose, daughter of King Albert. Mary was quiet, biddable and in appearance rather dowdy compared to the chic society women her elder brother was beginning to associate with. 'Don't you think she would be quite attractive if only she was allowed to dress decently & cultivate a proper chic straight figure which the poor darling isn't!!' wrote the Prince of Wales to Freda about his sister in 1918. Eve, whether through instinct or through a source close to the Palace, attributed the Princess's appearance 'in a really quite modish grey coat and skirt (and grey shoes and stockings to match!)' which she wore to a matinee in March 1918 to her stylish brother's influence. 'One had never seen her before in much the same clothes as we all wear, and – well, clothes do make a difference, of course, and we were wondering whether it was the

Prince. The brother and sister have been about together such a lot during HRH's last leave, and brothers are so particular, aren't they? Also, one must keep one's end up against the sort of programme crowd that contains Lady Rosemary Leveson-Gower, Lady Irene Curzon etc.'

It wasn't something that bothered magazines like *The Queen*, which loved the Princess's wholesome image. Better still, her war activity was exemplary. Rarely far from her mother's side, she involved herself in hospital and charity work and trained as a VAD nurse, passing with honours, though, unlike her brother, she was not allowed to go to France to put her training into practice and was instead posted to Great Ormond Street Children's Hospital. At Christmas 1914, she launched a national appeal asking for contributions for a Christmas gift for all those serving with the armed forces with tremendous success. In the end, 'Princess Mary's Gift Box', a small, embossed brass box containing either cigarettes or chocolate along with a photograph of the Princess, was sent to 350,000 recipients.

Princess Mary would have made her 'debut' in 1915 but the suspension of court presentations and curtailing of the traditional events associated with the Season meant that she, along with many other high-born young ladies, missed out on this rite of passage. To complain about it would have been churlish, but *The Queen* magazine, which reported on the courts every year, mourned the lack of the courts and the associated season wistfully.

'Had it not been for the war the present season would have been an unusually brilliant one. The King's fiftieth birthday will fall on June 3. Three weeks later comes the twenty first birthday of the Prince of Wales. And there would have been, under normal circumstances, the coming out of Princess Mary. However it is not much use to think of what the Season might have been.'

Many other members of the royal clan contributed to the war effort. Despite her advancing years, Queen Alexandra was patron of numerous charities and a regular visitor at concerts, hospitals and canteens, occasionally insisting on pouring tea out for unsuspecting soldiers at buffets during visits. Of the same generation, the King's aunt, Princess Louise, and his uncle, the Duke of Connaught, regularly visited hospitals and factories and were patrons of various causes. The Duke's elder daughter, Margaret, known as Daisy, was Crown Princess of neutral Sweden but his younger daughter, Princess Patricia of Connaught, was a high profile and popular figure who, following her father's Governor-Generalship of Canada, took a particular interest in the welfare of Canadian troops. Princess Arthur of Connaught, Duchess of Fife, fulfilled an ambition to be a nurse, working at St Mary's in Paddington. Princesses Helena Victoria and Marie Louise were also very active, the latter establishing a hospital for the poor in Bermondsey in 1914. There were also a number of high profile foreign and exiled royalties who had made their homes in England and worked for the allied cause.

Manuel II, the exiled King of Portugal, was a regular face at theatrical first nights or tennis tournaments but also set up two

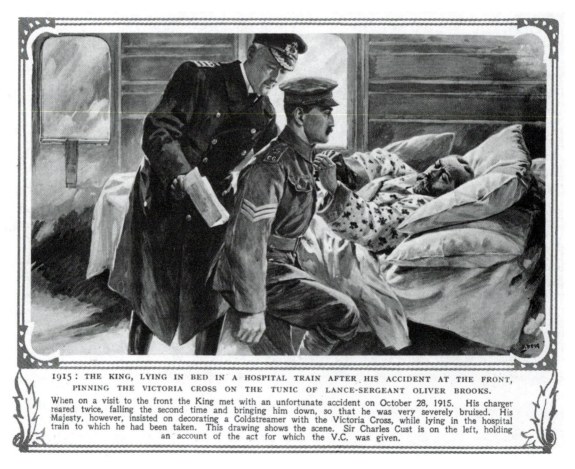

1915: THE KING, LYING IN BED IN A HOSPITAL TRAIN AFTER HIS ACCIDENT AT THE FRONT, PINNING THE VICTORIA CROSS ON THE TUNIC OF LANCE-SERGEANT OLIVER BROOKS.

When on a visit to the front the King met with an unfortunate accident on October 28, 1915. His charger reared twice, falling the second time and bringing him down, so that he was very severely bruised. His Majesty, however, insisted on decorating a Coldstreamer with the Victoria Cross, while lying in the hospital train to which he had been taken. This drawing shows the scene. Sir Charles Cust is on the left, holding an account of the act for which the V.C. was given.

Bedridden on a hospital train due to a fractured pelvis after a fall from his horse during a visit to the Front, King George V nevertheless carried on his duties. Here he is pictured pinning the Victoria Cross on the tunic of Lance-Sergeant Oliver Brooks. (Illustrated London News/ME)

hospitals for wounded officers in Brighton. His mother, Queen Amelie, was a leading figure in the Red Cross society, and devoted time each week to working at the 3rd London General Hospital in Wandsworth. Up in fashionable Harrogate, Grand Duchess George of Russia, sister of King Constantine of Greece, set up two hospitals for soldiers where she worked with her daughters, Nina and Xenia. She had the fortune to be stranded in England when war broke out – her husband was arrested by Bolsheviks and shot in January 1919. Grand Duke Michael Mikhailovich, banished from Russia after making a morganatic marriage, lived in exile on the Riviera and in England where he and his children were a glamorous addition to society. They lived in some style, renting Kenwood House for much of the war. In 1917, Eve reported they were leaving the house in Hampstead 'and will probably return to Claridge's where, I suppose, you can live cheaply by comparison'. But despite their lavish lifestyle, Grand Duke Michael and his family were part of the philanthropic movement that swept through society. The girls, Nada and Zia, lent their talents to charity matinees, bazaars and tennis tournaments and both married well – Zia to Sir Harold Wernher, while Nada married George Mountbatten, eldest son of the former First Sea Lord. In October 1918, their brother Count Michael de Torby held a fashion show at court dressmakers Reville and Rossiter which attracted a sizeable portion of society, with proceeds passed on to the Officers' Families Fund and Lady Beatty's Jutland Fund.

It would be 1918 before those members of the Romanoff dynasty who were exiled in Britain would realise quite how lucky they were. The fate of the Tsar, cousin to the King, and his family could not have been predicted when Eve discussed their being put under house arrest at Tsarskoe Selo in 1917:

And what they're going to do with all those Grand Duchesses. Goodness only knows! They would have come to England, I suppose, the home and haven of all distressed royalties. But their mother's pro-Hunism will rather interfere with that scheme, and might be a rather awkward situation for us as Allies. Still, after all, England's great enough to do anything, and if they did come it would be a parallel to the case of King Manuel, who's the dispossessed ruler of another ally and also married into a German family.

In hindsight, Eve's comments have a particular poignancy. It was indeed an awkward situation and it was the King himself who, despite his close ties with his cousin Nicky, began to have doubts about the wisdom of welcoming an autocratic ruler, with no visible means of financial support and a German wife (again, another cousin), into his country. The British royal family had led a scrupulously blameless existence during wartime and had held onto their throne while all around Europe other monarchs were tumbling from theirs, but there was no room for complacency, or for introducing a fly into the ointment. The King was alert to anti-monarchy rumblings. There were Socialist meetings at the Albert Hall and H.G. Wells had written to *The Times* suggesting it was time for Britain to cast off 'the ancient trappings of throne and sceptre'. The invitation to the Tsar and his family sent by Lloyd George's government was retracted. They felt sure they would be able to find sanctuary in either France or Switzerland. But they did not. Transported to Ekaterinberg in Western Siberia in April 1918, the entire family were shot and killed by their Bolshevik captors on the night of 17 July 1918. When the King learnt the full horror of his cousin's murder, he was distraught. 'It is too horrible and shows what fiends these Bolshevists are', he wrote in his diary. How much his distress was due to the guilty knowledge that he chose to save his throne rather than save his own relatives can only be guessed at.

Another cousin, closer to home, made the ultimate sacrifice. Prince Maurice of Battenberg was the youngest son of Princess Beatrice, and the youngest grandchild of Queen Victoria. Handsome, dashing and popular, Maurice slotted comfortably into the social scene, causing ripples of excitement when he appeared at balls during the 1914 Season. Photographs of him from this period show him at the races or at Cowes, top hat cocked at a rakish angle, cigarette in mouth, or looking natty at Cowes. His penchant for fast cars led to several brushes with the law, including two speeding fines, but a streak of recklessness only enhanced his charms. He joined the King's Royal Rifle Corps in 1911, and it is characteristic that he was among the first to go to France, departing with his regiment on 12 August, just a week after the declaration of war. He took part in the Retreat from Mons and survived a number of near misses, including, reported *The Bystander* on 7 October, 'a narrow escape from death, a bullet from a German rifle passing through the peak of his cap'. The men each side of him were hit, one fatally. His luck ran out on 27 October. While leading an advance during the 1st Battle of Ypres, he was hit by a shell and died within minutes. In *The Tatler*'s 28 October issue it was noted by Eve that Maurice had been mentioned in General French's despatches. By the next week, she was writing, 'Poor Prince Maurice of Battenberg was only twenty-four' (in fact he was twenty-three) – at the very outset of 'the morn and liquid dew of youth'. Maurice was buried in Ypres cemetery, his mother, Princess Beatrice, refusing Lord Kitchener's offer to bring her son's body home. She took solace in her continuing hospital work where she met and felt some solidarity with the many other women who had lost or had sons maimed in the war.

'Nothing could touch and help me more to bear this great trial, than to know that others feel for me', she wrote. 'To lose a beloved promising young man is a terrible trial, but I can look back with pride on him, and on his work nobly fulfilled, and life willingly given for his King and Country.'

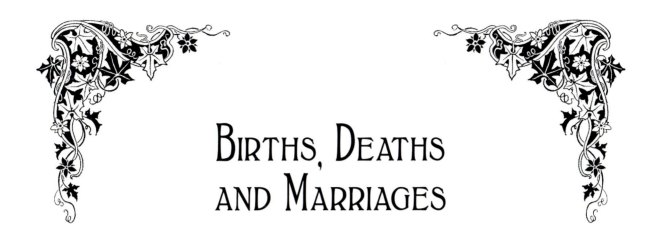

Births, Deaths and Marriages

On 9 September 1914, *The Tatler* published its first photographs of casualties in the war. There was Lieutenant G.C. Wynne of the Yorkshire Light Infantry, Major Foster Swetenham, 2nd Dragoons (Royal Scots Greys) and Lieutenant M.W. Broadwood of the West Kent Regiment, son of Mr Francis Broadwood of Hamptons. A few pages later, six more portraits of missing, wounded or dead soldiers appeared along with the words 'Though They Fell, They Fell Like Stars.' Included was Lieutenant Robert Cornwallis of the Coldstream Guards, 6th Viscount Hawarden, who died of wounds received at Landrecies, Mons at the age of twenty-three and the Hon. Rupert Keppel, third son of Lord and Lady Albemarle, who was wounded and taken prisoner-of-war. *The Sketch* reported that the Hon. Archer Windsor-Clive, son of Lord and Lady Plymouth and a first-class cricketer at Eton and Cambridge, had died of wounds received during the retreat from Mons. They were to be the first of many. Thereafter, the Roll of Honour added to this sorrowful tally every week.

The significance of these pictures was not lost on Eve, who temporarily abandoned the usual frivolous gossip to reflect on this sudden, heartbreaking reality: 'To die in the flower of their manhood, to fall in the shambles of war just when life is so full, so utterly worth living – for the women who have brought them to manhood, for those who are sharing it with them, it's almost too awful, too bitter to be borne, be the glory what it may.'

This lost generation, the so-called 'flower of manhood' Eve mourned for, remains one of the most haunting legacies of the First World War: 270 peers or sons of peers were to lose their lives over the course of the conflict, along with hundreds more young men of officer class. These were boys who had been raised through a public school system that engendered a belief in chivalry, sportsmanship and the obligation of their class to lead by example. They were men educated at Oxford and Cambridge; an intellectual and physical elite expected to become the country's future. They were also conditioned to become the nation's protectors, with a network of Officer Training Corps at schools and universities, teaching drilling and training young men to a standard whereby they would be ready to lead in the eventuality of war. Coming from such a background, it was only natural that many members of the aristocracy would be among the first to join up, and would also be among the first to die. After one year, forty-seven eldest sons of peers had been killed. Out of the 5,650 alumni of Eton College who served in the war, a staggering 1,157 died in the war. Of the 838 men who had attended Balliol College, Oxford and joined up, 183 were killed.

Their loss is no more or less tragic than the deaths of the hundreds of thousands of men who also died but did not share the same privileged background. But the deaths of certain individuals, those well-chronicled personalities of the war who had an impressive share of intellect, social connections and good looks – among them poets, writers, lawyers, sportsmen – remain a totemic reminder of the futility and tragic waste of war.

By November, Eve was reporting, 'Nearly a thousand of our officers gone and the war not much more than just begun...' and in December, she conveyed the shock of many of her readers when she realised 'that already at least three peers and more than a dozen heirs to peerages have lost their lives in this war – not to mention the holders of innumerable other honoured and ancient names.'

Among this first tranche of casualties was Captain Riversdale ('Rivy') Grenfell of the 9th Lancers. Rivy, and his twin brother Francis, sons of Pascoe St Leger Grenfell, were the eighth and ninth children in a large family of fifteen. Together, they typified the gentlemanly ideal of the era. Both attended Eton, where they excelled at sport, particularly foot-

As casualties mounted abroad, preserving the health of the next generation became a preoccupation of home front Britain. It is interesting that this advertisement for Glaxo baby food ('Builds Bonnie Babies') ran regularly in the *Illustrated War News*, a weekly digest dedicated entirely to the conflict, published by the *Illustrated London News*. (Illustrated London News/ME)

ball and cricket, and where Francis was Master of Beagles and Rivy the Whip. They were fine horsemen, both playing polo with distinction for England. Francis followed a military career, receiving a commission first in the Seaforth Highlanders and then the King's Royal Rifles before joining the 9th Lancers where his horsemanship could be put to good use. Rivy chose the City but trained with the Royal Bucks Hussars and went to France as a captain in his brother's regiment. On 24 August 1914, Francis took the lead in an action that was to earn him the Victoria Cross, heading a charge against unbroken infantry at Audregnies and then helping to save the guns of the 119th Battery. It was the first VC of the war awarded to an officer. While Francis was recovering in hospital, he received the news that Rivy had been killed in action at the beginning of the Battle of the Aisne on 14 September. 'Poor Rivy Grenfell,' sighed Eve, 'the cheeriest and coolest of polo players, and most charming of gentlemen.' The following May, Francis was killed by shrapnel at Hooge.

Another attendee was Lord Desborough, uncle to Francis and Rivy and a father himself to three sons, Julian, Gerald ('Billy') and Ivo. Julian, an Etonian and Balliol man, combined a talent for writing and poetry with a bullish and muscular aptitude for sports, a combination that jars with our modern preconceptions about the First World War poets; his best-known work, 'Into Battle', is a paeon to the glory and righteousness of war. He boxed middleweight for university, rowed at Henley, won college steeplechases, and had a passion for hunting, learning stalking skills that would serve him well during his time at the Front. He found the war exhilarating, writing to his mother Ettie 'It is all the BEST fun. I have never never felt so well, or so happy, or enjoyed anything so much…' He was gazetted the DSO in January 1915 but then, on 13 May that year,

was badly wounded by a splinter shard which penetrated his brain while on a message-carrying mission. He died thirteen days later (and just two days after his cousin Francis) in No. 7 General Hospital in Boulogne, his mother, father and sister, Monica, by his side. The following month, society was shaken by the news that the Desborough's second son, Billy, had died leading his platoon in a charge at Hooge over open ground, in the face of fierce machine-gun fire. His body was never recovered.

'The saddest thing of the month so far has been, I think, the death of Lord Desborough's second son, Gerald,' wrote Eve on 18 August:

The death of Raymond Asquith (1878–1914), eldest son of the Prime Minister, at the Battle of Flers-Courcelette on 15 September 1916 sent shockwaves through society. His close friend Lady Diana Manners wrote, 'By his death, everything changed …' (Illustrated London News/ME)

The Tatler

Vol. LXV. No. 836.
London, July 4, 1917

REGISTERED AT THE GENERAL
POST OFFICE AS A NEWSPAPER

Price
Sevenpence

Mendoza Galleries

MRS. W. LA TOUCHE CONGREVE AND HER LITTLE DAUGHTER

Mrs. W. La Touche Congreve is the widow of the late Major W. La Touche Congreve, V.C., D.S.O., M.C., who was killed in action very shortly after his marriage. He was the son of Major-General W. N. Congreve, V.C., and, like his father, was in the Rifle Brigade. Mrs. Congreve was Miss Pamela Maude and is the daughter of Mr. Cyril Maude. Her baby is a god-daughter of Queen Mary's

Mrs La Touche Congreve (formerly Pamela Maude), wife of Victoria Cross recipient Major William La Touche Congreve, pictured on the front cover of *The Tatler* with her baby daughter, Mary Gloria, who was born eight months after the death of her father at Longeuval, France in July 1916. The La Touche Congreve family were exceptional in that Major Congreve's father, General Sir Walter Norris Congreve, was also awarded the VC during the Second Boer War. Pamela remarried in 1919. (Illustrated London News/ME)

He died very gloriously – just as, I am sure, his father and mother would have wished – leading an attack, and I believe, died almost instantaneously. So at least they were spared the dreadful time of waiting they had before the death of their eldest son … There is only one son left now, an Eton boy, who, luckily, isn't old enough for war just yet. If he were, I know Lord and Lady Desborough would send him as willingly as they sent the others. They are a couple of 'sportsmen', you know. At one time Lady Desborough used to be reckoned the luckiest woman in society – she had everything she wanted. So many of the people one envied have suffered terribly, but they have, at any rate, the right to be proud of their dead.

A photograph of Lady Desborough, with Billy and Ivo, together with an inset picture of Julian, was published in the magazine a week before. Above it were lines by Kipling: 'If blood be the price of admiralty, Lord God, we ha' paid in full.'

The Grenfell family's sacrifice epitomised the patriotism and courage expected of their class. They were, wrote the Marquess of Winchester, a 'symbol of that landed gentry who made England a nation of sportsmen, pioneers and warriors. When that type fails to be bred, but not until then, will England begin to sink downhill.'

Lord Kitchener, much affected by Billy's death, vowed to ensure the Desboroughs' youngest son Ivo would not be called upon to serve in the trenches, a vow upheld by his successor, Lord Derby. 'Our family has done its share,' wrote Arthur Grenfell, Lord Desborough's cousin, 'I don't think we should run the risk of getting wiped out as a clan, and I do hope you will manage to keep him at home.' Tragically, despite the string pulling that perhaps saved him from death in the trenches, Ivo was also to meet a premature death, in a car accident in 1926.

Another peer saved by family connections was John Manners, Earl of Granby, only son and heir (after the death of his elder brother in childhood) of the Duke and Duchess of Rutland. The Rutlands' circle suffered greatly during the war. Ego Charteris, Lord Elcho, heir to the Earl of Weymss, was the husband of the Earl's sister, Letty. He was killed in action on St George's Day 1916. A cousin, another John Manners, was killed in the retreat from Mons. And then an appalling tally of friends and acquaintances, all of them brilliant and promising young men, were to have their lives cut short. Patrick Shaw-Stewart, Edward Horner and Edward's brother-in-law, Raymond Asquith, the eldest son of the Prime Minister, all died. Of the latter, Eve wrote at length in September 1916: 'A dreadful loss, isn't it, poor Raymond Asquith. One had hardly quite realised it yet somehow he was a soldier – he hardly quite realised it himself … an immensely brilliant scholar with Balliol written all over him. And a most subtle lawyer, too, as well as a splendid talker and writer – you know how delightfully he wrote verse of the light and amusing kind.' His close friend Lady Diana Manners wrote, 'By his death everything changed, except the war that ground its blind murderous treadmill round and round without retreat or advance, with no sign of the beginning of the end.' Violet, Duchess of Rutland, surrounded by such tragedy, was determined her own son would not suffer the same fate. Through a wealthy American friend, George Moore, who was closely connected to the Commander-in-Chief Lord French as well as being head-over-heels in love with Diana, she arranged for the Earl to spend his war in a staff position at GHQ. It was a humiliating fix, the evidence of which the 9th Duke, as he became, went to great lengths to bury in later life.

As the war continued to reap its grim harvest, *The Tatler*'s focus fell upon the mothers and widows of the fallen. Even allowing for lapses of (forgivable) journalistic mawkishness, the stories are affecting in their poignancy. When the twenty-five-year-old Lord Petre of Ingatestone Hall in Essex died in September 1915 of wounds received in action, a photograph of his widow, the former Catherine Boscawen, was published along with the words, 'To the Men the Glory – To the Women – Waiting and Irreparable Loss.' Lord Petre's son and heir was just a year old and to add to the tragedy, his wife, pregnant with her second child, gave birth to his posthumous daughter just a few hours after her own father's death. Such emotional trauma seemed at times overwhelming, and yet there was an expectation that women must 'carry on' despite their grief. Kitty, as Catherine was known, set up a school at the hall to teach dairying to children, and in 1918 gave a practical exhibition of boot-repairing at the Rayne Woman's Institute in Braintree. She eventually went on to marry Major Sir Frederic Rasch. Ettie Desborough occupied herself by turning the family home, Taplow Court, into a rest home for Red Cross nurses.

Mrs Percy Wyndham featured on the front cover of *The Tatler* in September 1914 with news that she had been widowed. Her husband, known as 'Perf', half-brother of the Duke of Westminster, was killed on the 14th of that month during the Battle of the Aisne. It was another death that sent shockwaves through society. 'The Wyndham friends innumerable are grieving. Poor Lady Grosvenor, whose house in Park Lane is now a St John of Jerusalem centre, has lost husband and son within a year, and both were such favourites,' wrote Eve, and then a month later reported an interesting turn of events. 'By the way, several people – Mrs Percy Wyndham, I

hear amongst them – are sending out men to recover their dead. The spot where they fall is always marked wherever it's possible, you know. But I'm afraid there won't be many of our men brought home again this way.' In fact, Wyndham's grave, in a small wood near where he was killed, was lost without trace and his name is instead listed on the memorial at La Ferté-sous-Jouarre. Many families, though desperate to bring their loved ones back home to rest, acknowledged that repatriating bodies, when they could be found, was a luxury that had to be forgone. Even Princess Beatrice refused Lord French's offer to return to England the body of her youngest son, Prince Maurice of Battenberg. An exception was Lieutenant Norman Champion de Crespigny, one of the five sons of Sir Claude Champion de Crespigny of Maldon, Essex. Norman died gallantly on 1 September 1914, at Nery, near Compiègne, killed by shrapnel as he attempted to hold a strategic point against advancing Germans. He was buried where he fell but disinterred later and returned home to lie in the family mausoleum at Champion Lodge. The exhumation had been difficult, buried as he was in a grave with seventeen other soldiers, but identification was finally made by the name on the neckband of his shirt. Eventually, the scale of the slaughter necessitated a ban on the repatriation of bodies to Britain in March the following year, though interestingly Lord Petre's body was brought back home, perhaps because his death occurred away from the battlefield at Duchess of Westminster's No. 1 Red Cross Hospital in Le Touquet.

Wartime society did not expect women to accept widowhood as a permanent state and second marriages were common – sometimes, in more unfortunate cases, even third marriages. When Lord Northland, the only son of Lord Ranfurly was killed in action in 1915, it transpired he made a will that was more

The Hon. Mrs Lyndhurst Bruce, formerly the Edwardian actress Camille Clifford, pictured in *The Tatler* after the announcement of her engagement to Captain John M. J. Evans MC (inset picture). Her first husband, Captain the Hon. Henry Lyndhurst-Bruce, Lord Aberdare's son and heir, was killed in action in 1914. (Illustrated London News/ME)

THE CENTRAL FIGURE
Of the Greatest "Crime Passionel" in the Records of our Courts.

Malcolm Arbuthnot

LIEUTENANT DOUGLAS MALCOLM
WHO WAS FOUND NOT GUILTY FOR THE KILLING OF "COUNT" DE BORCH

The most dramatic domestic criminal case of our time ended on Tuesday last week with the acquittal of the subject of our picture for the murder of the creature who attempted to ruin the life of the wife he loved. The unwritten law was not relied upon by the astute Sir John Simon, counsel for the defence, but nevertheless the unwritten law prevailed in the hearts of the jury, who had, as the judge remarked, no evidence in support of the claim of "self defence," on which the defence rested. The sympathy and respect of all men and women remain with Lieutenant Malcolm, whose splendid conduct was throughout on a refreshingly high plane, even if one views with some apprehension the introduction of sentiment into the cold, clear system of British justice

Lieutenant Douglas Malcolm, pictured in *The Tatler* at the time he was found not guilty for the killing of Count de Borch aka Anton Baumberg, a dubious character, womaniser and possibly a spy for the Germans, who had seduced the lieutenant's wife, Dorothy. Despite originally vowing to horsewhip Borch beyond recognition, Malcolm had shot Borch and killed him. It was seen as a sensational crime of passion and Malcolm, a man in uniform and 'home from leave', had public sympathy. He was eventually acquitted. (Illustrated London News/ME)

magnanimous than many left by young husbands (Perf Wyndham had left £10,000 to his mistress, Leila Milbanke, wife of Sir John Milbanke VC, but had failed to provide for his wife Diana). Lord Northland left all his property to his wife, adding that he would consider it an honour rather than a slur on his memory if she chose to marry again. Lady Northland did marry again; this time to the Naval Provost-Marshal Geoffrey Mills in March 1917. Eve confided, 'a war widow's second mating was necessarily quiet, of course, though Mr Geoffrey Mills is too well-known and knows too many people to keep his doings a very dark secret long'. But by September *The Queen* magazine was writing, 'Deep sympathy is felt for Lady Northland at the loss of her second husband, Captain Geoffrey Mills, after a short but happy marriage of only five months.' Twice widowed by the war, she married Lieutenant Michael Wardell on 30 April 1918, who happily survived. Violet Astor, who married John Jacob Astor in 1916, was a war widow; her first husband, Lord Charles Petty-Fitzmaurice, had been killed in action in October 1914.

Eve's occasional reflections on the brutal, stark tragedy of war brought out an elegiac quality in her writing:

The angel of death is so busy reaping, and it's such a splendid, such a tragically youthful harvest that he's gathering in! They say war cleanses, washes away the clogging mists of peace, and I suppose it does – with tears. But oh, Betty, I wish it need never have been, don't you? So many broken

hearts, so many lonely homes, such anxious days, such bitter nights! And one can do so little; one can do, in fact, nothing at all – that's the hardest part of all, isn't it? Out there in France an in all the seas of the world our men are doing splendid things for us who sit at home so safely.

In fact, there was much that women could do, and one fundamental activity particular to their sex. They could have babies. Procreation was positively encouraged in an attempt to reverse the notable decline in population caused by the war. In 1916, Eve treated the unofficial order with her usual tongue-in-cheek humour:

Francis Grenfell VC, and his twin brother, Riversdale 'Rivy' Grenfell, officers in the 9th Lancers. Francis earned the Victoria Cross in the early weeks of the First World War – awarded for gallantry while saving the guns of the 119th Battery, Royal Field Artillery at Audregnies, Belgium. Rivy was killed shortly afterwards in September 1914. Francis was also killed in action in 1915. (Illustrated London News/ME)

The Sketch

No. 1124—Vol. LXXXVII. WEDNESDAY, AUGUST 12, 1914. SIXPENCE.

1. MRS. ERIC KING. 2. THE HON. MRS. EUSTACE MORRISON-BELL. 3. MRS. ROBERT BOGER.

THE WAR ADVANCES THE DATES OF MARRIAGES: BRIDES WHOSE WEDDINGS TOOK PLACE EARLIER THAN ANTICIPATED.

So many Navy and Army officers applied for special marriage licences on the outbreak of war that arrangements were made for the Faculty Office, in Knightrider Street, to remain open continuously, day and night, for a few days.——Lieutenant E. W. M. King, R.N., and Miss Violet Baldry were married at Harwich last week, at an earlier date than had been arranged.——The wedding of the Hon. Harriet Trefusis, youngest daughter of the Dowager Lady Clinton and the late Lord Clinton, with Captain Eustace Morrison-Bell, son of Sir Charles and Lady Morrison-Bell, took place last week a day earlier than was originally arranged, the bridegroom having to rejoin his regiment.—— The wedding of Captain Robert Albany Boger, Royal Engineers, and Miss Diane Curtis, took place by special licence last week instead of next October.

Photographs by Swaine and Lallie Charles.

Cover of *The Sketch* documenting the predicament of many couples who had to hasten their marriages because of war commitments. So many navy and army officers applied for special marriage licences on the outbreak of war that arrangements were made for the Faculty Office to remain open continuously, day and night. (Illustrated London News/ME)

But of course, the thing to do, I mean the chic patriotic "womanly" thing is to get married, and with all possible dispatch do your bit about the birth-rate. Nowadays a positive glow of conscious virtue and self-sacrifice illumines the path of the maternally patriotic ones, and you'd really think from the airs they give themselves that they really were doing it simply and solely for the good of the country and not a bit so's to provide a pretty plaything for themselves.

In July the following year, she continued:

This week they're busy telling us that having babies is the best way of all to serve one's King and Country. Will the Order of the British Empire be conferred on the most brilliantly prolific?

Even as early as August 1915, she was reporting that doctors were discussing the possibility of scientifically influencing the gender of babies – boy babies naturally being preferred. And she pointed out that wartime pregnancies seemed to be carried out with the minimum of fuss, so it was no real hardship for willing mothers-to-be:

Women go to the theatre and other shows right up til the moment they disappear temporarily from view – and it's a very short disappearance very often – and have things made nice and easy for them by chloroform, nobody minds so very much doing their duty by the State and all that sort of thing. I believe though, that scientists and other frumpy people are talking very seriously about the effect on the nervous system of the future generation due to

The wedding of Baroness Beaumont and the Hon. Bernard Fitzalan-Howard at St Mary's Catholic Church at Carlton near Selby which took place in September 1914. The bridegroom, who was a Lieutenant in the 1st Lovat's Scouts, was granted forty-eight hours' leave for the wedding and honeymoon. (Illustrated London News/ME)

this new fashion of "carrying on" to the last moment.

This unnecessary worry about the potential dangers of an active pregnancy to the unborn child reflected a general growing concern for the care and welfare of infants.

'If the war has done nothing else,' lectured *The Queen* in December 1917, 'it has made the nation at last realise the value of human life in general and that of the child – the country's hope for the future – in particular. Our birth rate, like that of all belligerents, is declining at an alarming rate, and it is therefore all the more necessary to save every baby that can be saved, and to see that it is capable of becoming a sturdy citizen of the future.'

Infant Welfare Centres, known as 'Mothers' Welcome', began to mushroom, growing from 400 in 1914 to 1,100 by 1917, caring for around 70,000 babies and children under school age. Day nurseries opened to provide quality care for the children of working mothers, particularly at munitions factories and other enlightened employers such as at Port Sunlight. A concern about good nutrition led to the establishment of such organisation as the National Milk Hostels Committee, which supplied fresh milk directly from farms to the hostels in order to provide for some 2,300 cases. *The Queen* magazine took a great interest in Baby Week, 'an event of national importance … awakening the national conscience on a vital matter' where each year a variety of exhibitions, demonstrations, sermons and shows focused on child-rearing and health. As part of Baby Week in 1917, Queen Mary opened an exhibition at Central Hall, Westminster, which included a 'guard of honour of 160 babies' and one exhibit showing an example of bacteria found on a 'horrid dummy'. *The Queen* met one particularly prolific procreator, mother of nineteen Mrs

Phillips, who showed her newborn triplets off, having incredibly given birth to another set only the previous year.

A number of well-known members of society made child welfare their particular area of interest – 'it's positively in the movement to be interested in the babies of the poor', commented Eve, somewhat sarcastically, in 1917. The previous year she had adopted a similar tone when commenting on 'a new baby-feeding scheme the Duchess of Sutherland is president of and Lady Howard de Walden and Mrs Sassoon vice-presidents. They're starting a centre where poor mothers of babelets can be taught how rich mothers feed the delicious babies we see every day in the parks and gardens.' Even in the basic skill of having babies, Eve observed, the aristocracy felt they could impart superior knowledge.

Having babies was impossible, however (at least in respectable society), without a husband – and that, as the war progressed, became an increasingly rare breed. By the end of September 1914, Eve was already remarking that the shortage of men under fifty was 'awfully marked everywhere already', and by August 1916 she was discussing a rather scandalous solution: 'And the future, you know, is really a pretty frightful problem, isn't it, for the mothers of many marriageable daughters? Polygamy's the one and only solution some people think, but I can't see it ever taking so to speak, can you? We want at least one man all to ourselves.' *The Queen* magazine quoted a young officer who, back from the front after being wounded, described himself in a letter to a friend on being asked out to a hen tea-party as 'feeling like a lion among a lot of Daniels', and the situation provided rich fodder for cartoonists who particularly delighted in the desperate idolisation young women displayed towards the dashing officer class.

The heightened emotions of wartime, the shortage of men, a 'live for the day' attitude,

No. 737, AUGUST 11, 1915]

THE TATLER

"If blood be the price of admiralty,
Lord God, we ha' paid in full."—*Kipling.*

Bassano and Maull & Fox

LADY DESBOROUGH WITH HER SONS—THE LATE HON. GERALD GRENFELL (ON LEFT) AND HER SURVIVING SON, THE HON. IVO GEORGE GRENFELL (THE LATE CAPTAIN JULIAN GRENFELL INSET)

The deep sympathy of all of us goes out to Lord and Lady Desborough in their recent loss of their second son, the Hon. Gerald Grenfell, who is seen above with his mother and surviving brother. Few parents have been privileged to suffer more greatly for their country and in the cause of humanity, as their eldest son, the Hon. Julian Henry Grenfell, D.S.O., a portrait of whom is inset, who was a captain in the Royal Dragoons, died of wounds in May last. Their surviving son is still at Eton. Lord Desborough is famous as a great sportsman, and both he and his wife are very popular, particularly in the neighbourhood of Taplow, their charming riverside home

b

Ettie, Lady Desborough, one of Edwardian society's most celebrated figures, pictured with her two elder sons, Julian (left and inset) and Gerald, known as Billy. Julian died after a shell splinter penetrated his brain in May 1915; Billy was killed in action in July 1915. His body was never found. (Illustrated London News/ME)

all created an atmosphere in which wartime weddings were carried out with what may seem indecent haste. 'War and weddings seem to go together. Mars and Venus sort of idea, I suppose,' observed Eve in July 1917 before launching into an amusing, marriage-themed Biblical spoof:

> The young men did hurry them away unto the war, and amongst the maidens there were many sad at heart.
>
> When the time drew nigh unto a young man that he must gird up his loins and go, then would he speak unto the damsel of his choice.
>
> He would say unto her. Thou knowest that there yet remaineth unto me only so many days; let us therefore arrange matters quickly that we be married.
>
> Because the time was short and it was her chance, she would answer and would say unto him. Thou art my lord, and whatsoever thou commandest, it shall be done.
>
> There were some that did marry for love and there were some that did marry for a pension, but there were some that did marry because it was a discreet thing to do.
>
> Every maiden did seek for to get her an officer, for these were great men whom the common soldiers did salute in the public places so that to walk with such a one was indeed pleasurable.
>
> The number of them that did marry was beyond anything that men could remember.

It was expected that weddings would be quiet, low-key affairs. The wedding of Lady Cicely Pierrepoint to Major Francis Hardy of the Coldstream Guards at the Guards Chapel in October 1915 had no reception and no bridesmaids, 'on account of the war'. Eve described the wedding of Lady Joan Stuart-Wortley to Mr Gordon Miles in March 1917 as having no cards, no reception and no wedding gown: 'one couldn't help thinking it was a bit more in the picture than the fancy-dress, pre-war-time, hang-the-expense ones we've had such a lot of lately.' In January 1915, the wedding of the Earl of Granby (by then serving on the staff of the GOC, North Midland Division) to Kathleen Tennant was billed as 'very quiet', though it

Lord and Lady Petre pictured in September 1913 at Tregye, Perranwell, Cornwall shortly after returning from their honeymoon. Lionel, born 1890, was the 16th Baron, and became a Captain in the Coldstream Guards. He was wounded near Arras in the late Spring of 1915 and died of his wounds in September leaving two children, one born posthumously. His wife Kitty (formerly Catherine Boscawen) carried on with her war work and eventually remarried, becoming Lady Rasch. (Illustrated London News/ME)

was still held at St Margaret's, Westminster, and the couple appeared on *The Tatler*'s cover. Many marriages took place quickly, during leave granted for such a purpose, such as that between Baroness Beaumont and the Hon. Bernard Fitzalan-Howard of the 1st Lovat's Scouts, who married and honeymooned during the groom's brief forty-eight hour leave in September 1914.

But marrying in haste for some often meant repenting at leisure. Nancy Cunard married a wounded Australian veteran, cricketer Sidney Fairbairn, in November 1916; a conventional union which was at odds with her own provocative and artistic lifestyle. The marriage lasted twenty months before the pair separated.

Absence of husbands away at the front could also inflame jealousies, real or imaginary. The case of Captain Douglas Malcolm (father of the film critic and journalist Derek Malcolm), who was tried and then acquitted of the murder of Count de Borch, aka Anton Baumberg, caused a sensation and a serious public debate on the role of men and women in modern-day relationships. Baumberg, a dubious character, a womaniser and possibly a spy for the Germans, had seduced the lieutenant's wife Dorothy while Malcolm was away serving at the front. Despite originally vowing to horsewhip him, Malcolm had instead shot and killed him. Public sympathy was largely with the man in uniform 'home on leave', and the judge, in an exceptional ruling, acquitted him on the grounds that it was a crime of passion. But it was the old-fashioned notion implied by the judge – that women needed protecting – that provoked such an outcry. Eve had her say on the matter:

> As I told you, what's amused people most was the idea that we females must be 'protected.' If not – well, you know what happens. The Worst! Amusing return to medievalism, isn't it? But what riled the whole sex worse than anything, of course, was the delightfully masculine idea that man is the keeper of woman's 'honour.' As if woman wasn't quite capable of keeping anything she wanted to keep.

The furore over the Malcolm case was indicative of changing social mores, and the growing independence of women. But marriage remained the expectation of most, even if the bitterly poignant reality of war was that many women would never find a husband. Despite a temporary upsurge in marriages when demobilisation released soldiers back to civilian life, there simply were not enough men to go round.

ENTERTAINMENT

'Seems war takes some forgetting, and the quickest way to forget is to go to the opposite extreme – light and love and laughter after darkness and hate and horrors.'

This was Eve, writing in her column in September 1916, a time when, two years into the war, the privations at home, together with the rising casualty statistics and frustrating stalemate on the fighting fronts, were beginning to take its toll on the morale of the British population.

Should we entertain in wartime? Should we still go dancing? Was it disrespectful to enjoy oneself when so many were not only sacrificing life's small pleasures, but also their own lives? These were questions posed regularly by writers in the press. Unsurprisingly, Eve, a good-time girl whose *raison d'être* relied on some continuing semblance of socialising and entertainment, was wholly in favour of living for the moment, though her conscience was frequently pricked. 'You don't think it's wicked to dance in war time, do you?' she confided to her correspondent, Betty. 'Lots do, I know, and sometimes I agree with them. But the truth is most of us just live these days to give all the pleasure we possibly can to our splendid fighting men, and they, you know, don't mind how bright and cheery things are here at home.' Not everyone agreed. Lord Northcliffe, through his paper, the *Daily Mail*, was a ferocious critic of those he viewed as flagrantly and selfishly disregarding advice on economy given by government ministers and committees. Eve quoted the paper in 1917:

'We are satisfied' thunders somewhat pompously the noble baron aforesaid's Tuppenny Tome, 'that there are whole circles in which the spirit of sacrifice is utterly unknown.' – and where no one's taking the very faintest notice of the exhortations of the Prime Minister and the Food Controller. It also thinks the greater the sinner the greater the sin – 'the more exalted the position of the offender, the greater the difficulty of instilling economy into those well-paid communities which are said to be 'enjoying the war.' It is a matter of life and death to this country that there should be no exceptions to the rule of self-denial … If nothing but the pillory will bring these thoughtless spendthrifts into line, then the pillory it must be.

The Queen magazine took a more balanced view, justifying entertainment as a philanthropic necessity. Mrs C.S. Peel, writing on the subject in April 1915, believed that 'When we entertain out of a true desire to help and cheer those who are sad, entertaining becomes right and proper, even in such times as these. To remain sane, brave, pitiful, yet calmly determined to do our part in the nation's work is the duty of us all, and I cannot think that the meeting of friends, the sympathetic desire to lighten, if even for an hour or two, the burden of those living in the shadow of death, the wish to give pleasure to those in humbler circumstances than our own, and to show hospitality to the nation's guests can never be anything but right and proper.'

The watchword, as with everything in wartime, was moderation. The war seriously interfered with the old way in which the upper classes socialised. Court presentations, when debutantes were presented to the King and Queen marking their official 'debut' in society, were suspended for the duration of the war, and the round of smart, social events making up the 'Season' from the Private View of the Summer Exhibition at the Royal Academy at the beginning of May to the races at Goodwood in July were either cancelled or were carried out without frills or extravagance. Gone were the lavish balls of the Edwardian era, and young ladies who would normally enjoy a round of parties to celebrate their 'coming out' had to make do with a modest dance to mark this milestone, or nothing at all. Many of the enormous mansions that would have usually hosted grand events were either closed for the war for reasons of economy or were else turned into temporary hospitals, charitable clubs for war workers or convalescent homes. There were alternative sources of amusement

of course – the constant round of wartime weddings, for instance, or the similarly ubiquitous charity matinee ('mat') performed by society ladies, usually dressed in historic costumes and striking solemn-looking poses in indulgently tiresome tableaux.

The Queen magazine's idea of entertainment were docile gatherings 'of the boy girl variety' at home, with the help of a pianist or gramophone (the Decca portable gramophone enjoyed popularity during this period), frugal rounds of sandwiches filled with sardine purée or potted shrimps (spread with margarine, not butter) and ginger beer or barley water to wash it all down. The magazine even suggested combining children's parties fuelled by honey sandwiches, hot potato scones and sultana cake ('with very little fruit and some potato') with those for wounded soldiers – not quite, perhaps, the kind of sophisticated entertainment the average British soldier might have been

The New Zealand tennis player and four times Wimbledon champion, Anthony (Tony) Wilding. Tall, athletic and with matinee idol looks, his winning streak at Wimbledon came to an end in 1914, but he did help Britain towards Davis Cup victory in America before heading back to Europe to join up. He was killed by a shell explosion during the Battle of Aubers Ridge in May 1915. (Illustrated London News/ME)

"Well, if you knows of a better 'ole, go to it."

The most famous cartoon of the Great War, Captain Bruce Bairnsfather's 'Better 'Ole' joke, along with his many other cartoons, in *The Bystander* spawned a stage play as well as merchandise and pottery featuring 'Old Bill' and his comrades. (Illustrated London News/ME)

fantasising about while in the trenches. In fact, a piece in *The Queen* magazine in 1918 claimed that ensuring wholesome amusements were available for young officers on leave was a way to avoid them following the lure of more unsavoury forms of evening entertainment. 'There have been quite a number of cases in which unscrupulous people have hired furnished houses in quite good localities in order to give dances for gain, lasting very often all night and partaking of the nature of an orgie,' it reported with all the indignation of a puritanical maiden aunt.

Nightclubs, then, were probably not familiar territory to staff of *The Queen*. But to the cosmopolitan readership of *The Tatler*, they had become part of London's nocturnal attractions. Clubs had begun to spring up in the years leading up to the war, inspired in part by the growing popularity of ragtime and jazz, as well as the craze for the tango in 1913. Venues opened offering thé dansants where the dance was demonstrated to patrons who could also receive instruction in not only the tango but other fashionable steps like the turkey trot and pigeon walk. One such club, Murray's, was opened in 1913 by a Canadian, Jack May, and flourished during the war years, 'nightly packed' as *The Sketch* described it, despite the 'present restrictions that they have to close at

A women's war workers football match held at Barnes in 1917. The team from Sterling (main picture) defeated the employees of Harrods by an impressive eight goals to two. (Illustrated London News/ME)

midnight.' It was so popular dancers had to take to the floor in shifts using a system outlined in the magazine:

> Mr Jack May, always to the fore to remedy our passing troubles, has inaugurated the happy idea of giving each dancing man either a red or white favour on entering the club, the colour to dance being clearly indicated, and now we dance each in our turn, and have even the accommodation in which to do our 'stunts' all up and down the floor, undisturbed by such trifles as heels and elbows which sadly impeded our progress before the new regulation.

Elsewhere, other nightclubs and restaurants enjoyed a similar boom, mushrooming across the West End and Soho until it was estimated there were 150 in operation in this area alone by the end of 1915. In December 1914, Eve commented on Prince's in Piccadilly looking 'almost like old times, but for the khaki … and the Four Hundred you know's been going strong all the time.' In March 1917, she wrote how restaurants were really 'more full than ever – at the Carlton all the celebs, like Mrs. Vernon Castle, with the cropped locks, and other theatrical people, as well as such about-town Royals as for instance, King Manoel and the Connaughts.'

This lively nightlife scene continued to thrive despite shortened licensing hours, measures put in place by the government in 1915 under the Defence of the Realm Act to counteract the effects drunkenness was having on industrial production. The new laws, dubbed the 'beauty sleep order' by revellers, extended to all licensed premises, and so, after 10 p.m., patrons of Ciro's, Prince's and other clubs switched to ginger beer and barley water, or else enjoyed an illicit drink out of innocent looking teacups. Ella Hepworth

Dixon remarked on the surprising effect on the upper classes in *The Sketch* in 1915, claiming they were 'becoming so temperate as to be well-nigh 'total abstainers'. Society has taken to soda-water – or, as a wild dissipation, to cider – with an enthusiasm which was hardly to be expected. One may say that this abstemiousness is forced upon them after ten o'clock, but the fact that the smart restaurants are crowded after the theatres, and that the Savoy nightly sees crowds supping as usual, chatting in the lounge, and dancing light-heartedly in the adjacent ball-room on nothing more exciting than ginger-pop, is a tribute to our national cheerfulness and capacity for restraint.' She described the sight of 'our Happy Warriors, back from the trenches, dancing till the small hours, and even looking on at dancing with nothing more stimulating than coffee and cigarettes. If we could induce the masses to follow this fashion we should be a regenerate nation.' Blanche in *The Bystander* observed wryly that officers on leave had a more exhausting time on leave than in the trenches, being dragged from the Savoy Grill, then to the theatre to see *Peter Pan*, before ending up at the Four Hundred, 'where they drink lemonade, bottles and bottles of it. And "night club cup", 5s. a glass, jugs and jugs of it.' London's carefree nightlife had its critics. In 1918, *The Bystander*'s Blanche recounted the comments of the editor of the American magazine, *Ladies Home Journal*, who had felt the city's social scene was 'morally crucifying' the wholesome American soldiers by then based in London.

Theatre auditoriums were packed during the war and although it was not particularly a golden age in terms of quality (few dramatic masterpieces were written during this period), still thousands flocked to the theatres. There had been an initial abstinence from theatre-going on conscientious grounds at the outbreak of war but soon it was realised, explained

A young girl hosts a garden party picnic for wounded soldiers in lieu of receiving any birthday presents. *The Queen* magazine frequently suggested combining children's parties with entertainment for wounded men, a concept that seems to have worked rather splendidly in this case. (Grenville Collins Postcard Collection/ME)

The Sketch in 1915, 'that such abstention was the cause of much hardship and unemployment in Theatre-land', and that 'a visit to the theatre was an excellent moral tonic and gave relief to strained nerves'. Revues and musicals, rooted in the Edwardian tradition of the music hall, offered light-hearted respite, trading in spectacle and laughter rather than tragedy and contemplation. 'The men must have music, laughter, and how they laughed', reminisced the actress Elsie Janis. 'The men must be made to forget it, and they were.' Many shows were topical, with names such as *Business as Usual*, *The Munitionette*, and *Tommy Atkins*, which was put on at the Lyceum as early as September 1914. Topical was fine, but only when it explored the lighter side of war. According to 'Jingle', *The Bystander*'s theatre correspondent, writing in August 1915, 'a

noticeable factor of the present condition of the theatrical world is the unpopularity of the war play – that is, the play dealing with in a more or less realistic fashion with the dismal state of affairs.'

Stages around the country often doubled up as recruiting platforms. Vesta Tilley had made a name as a male impersonator in the late Victorian and Edwardian era, and continued to plough the same furrow during the war, portraying the archetypal British Tommy in a variety of military costumes, a role she executed with boyish charm despite being over fifty years old by this time. Dubbed 'Britain's best recruiting sergeant', her repertoire of patriotic songs included 'Jolly Good Luck to the Girl Who Loves a Soldier' and 'Six Days Home on Leave', which she performed at the London Coliseum in January 1917. *The Tatler*

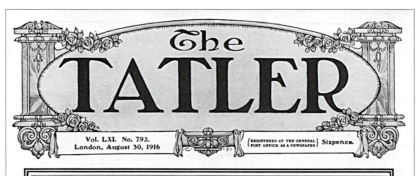

The TATLER

Vol. LXI. No. 792.
London, August 30, 1916

REGISTERED AT THE GENERAL
POST OFFICE AS A NEWSPAPER | Sixpence.

"BASIL HALLAM"
(THE LATE CAPTAIN BASIL HALLAM RADFORD)

Captain Radford, who was better known on the stage as Basil Hallam, got a commission in the R.F.C. (Kite Balloon Section) not long ago, and has recently been killed in action. He made a name for himself by creating the character of Gilbert the Filbert in "The Passing Show" at the Palace Theatre, a part he got through Miss Elsie Janis' kind offices, as he had not been in revue before that appearance. He met Miss Janis when he was in America playing in Mr. Cosmo Hamilton's clever little piece, "The Blindness of Virtue," and when Miss Janis came to England to play in "The Passing Show," she it was who suggested he should go into revue. The result we know. He successfully created a type which went out when war came in

Basil Hallam, born Basil Hallam Radford (1889–1916), English actor and singer, best known for his role of Gilbert the Filbert, Colonel of the Nuts in the 1915 revue *The Passing Show* with Elsie Janis. Basil joined the Royal Flying Corps in the Army Kite Balloon Section. He died in August 1916 as his balloon drifted towards enemy lines and his parachute became entangled in the rigging. (Illustrated London News/ME)

pictured her on their cover at this time writing with admiration: 'Miss Tilley is undoubtedly the best male impersonator the "Halls" have ever seen, and is a great favourite practically all over the world.'

New plays and revues proliferated. Many were fleeting but a handful enjoyed phenomenal success, as did their stars, often adopted as unofficial mascots by the troops. *Peg O' My Heart*, written by J. Hartley Manners and starring his wife, American actress Laurette Taylor, had enjoyed a successful run on Broadway from 1912 to 1914, before moving to London's West End in 1915. 'The play itself is not exactly a masterpiece,' wrote *The Bystander*, 'but Miss Laurette Taylor who plays the title role is a little lady of genius.' *The Sketch* was delighted to report the show's leading lady had written a letter addressed to 'The Dear British Public', which was inserted inside the audience's programmes each evening, conveying her hope that the *Day* would

arrive quickly 'when your Armies will return victorious and I can shout with you!' In the same year, *The Passing Show*, starring another American, Elsie Janis, together with her British co-star, Basil Hallam, featured the pair in a series of sketches. One of their songs, 'I'm Here and You're Here', was adopted as a favourite among soldiers. Janis, dubbed the 'sweetheart of the AEF' (American Expeditionary Force), had planned to marry Hallam, whose character, Gilbert the Filbert, Colonel of the Nuts, lampooned the much-derided 'k'nut', the nickname given to the raffish swell of pre-khaki days. The charming and mild-mannered Basil gained a legion of adoring fans, among them Lady Diana Manners, who admitted in her memoirs, 'I should have liked to have danced all night with Basil Hallam, being a little in love with him.' When Gaby Deslys replaced Elsie as his leading lady in *The Passing Show*, Basil himself fell under the French lady's irresistible spell, an indiscretion which Elsie, over in America at the time, treated with an indulgent understanding. Having tried to join up in the first week of the war, Basil had been rejected due to a smashed instep from his schooldays, and despite his success on stage he keenly felt the criticism he might invite, being a young man treading the boards at a time when most of his age were fighting for King and Country. Comments such as those by *The Sketch* in 1915, speaking about members of the Garrick Club who had joined the colours: 'There is no lack of ardent patriotism in Stage-land though the mincing young chorus-man of the musical-comedy theatres is still an offence,' must have

The actor Arthur Bourchier looking most convincing in the role of Old Bill, the curmudgeonly cartoon character created by Captain Bruce Bairnsfather in *The Bystander* and brought to life on stage in 'The Better 'Ole' by Bairnsfather and Arthur Eliot, produced by Charles Cochran and staged at the Oxford Theatre in 1917. (Illustrated London News/ME)

cut deeply. In June 1915, he was accepted by the Kite Balloon Section of the Royal Flying Corps, gave in his notice and enjoyed a standing ovation at the end of his final performance. A year later he was killed, trying to escape from his balloon as it drifted towards enemy lines. Diana Manners received a letter from Raymond Asquith who had witnessed Hallam's fall to his death, '… killed before my very eyes by falling 6000 feet or so from an escaped balloon. He came to earth in a village ½ a mile from where I stood … shockingly foreshortened, but recognisable by his cigarette case.' His comrade who had also jumped from the balloon and survived had given a far less upsetting account to Elsie, describing how Basil had encouraged him by saying, 'Let's jump for it! Let's sit on the edge of the basket and count three!' 'I never thought,' wrote the young man, 'it would be "Gilbert the Filbert" who would give me the courage to face death.' Poor Basil. In contrast to the infamous character he played, he had done his duty and paid the ultimate price.

On 3 August 1916, the most popular show of the Great War opened at His Majesty's Theatre. Written by Oscar Asche, *Chu Chin Chow* was a kind of adult pantomime based loosely on the story of *Ali Baba and the Forty Thieves*, its oriental theme undoubtedly influenced by the Ballets Russe staging of Scheherezade before the war. Eve, speaking of the British audience's desire for 'plenty of noise and legs and sentiment, and no tiresome problems or tragedies', gave the following verdict:

Chu Chin Chow's great, but it was funny to hear musical comedy songs and see legs and shoulders and nearly everything else galore at His Majesty's. And dancing – not the Margaret Morris or Greek-vase kind either! But the dresses are just too utterly lovely for words. Poiret and the far,

far East mixed, you know, with a dash of Bakst and the Russians, and for faces – London's prettiest.

Among the pretty faces was the dancer, Dacia, a frequent pin-up in *The Tatler* and *The Sketch*. *Chu Chin Chow* ran for five years and 2,238 performances playing to an estimated audience of 2,800,000 attracted by the spectacular stage sets, the live animals (including a camel) but most of the all, the exotic and revealing costumes worn by cast. To keep the show fresh, new costumes were introduced at intervals with photographs published in magazines of the fantastical and scanty creations. 'Very suitable for the sultry climate of Baghdad', wrote *The Tatler* in September 1917, with a palpable leer, when it featured six photographs of the latest designs. Little wonder that *Chu Chin Chow* was an essential destination for soldiers when on leave in London. Rivalling *Chu Chin Chow*, *The Bing Boys are Here* was another smash hit and included the song 'If You Were the Only Girl in the World'. Starring George Robey, Alfred Lester and Violet Loraine, it spawned spin-off variations later in the war – *The Bing Girls are Here* and *Bing Boys on Broadway*.

But perhaps the show with the deepest connection to the war opened in 1917 at the Oxford Theatre in London. *The Better 'Ole*, produced by impresario Charles Cochran, brought to life on stage one of the most famous cartoon characters of the Great War. Captain Bruce Bairnsfather was a familiar name to readers of *The Bystander*, which had first begun to publish his cartoons depicting trench life in 1915. Central to his weekly drawings was a curmudgeonly, walrus-moustached old soldier known as 'Old Bill', combining the wise cracking cynicism and resigned stoicism of the typical British Tommy. Bairnsfather's characters had already featured in a short revue sketch in

NEW DRESSES FOR "CHU CHIN CHOW"
Very Suitable to the Sultry Climate of Old Bagdad.

Photographs by F. W. Burford

THE COSTUMES OF SOME LOVELY HOURIS WHICH WERE INTRODUCED UPON THE ANNIVERSARY OF THE FAMOUS PLAY AT HIS MAJESTY'S

Mr. Oscar Asche's great reconstruction of the days of Haroun al Raschid, "Chu Chin Chow," reached its first anniversary last Friday week and is still drawing crowded and delighted audiences to His Majesty's and may yet see its third birthday. Mr. Oscar Asche is one of the greatest manufacturers of Eastern atmosphere that the stage has ever seen, and fanciful as some of his colour schemes may perhaps sometimes appear they are not very far wide of things that can be seen to-day in almost any of the big native cities of Ajmere and Rajputana

A selection of mannequins showing the latest costumes from the show *Chu Chin Chow*, which opened at His Majesty's Theatre in 1916 and ran for five years and more than 2,300 performances. The show was one of the major theatrical successes of the First World War and was particularly popular with soldiers on leave due to the scantily clad slave girls in the cast. (Illustrated London News/ME)

MISS VESTA TILLEY

Who is delighting the London Coliseum audiences with her new song, "Six Days Home on Leave," a new and novel song-scena depicting the return of a Tommy from the front. Miss Tilley is undoubtedly the best male impersonator the "Halls" have ever seen, and is a great favourite practically all over the world

Music hall star Vesta Tilley (1864–1952), whose speciality was male impersonations. During the First World War she earned the nickname 'Britain's best recruiting sergeant' with a number of patriotic war songs she performed at various shows and revues. Pictured here in the role of Tommy home from the front at the London Coliseum, where she delighted audiences with the song 'Six Days Home on Leave'. (Illustrated London News/ME)

Flying Colours at the Hippodrome in 1916. *The Better 'Ole*, named after Bairnsfather's best-known cartoon, was co-written by him and Arthur Eliot and starred Arthur Bourchier as a larger-than-life Old Bill. Unsurprisingly, *The Bystander* went to town promoting the show with sketches by their theatrical artist Norman Morrow, but even *The Queen*, not a great reporter on the world of the stage, featured photographs of scenes from the play. *The Better 'Ole* ran for 833 performances in London and the following year, Welsh Pearson brought the story to the cinema screen. Kensitas Cigarettes used a picture of Bourchier in character for their advertisements with the tagline: 'If you knows a better cigarette, go and smoke it.' It was a slogan that was probably recognisable to every single member of the population.

The popularity of *The Better 'Ole* reflects the influence and impact of illustration in a period before television or radio. Pictures by 'special artists' were still used frequently in news magazines, their composition and clarity of reproduction often giving a better impression of events than photographs. Alongside Bairnsfather, there was a whole host of illustrators and cartoonists whose work was familiar to the British public and whose humour struck a chord, crossing class barriers and creating a shared national characteristic – an irrepressible sense of humour in a crisis. William Heath Robinson, published in *The Sketch* and the *Illustrated Sporting & Dramatic News*, drew numerous cartoons throughout the war offering crackpot solutions employed by the dastardly Hun to defeat the British, from using oversized magnets to ping away their uniform buttons to piping laughing gas into the trenches to render them incapable of nothing more than a giggle. No offence was caused by Heath Robinson's light-hearted vision of war; if anything – as with all forms of entertainment – it offered some relief

to the all-too-present stark reality. Other illustrators, famous names such as George Studdy, Bert Thomas and Alfred Leete (who had drawn the original 'Your Country Needs You' Lord Kitchener design for the cover of *London Opinion*) variously poked fun at stereotypes of profiteering shopkeepers, opinionated clubmen, working-class East Enders, 'shirkers', rookie recruits and of course the enemy, who was caricatured and belittled in a number of infinite ways. Romantic themes were also popular; Lewis Baumer, Claude Shepperson and Edmund Blampied often drew pretty girls, fashion puns or sorrowful partings between sweethearts. *The Sketch* magazine in particular championed the work of numerous artists and in Britain, pioneered the pin-up genre, publishing, in an exclusive deal, the work of Raphael Kirchner, whose sensual, coquettish Kirchner Girls were a sensation, and particularly popular with troops at the front who used them to enliven the walls of dug-outs. *The Sketch* published one letter of gratitude, after one of his most popular pictures had been published:

> Dear Sketch,
> I feel that a special vote of thanks should be rendered to your excellent publication in general, and Mr. Raphael Kirchner in particular, for the coloured supplement of 'A Duck's Egg' hatching out on March 31. No officers' mess in the North of France is to be found without one or more of your cheering productions on its walls...

Kirchner's pictures were exhibited at the Bruton Street Galleries in 1915, one of many exhibitions during this period. Attending museums and exhibitions was a reasonably priced, often educational activity – in Kirchner's case, a particular kind of education! They could also be visited via public transport, in daylight, and were unconcerned

'Not during the war, thank you'. A British bulldog refuses a tankard of frothy beer on the front cover of *The Tatler*, a metaphor for the government's measures to curb drinking in April 1915. (Illustrated London News/ME)

by the curtailed licensing hours affecting other forms of entertainment. *The Graphic* Galleries at 190, Strand (run by *The Graphic* magazine, parent to *The Bystander*), held a Bairnsfather exhibition in the spring of 1916, an event that was publicised in *The Bystander* notifying readers that a certain number of originals by 'the soldier who has made the Empire laugh' were available to buy, and that entry was free of charge. A charming sketch made from inside the gallery, and showing a crowd of passers-by enjoying a spontaneous chuckle at the pictures on display, appeared in the magazine the following week. The Dutch cartoonist Louis Raemaekers had his pictures on display at the Fine Art Gallery in New Bond Street in July 1915, paintings by various members of the Artists' Rifles were the subject of another at the Leicester Galleries in January 1916 and Paul Nash, one of the official war artists, held an exhibition at the Goupil Gallery in 1917. Eve was surprised by what she saw there:

Talking of exhibitions, it's becoming quite the fashion for artist men who've been 'out there' to give shows of their war pictures when they come back. But it isn't all of them who've done their 'impressions' actually in the trenches, under fire, like Mr. Paul Nash of the Hampshires, whose clever sketches of Ypres Salient are now on view at the Goupil Gallery – impressions, too, that are distinctly intriguing. I hadn't imagined, for instance, that 'over there' there was still colour. One pictures the Front one dreary waste of mud-tones.

There was more colour at the Grafton Galleries in March 1918 with an exhibition of war photographs, the private view of which was attended by the royal family. In May the display moved to the People's Palace in Mile End, where it was opened by Princess Patricia of Connaught and allowed the dramatic images to be seen by more than just the upper-class patrons of Mayfair galleries ('the East-Enders are crowding to see them as eagerly as the West-Enders to the Grafton Galleries,' observed *The Bystander*). *The Sketch* reported on the thought-provoking impact of the images:

Everybody is talking about the wonderful realism of the coloured battle photographs on view now at the Grafton Gallery… There are two pictures of German wire which beggar description in their sinister immensity. For anyone who imagines they know what war, fear, or discomfort means in this country – and to many others – one may earnestly recommend a visit to the exhibition.

Society was out in force in December 1917, when a 'Loan Collection' on display at the Grosvenor Galleries, comprising paintings of prominent figures by smart painters such as Ambrose McEvoy, gave everyone a chance to gawp at each other. Eve described some of the portraits on display: 'Lady Cynthia Asquith looks soulful, and the Duchess of Marlborough as usual chic personified, in marvellous pearls and faint clouds of ethereal chiffon, and Lady Diana Manners, in pink, is good. But then, as a bored young wench at the Private View remarked, "Diana's so easy to do".'

In March 1917, Eve reported on a more unusual exhibition at the Victoria and Albert Museum, one to appeal to those of a nosy disposition: 'Reminds me, there's been a regular pilgrimage down to the old Victoria & Albert to see the lovely furniture that the owners of Montagu and Devonshire and Grosvenor houses have sent along there for safe-keeping while their houses were in the hand of the barbarians – or rather, VAD's, food controllers and Labour ministers.'

The idea of being able to see the contents of some of London's most exclusive residences was clearly a crowd-puller, though what to do with the art of the nation was an issue of concern. *The Queen* reported in December 1915 on the distribution of national art treasures to provincial galleries around the country in case of air raid damage, though it clearly thought this was a delayed reaction, adding sniffily, 'It is rather remarkable that the nation should have waited a year and a half to take such elementary precautions.'

Art gallery and museum-going was one leisure pursuit to escape taxation and the consequent price hikes during the war, although a number closed temporarily during the war.

Cinemagoers suffered an additional 2*d* on 6*d* tickets and 1*d* on cheap seats but it did not seem to discourage the public. The 3,000 cinemas around the country in 1914 had, by the end of the decade, grown to almost 4,000 and the stars of the silent movies, Douglas Fairbanks, Mary Pickford and particularly Charlie Chaplin, became popular icons of the period. Among the films Chaplin appeared in at this time was the war-themed *Shoulder of Arms* of 1918, which bore all the hallmarks of Bairnsfather-style trench humour. *The Tatler*'s Eve was even brought to life on-screen in a series of twelve short comedy films, 'The Adventures of Eve', starring Eileen Molyneux, with wartime titles such as *Eve Adopts a*

Eve and the reckless one arrive at the pictures, and are swallowed up into an impenetrable and sympathetic darkness—

Eve and her beau, Reggie, are shown the way into a cinema by an usherette and are pleasantly surprised to see how dark – and private – the auditorium is. Cinemas were considered potential dens of iniquity during the First World War! (Illustrated London News/ME)

'Gods and Fighting Men' by Edwin Morrow. A quietly moving illustration from *The Bystander*, January 1916, showing khaki uniform predominating in the upper circle as soldiers watch the opera from a high vantage point. (Illustrated London News/ME)

Lonely Soldier and *How Eve Helped the War Fund*. In August 1916, a quite different sort of war film was released. *The Battle of the Somme* mixed real footage filmed by official cinematographers with staged scenes to produce a powerful documentary that brought the brutal reality of war to the civilian population. It was seen by two million people. In *The Tatler*'s 'Bubble & Squeak' column in January 1917, the national ability to see the lighter side of everything was conveyed by a story of a conversation overhead in a Glasgow cinema between a Highlander and an English Tommy:

> When they came to the part showing the English regiments going over the parapet, Tommy turned to the other and said, 'Where are all the Jocks now, the men who get the name for doing all the fighting?' 'Awa' ye eeediot,' was the reply. 'They're up in the front line haudin' the Germans back tae let the English chaps get their photo ta'en.'

If theatre, cinema and art thrived, despite the impediments caused by war, sport fared less well. Football, which since the formation of the professional football league in 1898 had attracted enormous spectator numbers, was the subject of controversy. On 25 November 1914, *The Tatler* ran a picture showing a typical football crowd at a Saturday afternoon match between Fulham and Clapton Orient. *The Tatler* was unusually opinionated about the scene:

> A close examination of the latter picture shows that the crowd is composed of young men who, decorated with patriotic flags in their buttonholes and singing patriotic songs, march boldly forward – to see other men footling at football. Why can they not listen to the now silenced call of the grand

old man we buried last week and serve their country in the ranks of the new army?

In its next issue, the magazine quoted a letter from the front which strongly demanded: 'A law should forbid a football being kicked.'

'The grand old man' mentioned was the recently deceased Lord Roberts, who, in a speech to the Special Service Battalion in London, famously said, 'This is not the time to play games.' The pressure on both players and spectators to abandon the sport was immense; *Punch* commented with cartoons and *The Bystander* published a photograph showing a disturbance at a match at Fulham in October 1914, when Frederick Charrington, a member of the famous brewing family, made a vociferous protest at half-time. The magazine also reported on a visit by Robert Baden-Powell to Tottenham Hotspur in the same month to open the shooting range they had just built underneath the stands. Not one to pass up the opportunity to speak on the country's dire need for men to enlist, the General spoke to the assembled 15,000 men on the fact there was a game far more worthy of their attention – 'a man's game full of honour and adventure for those with grit in them.' 'The chance', he reminded them, 'may never come again. We can do our football when we have done the war.' The Tottenham Hotspur chairman was reported to look somewhat uncomfortable. Eventually, in spring 1915, the football league's fixtures were cancelled and activity was suspended for the remainder of the war. Those who suffered withdrawal symptoms from the beautiful game could enjoy instead inter-regimental and military matches, or women's football, which flourished during this period with teams made up of women workers from munitions and other factories.

Some professional football players had already been released from their contracts, like the Bradford player Donald Bell VC, who joined the West Yorkshire Regiment and died during a heroic defence of Contalmaison on 10 July 1916. His story, as with many others, transferred the role of sport to the front where the skills, strength and courage of elite sportsmen embodied the very best of the nation and set an example to all. There was the legendary attack of the East Surreys at Montauban where Captain Nevill, who was killed during the action, famously encouraged his men to dribble footballs towards the German trenches, and the truce between British and German soldiers up and down parts of the front on Christmas Day 1914 sportingly involved a game of football in some parts. Both incidents were recorded in the illustrated papers with pictures that would inspire readers at home; Captain Nevill's exploits were immortalised in the *Illustrated London News* by Richard Caton Woodville, a military artist famed for painting heroic charges and derring-do in the best *Boy's Own* tradition.

The football league had been criticised for its tardy reaction to the call for recruits, but other sports were quicker to respond. By the end of November 1914, *The Times* was reporting that every England Rugby international had joined the colours. *The Sketch* published two double-page spreads in March 1915, one showing the portraits of 76 Cambridge Blues who had enlisted, another a week later with the same

Decca gramophones advertised in magazines such as *The Sketch* throughout the war, depicting life in the trenches (and the joy brought there by their music). In this post-war advertisement, published in February 1919, the mood is joyful and optimistic but is also indicative of the modest entertainment enjoyed at home in place of the lavish balls and parties of pre-war days. (Illustrated London News/ME)

number of Oxford University's finest sports-men. The *Illustrated Sporting & Dramatic News*, a high quality paper established in 1874 and covering sport and theatre, devoted space each week to 'The Sportsman's Roll of Honour'. It makes sobering reading. Week after week, photographs of fallen sportsmen were published, county and international players; the country's sporting elite, many nurtured on the playing fields of England's public schools. There was the Rugby International, Edgar Mobbs, who raised his own sportsman's battal-ion (Mobbs' Own) for the Northamptonshire Regiment and was killed in action at Zillebeke in July 1917 during the Third Battle of Ypres. Also from the Northamptonshire Regiment

was Captain Anketell Moutray Read VC, the athlete and heavyweight boxer killed near Hulluch, France in September 1915. From the polo world, a sport unsurprisingly the preserve of the upper classes, there were numerous cas-ualties including Francis Grenfell VC, his twin brother Rivy and the celebrated Leslie Cheape, who had helped England to a historic win over America in the Westchester Cup just weeks before the outbreak of war, killed in Egypt in 1916. Another great loss was the New Zealand tennis player, Anthony Wilding, Wimbledon Champion from 1910 to 1913. Wilding, 6ft 2in, athletic and with charm to match his matinee idol looks, moved effortlessly in high society. He was close to former Prime Minister Arthur

Having already found fame on the stage, Eve was next to conquer the cinema screen. In 1918, the Gaumont Film Company produced twelve silent short films called *The Adventures of Eve* starring actress Eileen Molyneux in the title role. The films were written by Annie Fish and followed a number of war themes such as 'Eve Helps the Censor' and 'How Eve Helped the War Fund'. (Illustrated London News/ME)

Balfour, whom he coached, and was engaged to the celebrated American actress Maxine Elliott. The news of his death – he died near Neuve Chapelle on 9 May 1915 during the Battle of Aubers Ridge – sent ripples of shock through society. 'Just now it is the deeds in the Greatest Game of all that count,' wrote the *Illustrated Sporting & Dramatic News*, reporting on his death. 'Nobody who knew the man expected aught else of Tony Wilding. He belongs to the numbers of those Sons of Empire who will not be soon forgotten.' Three months earlier, the Olympic hurdler Kenneth Powell, who had been Wilding's doubles partner in tennis during their time at Cambridge, featured on the front cover of *The Sketch*, with news that he had been killed near Ypres on the 18 February.

While Britain's sportsmen succumbed to the carnage of war, again, the question of whether it was morally right to continue with sport at home was debated. The tennis world did not hesitate and in January 1915, *The Queen* magazine briefly reported: 'The committee of the All-England Lawn Tennis and Croquet Club, having considered the position arising from the war, has decided, for the present, to make no arrangements in connection with the championships in 1915.' But whether playing tennis at home was acceptable (an activity only open, after all, to those who actually owned or had access to a tennis court) posed another moral dilemma. 'There is probably not a single court in this country that will not lack some familiar player, some one among the many thousands of men who have left their rackets behind them and gone to other fields. But one does not see that there is any reason for the feeling expressed in some places that there should be no tennis playing at all this year. Of course, there cannot be tournaments. But games on peoples' own courts cannot, we think, be in any sense either deplorable for the players or offensive to other people. There must be much less tennis than in other years, but people may as well have what they can.' It concluded that although there could not possibly be tournaments – and 'tennis as a social affair would certainly be rather an outrage' – keeping fit was a patriotic duty. 'We fancy that people who do play tennis this summer will turn out to be more useful after all those people who on purely theoretical grounds decline to play at all.'

The continuance of racing, whose fixtures underpinned the social season, was the subject of fierce debate within Society. *The Sketch* recorded a meeting of the Jockey Club on 16 March 1915 at the town house of Lord Derby. Its decision was to continue with racing, but, with the King already announcing he would not attend Ascot that year, 'the social element would therefore be eliminated.' There was also controversy over the Grandstand at Epsom, which had been converted into a hospital for wounded soldiers. When it was proposed that two of the four rooms given over to this purpose would be commandeered as luncheon rooms on race days, the Duke of Portland scratched all his horses for all the engagements that year in protest, declaring it would be deplorable if wounded soldiers were turned out and it would be better to abandon the meeting altogether. The Director-General of the Army Medical Service made assurances that this would not be necessary but the Duke's strong reaction proved where it was felt priorities should lie, even to those with a vested interest in the sport. Racing limped on for a time but organised meetings were eventually abandoned, much to the chagrin of Admiral Sir Hedworth Meux who, gossiped Eve in 1917, 'says it's nothing to do with oats at all, but just because some of the War Council – the P.M., Mr. Bonar Law, Arthur Henderson and milord's Milner and Curzon to wit – don't approve of the sport of kings,

A humorous illustration by *The Bystander*'s theatrical artist Norman Morrow demonstrating the tastes in theatrical entertainment during the war. While the public enthusiasm for tragedy and war plays had dwindled, musical revues with pretty girls, dancing and lavish costumes flourished. (Illustrated London News/ME)

anyway in war time.' Petrol shortages meant it was difficult to travel to events, and with many able jockeys leaving the turf to join up, the sport would have been limited anyway – though the legendary Steve Donoghue, declared unfit for service, nevertheless rode Gay Crusader to win the Derby twice during the war, in 1915 and 1917. On 16 September 1914, *The Tatler* carried a photograph of jockeys who had all become troopers in the 19th Hussars, among them Percy Woodland, who had won the Grand National in 1903 and 1913; George Byng; Lord Torrington, the gentleman jockey and racehorse owner; and Herbert Tyrwhitt-Drake, who was killed in action in March 1915.

Hunting, an integral part of upper-class life, continued on for much of the war, supported in part by Lord Derby, who called for hunts to be protected in December 1915 and for those involved in the care of the horses to be exempted from conscription, all in order to maintain a steady supply of cavalry chargers as requested by the War Office Director of Remounts. For many this was not regarded as sufficient justification; the policy was reviewed two years later and the exemption withdrawn. But the romance of the hunt remained a potent symbol of traditional British values, something to uphold and cherish despite the war. The wife of Major Richard Selby-Lowndes was pictured in *The Illustrated Sporting and Dramatic News* in November 1915, acting as Master in the absence of her husband at a meet of the Whaddon Chase foxhounds near Leighton Buzzard. Mrs W.F. Inge took over the Atherstone county hunt formerly hunted by her father, while Mrs Ralph Lubbock headed the North Hereford hunt. Pictures of a group of army officers who had, with the permission of the military authorities, shipped over a pack of beagles so they could enjoy some hunting in their leisure time appeared in several

magazines, including on the front cover of the *Illustrated London News*. The pack had been lent to Lieutenant Charles Romer Williams of the 4th Dragoon Guards while home on leave for hunting hares 'as a change from herr-shooting!', chortled *The Sketch*. 'We Don't Care for the Shells and the Shot, And We-ll All Go A-Hunting To-day,' wrote *The Tatler* with bravado across the photographs.

Travel and holidays abroad, which, prior to the war, had punctuated the annual timetables of the wealthy, were still taken, though the once popular spas of Germany – Marienbad, Carlsbad and, a favourite of the late King Edward VII, Baden Baden – were ceremoniously crossed off the map. Instead, the spa at Harrogate enjoyed a renaissance. 'I had never been to Harrogate,' wrote Silas Dark in *The Sketch* in July 1916, 'but any misgivings I have had that things would not be done as well as at Continental spas … were disposed of on entering the Royal Baths'. Around the same time, Eve reported that 'lots have gone to Harrogate, of course – now there aren't any Bads to visit, people do. Queen Alexandra was up staying with the Grand Duchess (Grand Duchess Marie of Russia who ran two hospitals in the town) for a long week-end.' It was still possible to travel by train down to the Riviera early in the war, to Nice or Monte Carlo, where some of the luckiest wounded officers found themselves in hospital, but the closer fashionable French resorts were transformed. 'All the great hotels, and even the Casino – where we wore our frocks and lost our francs – are turned into hospitals,' wrote Eve in November 1914, adding that 'Dinard and St Malo were also full of woun2deds.' So too was 'nearby homely Brighton', which could list among its visitors such scions of society as 'Mr Asquith … the Duchess of Marlborough, who's got a house there somewhere on the front, and several

Americans, and the de Traffords, and such war philanthropists as Lady Dudley and King Manoel, who "runs" two of the many convalescent homes for officers there.' Eve confessed to finding the Brighton scene a little too depressing to be an enjoyable getaway destination – 'So many broken men, so many splendid young bodies maimed and spoiled beyond repair.'

Life – and life's pleasures – went on during wartime, but the spectre of war was never far away.

Aftermath:
Peace, Celebration
and Remembrance

'Whereby our dead shall sleep
In honour, unbetrayed
And we in faith and honour keep
That peace for why they paid'
(Rudyard Kipling)

'Hostilities to cease at eleven' – that was the magic key which opened the floodgates. To think – just to think – that with the stroke of eleven the lads 'out there' would be safe from wounds and death, and that, after all they had endured, they would come home to share the victory they had won. The very thought had its delirium; and as the hour struck we stood with bared heads and gave thanks to the God of Battles, who was also the God of Life. The guns of death were silenced with the first golden stroke from the bell-tower … Could the dead hear it, we wondered – our gallant dead? Was there joy in their souls also in the land where soldiers rest?

The staff of *The Bystander* offices, situated in Tallis Street, just off the main drag of Fleet Street, were ideally placed to describe the wave of rejoicing that swept through London as finally, after four long years, news of the Armistice 'rushed down on the Strand like a tornado'. In its previous issue, as Europe stood on the cusp of peace, it had debated in its leader column the proper way to act when the much-anticipated moment finally did arrive. 'Should we shout?' it asked. 'We have never shouted during this war. Even our church bells have been dumb … How can one cheer when one thinks of those silent figures with their faces to the sky?'

But when the news came, it admitted that all sombre intentions were lost: 'After all, we did cheer and sob and thank God with a fervour such as never before had swayed us.' It described how the city erupted into celebration, how 'one moment it was the wonted place, with its ordinary, passing crowd. The next it was a howling arena into which had tumbled from shops and great buildings a frenzied, shrieking mob – an amazing transformation. "Germany has surrendered." "The war is won." "My lad is coming back." Nothing even like the scene can have been witnessed before. We stolid English folk flung reserve to the winds.' Not far away was Constance Peel, by now an employee of Lord Northcliffe at the *Daily Mail*, who was at work when the news came through:

We opened the window wide and could hear cheering and immediately somewhere near a wheezy old gramophone began to play "God Save the King". I longed to go into the street but could not, for whatever happens, newspapers must go to press. I was correcting proofs and my eyes kept

filling with tears, tears for those to whom peace had come too late to save some one dearly loved. By the time my work was over, it was five o'clock and raining heavily.

Thousands made their way towards the Mall and to Buckingham Palace, where the King and Queen appeared on the balcony to acknowledge the crowds and to join with them to sing 'The Old Hundred', 'Home, Sweet Home' and 'Auld Lang Syne'. At the Comedy Theatre that evening, such was the excitement of some of the young men in the audience, they climbed over the orchestra rails and onto the stage to dance, much to the amusement of the actors and actresses performing. Around London, prominent members of society mingled with the crowds and were spotted by press photographers. *The Tatler* printed pictures of F.E. Smith with his wife and small daughter, Lady Milbanke, whose husband, a VC winner from the Boer War, had been killed in action at Gallipoli, and, seated on a captured gun on display in the Mall, Mrs George Keppel, mistress of the late King Edward VII. Lady Diana Manners, who had lost so many dear friends in the war, wrote in her memoirs that with so much bitter loss it was 'unnatural to be jubilant', and spent Armistice night dining quietly at the Ritz with her mother before slipping away to be with her future husband, Duff Cooper, who was bedridden with the influenza that was spreading through England and Europe with devastating speed. *The Bystander*'s jubilation was tempered by the sad news that one of its writers, 'Jack Johnson', who had written the 'Letters from Flanders' column throughout the war, had passed away of pneumonia as a result of influenza on very day of the Armistice itself. Two more *Bystander* contributors would succumb to the epidemic: Alexander Gray, who had written on motoring, and Frederick George Aflalo, who

Prince John, the youngest child of King George V and Queen Mary, had suffered from epilepsy since birth. He never reached adulthood and died on 19 January 1919. (Illustrated London News/ME)

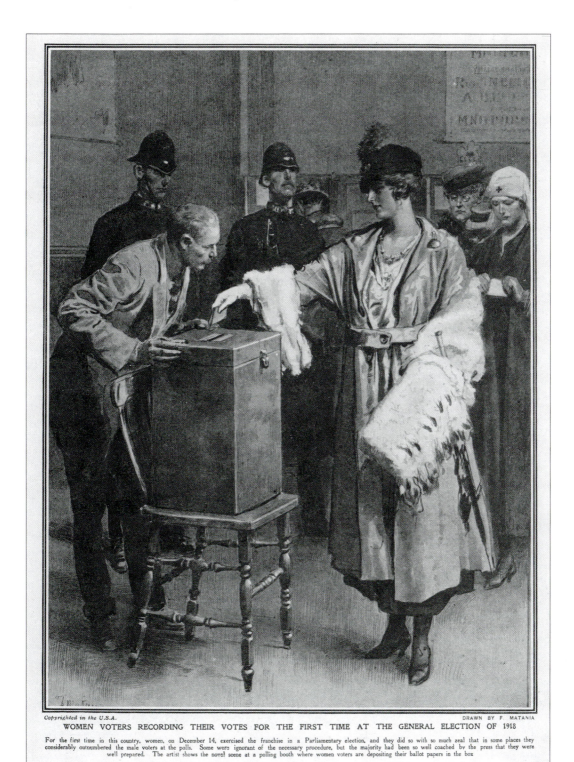

Copyrighted in the U.S.A. DRAWN BY F. MATANIA

WOMEN VOTERS RECORDING THEIR VOTES FOR THE FIRST TIME AT THE GENERAL ELECTION OF 1918

For the first time in this country, women, on December 14, exercised the franchise in a Parliamentary election, and they did so with so much zeal that in some places they considerably outnumbered the male voters at the polls. Some were ignorant of the necessary procedure, but the majority had been so well coached by the press that they were well prepared. The artist shows the novel scene at a polling booth where women voters are depositing their ballot papers in the box

After years of campaigning by the female suffrage movement, women were able to vote for the first time in 1918. But this breakthrough came with limitations. Only women householders and university graduates over the age of thirty qualified, meaning that the thousands of women who had swelled the wartime workforce and had served their country were still too young to vote. They would have to wait another decade before achieving electoral parity with men. (Illustrated London News/ME)

occasionally wrote for the magazine on fishing and big game shooting. The magazine had suffered the loss of one of its writers in action too, H.H. Munro, who wrote under the pen-name 'Saki'. He had enlisted despite being over age and was killed on 14 November 1916.

For Eve too, there was contemplation and ambivalent feelings of joy and sadness. 'My Dear Betty, – So it is over. Over at last. The captains and the kings depart … 'Specially the kings, by gum, 'spesh'ly the kings! They are behind us, the weary years, these tragic, terrible years of war, so full of pain, so sad and bitter – and yet, how glorious.' Blanche's column in *The Bystander* was muted too. She acknowledged how those, like Diana Manners, 'who mourned our fallen conquerors, had kept at home and hid their grief, of course, for to the stricken soul how impossible is London, the gay, the sparkling.' The author of 'The Way of the World' column in *The Sketch* had his own poignant story to tell:

There was a sad side to the rejoicings. I was made to realise this only a few minutes after the victory guns had ceased to growl. I had got into a 'bus at Chancery Lane. Just opposite me there was a woman dressed in black. Crowds were surging along the street waving flags and shouting. Girls were laughing, boys were cheering and everybody seemed as happy as the day is long. But this woman, as she looked out upon these merry, cheering crowds, was crying bitterly. At Charing Cross she got out of the 'bus. Then the little conductress turned to me. 'She lost her boy only last week,' she said, and I noticed there were tears in her own eyes.

By *The Bystander*'s next issue, Blanche was feeling irritated by what she viewed as an extravagant prolonging of celebrations. 'For whatever else there was, there was certainly no dignity about the way, in the streets of the great cities, England took her peace!' In London, she claimed, 'it took the lighter spirits no less than the whole of the week to scream themselves hoarse and walk themselves footsore and lull their ardour for "celebrating"'. She referred specifically to the German guns, which had been burned and broken by the crowds, and wondered how the regiments in France, for whom such trophies had been hard-won, might feel about them being 'destroyed and damaged to make some maffickers' holiday.' ('maffickers' – from the verb 'mafficking' was used to describe the type of excessive celebrating seen in London after the Relief of Mafeking during the Boer War). Worse still were the 'better-class' joy-makers who had thrown champagne bottles through windows and danced on the tables in restaurants. All the same, she was as keen as anyone to attend the Victory Ball at the Albert Hall, scheduled for 27 November with all proceeds going to the Nation's Fund for Nurses.

The attendees of the fancy dress Victory Ball read like a who's who of London society, at least those who had been able to secure one of the 4,000 tickets. The event was dreamt up by Mrs Edward Hulton, wife of the newspaper proprietor, and Miss May Beeman, and supported by notable women such as Hazel, Lady Lavery and Lady Idina Wallace. The focal event of the evening was a symbolic procession arranged by renowned pageant master Mr Louis N. Parker and headed by (who else but) Lady Diana Manners, wielding a trident as Britannia. She was followed by the Duchess of Westminster as England and Mrs Hulton as Peace, who entered in a chariot, releasing

Opposite: Astonishingly, the influenza pandemic of 1918 and 1919 claimed more lives globally than the war itself. This Heath Robinson cartoon, published in *The Bystander* in April 1919, suggests a fresh air bedroom to avoid contagion. (Estate of Mrs J.C. Robinson/Pollinger Ltd/ILN/ME)

doves among the flag bedecked hall. Miss Louis Duveen came as France, Mrs Lionel Harris in a costume redolent of the Statue of Liberty, and the actress Doris Keane wore a 200-year-old lace shawl she had bought in Granada, weighing 5st and of exquisite workmanship. Irene Castle sealed her reputation as a world leader of style by donning a rakish costume of frock coat and boots worn with a turban from which soared two arching feather plumes. She was, declared *The Sketch*, 'an object lesson in the art of wearing fancy dress'.

The Victory Ball's success was marred when news filtered through that the twenty-two-year-old actress Billie Carleton had died the following day, apparently of a cocaine overdose. Carleton had begun to enjoy some theatrical success in 1917 and 1918, with roles in *The Boy* and *Fair and Warmer*, garnering favourable reviews. After appearing at the ball in a transparent costume of black georgette designed by her friend and sometime drug dealer Reggie LeVeulle, she had returned to her flat at Savoy Court Mansions in the early hours and gone to bed. At some point the following afternoon, her maid had discovered her dead. The inquest that followed caused a sensation, revealing as it did a sordid underworld of drug-taking, opium dens and 'orgies'. It was a tragedy that both repelled and fascinated society and was an event that had far more in common with the louche fast living that would be associated with the 1920s and a prime example of the modern world preying on the innocence of young women. *The Tatler* remained tight-lipped about the subject. It featured a photograph of the actress but said nothing more other than a brilliant career had ended in tragedy.

While London celebrated victory, the Royal family took a more dutiful approach to the end of war. After attending a service of thanksgiving at St Paul's Cathedral on the 12 November, *The Sketch* noted that 'Princess Mary set and fixed a fashion of persisting seriousness when, instead of staying at home to share in Peace festivities, she started for France in her VAD dress to visit the hospitals worked – if one may not say manned – by women.' The King, Prince of Wales and Prince Albert all followed her to France where inspections, hospitals and award ceremonies all required a royal presence. Prince Albert, now in the Royal Air Force, flew over to France with his friend Commander Louis Greig.

As Eve had noted in her own peace soliloquy, war had had a corrosive effect on Europe's royal families, but for those who remained, peace meant the chance to travel freely once more. The elder daughter of the Duke of Connaught, Princess Margaret ('Daisy') of Connaught, the Crown Princess of Sweden had been unable to travel back to England during the war, even for the funeral of her mother in 1917, though she had spent the war working indefatigably for worthy causes. On 19 January 1919, she arrived in London at Liverpool Street Station with her youngest daughter Ingrid, but the event was overshadowed by the death that same day of Prince John, the youngest epileptic son of the King and Queen. Daisy stayed for her sister Patricia's wedding to Commander Alexander Ramsay on 27 February at Westminster Abbey, an event that drew thousands of well-wishers to the streets to cheer the popular Princess Pat. The renouncement of her royal title – she became afterwards Lady Patricia Ramsey – signalled a significant shift in the British royal family's adaption to the modern age. Her decision, observed *The Bystander* approvingly, marked 'a change between the pre-war order of thought and the outlook of to-day, sharply and irrevocably.' Within the next few years, two of the King's children, Princess Mary, in 1922, and Prince Albert, the future King George VI, would marry commoners.

Queen Maud of Norway, the King's youngest sister, could also, at long last, return to England to see her family. 'Queen Maud of Norway has lost no time in paying a visit to her girlhood home. Her coming is, of course, an immense joy to Queen Alexandra, as well as to the King and her sisters, for the warm affection uniting the Royal family is a matter of common knowledge. Indeed, one of the personal trials the war has brought to Queen Alexandra has been this enforced separation from her youngest daughter. Five years is a long time, and it has seen the passing of Prince Olaf from a fascinating small boy into something very near, at any rate, to the dignity of manhood', wrote *The Queen* on 21 December 1918. It also predicted hopefully that once the King and Queen had returned from their 'well-earned rest at Sandringham' over Christmas, the court presentations would once more be resumed at Buckingham Palace. 'It is now four and a half years since any such functions have been held, and it will take a very long time to work through the long list of those waiting to be presented at Court. Apart from the immense number of young girls who have grown up since 1914, there has been an unusual number of war-time marriages, which means a huge list of brides.' In fact, *The Bystander* reported, 'there will be no Court functions so long as we are in the armistice state', and to deal with the sheer numbers, debutantes of 1919 were dealt with en masse at garden parties. Evening courts were not re-introduced until the following year.

The Bystander was just as keen to see reconstruction in the world of sport. Writing in the magazine, Captain H.S. Scrivener, a former tennis player, suggested that sport did not

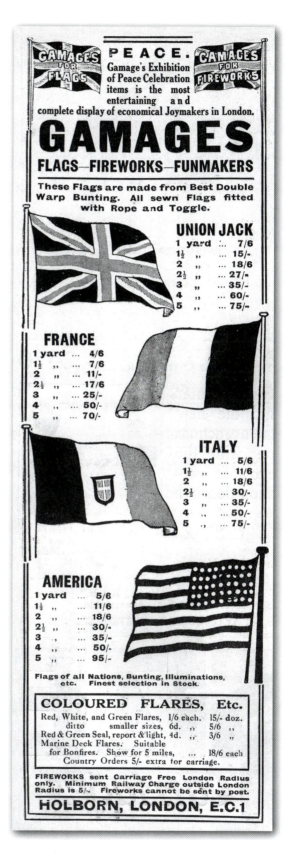

Gamage's in Holborn promoting its 'Exhibition of Peace Celebration' items in July 1919. On offer were flags, bunting and flares for the peace celebrations that summer. Ever observant of thrift, *The Queen* magazine printed a pattern for sewing one's own Union Jack flag around this time. (Illustrated London News/ME)

have to be carried out with elaborate expense and that post-war, it would be based on 'good fellowship rather than the limelight'. Those sportsmen who had survived 'will come back, and will bring with them a whole crowd of recruits from the navies and armies of Great Britain and her colonies, who, perhaps, before the war, had no liking or desire for sport, but whose training and life as soldiers and sailors have taught them the value of physical culture and the benefits, both mental and bodily of athletic pursuits'. The article was hauntingly accompanied by a number of portraits of fallen sportsmen; Tony Wilding the tennis champion, the polo player Francis Grenfell, the Oxford and England rugby three-quarter Ronald Poulton-Palmer and Kenneth Hutchings, the Kent and England cricket batsman, among them. A racing article in January 1919 reported that the Grand National would be run at Aintree at the end of March and that the Derby would return to Epsom. An advertisement for W. Abbott & Sons football boots appeared hopefully in *The Sketch*, suggesting them as the ideal gift for officers to present to their men. 'Tommy will find time hangs badly waiting demobilisation and he loved Football, but he cannot get Football Boots. Have a whip round in your mess, and send us an order for sufficient to equip a team of your own.'

Demobilisation was indeed a long-winded process. Some units remained to police the Rhineland region, where they were joined by regular soldiers, but for most men, their demobbing date depended on their assessed value as workers. Priority was given to civil servants who would administrate the return of the others. After that came 'pivotal men', the job creators, and then 'slip men' (those who had notes from employers promising a position). The system was frustratingly flawed, allowing as it did more recent recruits to return home before long-serving soldiers, who instead spent weeks and even months waiting to be released. 'The hustling Geddes (Sir Auckland Geddes, responsible for winding up the Ministries of National Service and Reconstruction) will need a sabre to sunder the red tape,' observed *The Bystander* sagely, 'yet from the War Office standpoint there is much to to be said. The condition of Germany, not to mention Austria, makes a swift and

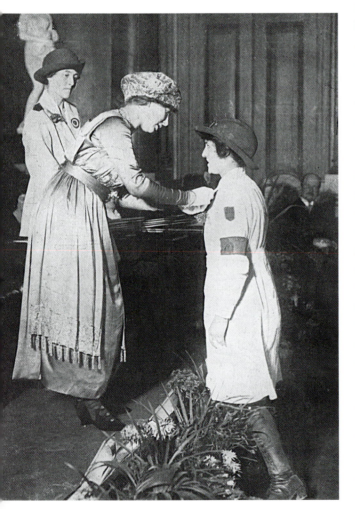

Farewell to the land girls. Princess Mary presenting medals to members of the Women's Land Army in December 1919 at the Draper's Hall, at their last rally before demobilisation. Fifty-five women were awarded Distinguished Service Bars for deeds of bravery whilst in charge of horses, cattle and the like. Pictured is Miss Ascanio receiving her medal from the Princess. (Illustrated London News/ME)

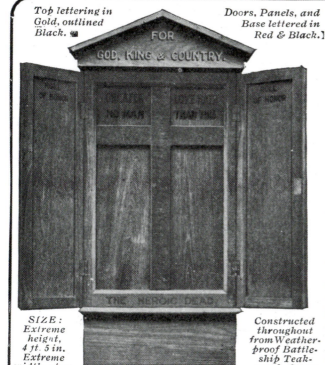

As every town, village, school and organisation sought to remember their dead, finding a dignified and lasting tribute to men who had given their lives for their country became a priority. This advertisement from October 1918 suggests war shrines made from reclaimed materials of HMS *Britannia* as a fitting memorial 'to the Patriotism of Britain's Sons'. (Illustrated London News/ME)

wholesale demobilisation unthinkable.' For those returning to Blighty and to civilian life, all was not a bed of roses. Wartime rationing and controls continued for up to a year after the Armistice. In the case of sugar, rationing was not lifted until November 1920. *The Queen* magazine published instructions for making a Union flag for the peace celebrations because of a dearth in the shops 'and those which can be got are very costly', and in her letter about New Year's Eve that year, *The Bystander*'s Blanche complained at the extortionate prices charged by restaurants: 'Seems as though being a restaurateur in this peace year of 1919 is going to be an even fatter job than it was in the war years, 1914–1918, what?'

While 11 November 1918 may have marked the end of fighting, in many ways Britain was in a state of flux as it struggled to reconcile the persistent economic conditions caused by war with society's desire for change. Industrial workers, essential during war, either found themselves unemployed, or those who remained sought to demand better pay and conditions. Through 1919, there was an average of 100,000 workers on strike on each day of the year. 'We read of bakers' strikes, transport strikes, dairy strikes, police strikes, engineers' strikes and last, though not least, servant strikes, here in England now; of one munition area alone, where 20,000 personas are receiving "unemployment donation"', wrote Blanche at the beginning of February. 'Course, what we're banking on is the hope that the good, old feudal spirit still prevails, and there remains, at any rate, SOME faint essence of the good old times when a gentleman was a gentleman and the rest of the world mere churls; but the hope, I confess, is a slender one. "Wait till the war's over and there's no more work for them, THEN there'll be servants all right!" choired the optimists these four years. But the war's over, the war work-

ers work no more, and the verdict is: "Sooner starve than be a servant!"' For women who had enjoyed the comparatively high wages of factory work during the war, a return to service did not appeal, and besides, middle-class households who before the war may have employed household staff could no longer necessarily afford such a luxury.

'We hear a good deal about the pinch of poverty felt by munition workers and other who have exchanged hard work and high wages for an unemployment benefit of 25*s* a week. This sum is two and a half times as much as the average wage of a working woman before the war,' pointed out *The Queen* magazine, even though it could now only buy simple food and lodging.

Eve talked of the same reticence of the working classes to return to service when she ruminated on the expectations of women war workers now that the war was over. 'And millions of women to keep occupied somehow – 'cos you don't suppose they're going straight home to dust the baby and buy the cabbages after four years of flapping, short-skirted and crêpe-de-chine-shirted, in Whitehall, basking in the bright rays of Brass Hats and Scarlet Tabs, and lingering in the languor of long lunches with temp. Left'nant. If that won't be the prob. of post-war probs, I don't know what will be, d'you? Course, what we OUGHT to do is to produce a new kind of DORA to herd all the Flossies back into the fold of domestic service – which is where most of 'em came from, or ought to, and where they should be replaced, gently but firmly as soon as poss.'

Lady Londonderry, Commandant of the Women's Legion, explained in a piece she wrote for *The Queen* in February 1919 how the Legion was forming a new household service section to train up members who had formerly worked as mechanics and clerks. 'By raising the status and dignity of domestic

IN LONDON ON VICTORY DAY.

LADY HONOR WARD AND MRS. DUNVILLE

Lady Honor Ward (in centre), who is Lord Dudley's eldest daughter, is here seen in front of Buckingham Palace with Mrs. Dunville on Victory Day, November 11

SIR HERCULES LANGRISHE AND LADY MILBANKE

Sir Hercules Langrishe and Lady Milbanke were among the numerous victims of the camera barrage in the Mall on Victory Day last Monday

SIR F. E. AND LADY SMITH AND THEIR DAUGHTER

The Attorney-General, like many other gallant members of his profession, has served with distinction in this war, and was with the Oxfordshire Yeomanry in 1914

MRS. GEORGE KEPPEL, LADY GAINFORD, AND LADY JOAN COMBE

An interesting group photographed sitting on one of the numerous German guns on view in the Mall. Lord Gainford was formerly Mr. Joseph Albert Pease

The Tatler featured snapshots of prominent members of society out in London to celebrate the signing of the armistice on 11 November 1918. Among the personalities captured were Mrs George Keppel (former mistress of King Edward VII) sitting on one of the numerous German guns on view in the Mall and F.E. Smith (Lord Birkenhead), the Attorney-General and best friend of Winston Churchill, with Lady Smith and their daughter, the future Lady Pamela Berry. (Illustrated London News/ME)

A BRILLIANT CAREER
Ended in Tragedy.

Miss Compton Collier, insets Bertram Park

THE LATE MISS BILLIE CARLETON

The death of Miss Billie Carleton under such tragic circumstances has caused much grief, both in the ranks of the profession and amongst her many friends off the stage. Miss Carleton may be said to have graduated in musical comedy and revue, but more recently she gave us proof of her talent in another direction, and made distinct successes in " Fair and Warmer " at the Prince of Wales' and " The Freedom of the Seas " at the Haymarket. She will be much missed. The inquest, which was opened last week, will be continued on Thursday

The death of the young actress Billie Carlton, found dead apparently of a drug overdose the morning after the Victory Ball at the Royal Albert Hall, cast a shadow over celebrations and revealed a dark underbelly to London's social scene. (Illustrated London News/ME)

service we hope to induce them to return to duties which need in no sense be degrading, and at the same time to help to supply a pressing need of the community.'

After years of campaigning for equal suffrage, the General Election at the end of 1918 saw women able to vote for the first time. But it was on limited terms. Women voters had to be over the age of thirty and to be either householders or married to a householder. Those paying rents of £5 a year or more and university graduates also qualified, but in reality, the majority of newly enfranchised voters were those whose focus lay with home and family. It was a patriarchal sop, but it was a start. Even so, the thousands of women who had swelled the wartime workforce and served their country were still too young to cast their vote. The performance of women candidates in the polls was disappointing. *The Queen* magazine noted that in only three cases did female candidates receive more than one third of the total votes from members of their own sex; one of these being Christabel Pankhurst, standing for the Women's Party. 'In other cases the proportion was deplorably low. Mrs Pethick Lawrence received less than one-quarter at Manchester, namely, 2,985 where there were 13,161 women voters on the register. Miss Markham received 2,000 votes at Mansfield, where there were 14,861 women voters.' *The Bystander* was dismissive, merely commenting on women's 'electoral unattractiveness'. Keble Howard, writing in *The Sketch,* merely wondered, laconically, why women had wanted the vote – 'For my own part, I don't think votes have much to do with the government of the country' – adding proudly, 'I myself have been entitled to the vote for the last twenty years, but have never once voted.' Both magazines chose to ignore the achievements of Miss Kate Edmonds, who was elected Britain's first woman town coun-

cillor in Plymouth by a large majority of 661. In her acceptance speech, she said: 'I am not going to take this as a personal triumph but as a tribute that you wish to pay to my sex for what they have done in the war.' The following year, after winning an October by-election in Plymouth Sutton, society hostess Nancy Astor became Britain's first female MP. But it was not until 1928 that women aged twenty-one and over finally gained electoral parity with men, and despite the convulsion of war, on being demobilised, many women reverted to their traditional roles of wives and mothers.

Finding employment for thousands of wounded men, many of them amputees or blinded by their injuries, was another ongoing concern. *The Queen* wrote of one young officer, Douglas Hope, son of Mr and Mrs Hope of Belmont, who 'had the misfortune to lose both his eyes through a shot from the enemy.' After being nursed back to health at Princess Christian's Hospital in Grosvenor Place, he was shortly to go to St Dunstan's, 'where he intends to learn how to occupy himself, and still to live a busy, useful life, as so many other officers have done who have suffered cruelly owing to the loss of eyesight in this terrible war.' Writing in *The Queen* in November 1918, the Marchioness of Carisbrooke emphasised that it was not by charity that the nation could show their gratitude to wounded men, but by 'showing them the dawn of new possibilities'. As patron of the Disabled Soldiers Embroidery Industry, she explained its object was to teach totally disabled men (those who could not leave their homes to work) embroidery of all kinds: church embroidery, badge embroidery, chair seat and back embroidery, even embroidery on dresses. Already, she wrote, the organisation had received several orders, including one from the Young Women's Christian Association for regulation hat bands. The Women's Legion also turned

"FROM KHAKI TO MUFTI"

MOSS BROS. & CO. LTD.

WELCOME BACK

the thousands of Officers they have equipped with KHAKI—and they inform them that they hold the LARGEST, MOST VARIED, and UNEQUALLED STOCK OF MUFTI IN LONDON, nearly all of pre-war materials.

Mufti Outfits for Town and Country Wear. Hunting and Racing Kit of every description kept in stock.

MOSS BROS. & Co., Ltd.,

20 & 21, KING ST., } COVENT
25, 31 & 32, Bedford Street, } GARDEN W.C.2

'Phone 3750-1 Gerr.   Tel. Add. "Parsee Rand, London."

After four long years of khaki being 'the only-wear', this advertisement for men's outfitters, Moss Bros, marks the transition of men's clothing from uniform back to civilian. The firm welcomes back 'the thousands of Officers they have equipped with khaki' and they inform them that they hold the 'largest, most varied, and unequalled stock of mufti in London'. (Illustrated London News/ME)

its attention to the training and employment of disabled soldiers and sailors. The Broderers' Company presented the Legion with a school in London where the men could work on gold and silver embroidery for naval and military purposes. Nationwide, eleven branches of the Lord Roberts Memorial Workshops trained and employed men in carpentry and other skills. In other cases, officers who had gone straight from school to military service found themselves poorly qualified for the kind of employment they were expected to fulfil in civilian life and took up further education, or were educated as they recovered. At the Kitchener House Hospital for Wounded Officers, also in Grosvenor Place, officers had the benefit of lectures and demonstrations to enable them to take special positions

in science and industry when they returned to civilian life. For some of 'modest means' there were opportunities around the Empire. Inspired by posters that promised farms and lands at a bargain price, some chose to make a new start and emigrated to Canada, South Africa or Australia.

As Britain looked forward to a new future, however fractured and imperfect, there was one subject on which the nation agreed: that there should be a fitting tribute and lasting monument of remembrance to those who had given their lives during the conflict. Around the country, towns and villages began to plan their own memorials to the dead. In January 1919, a full-page advertisement in *The Bystander* carried a photograph of the war memorial made for the tiny village of Harvel in Kent by a local

FANCY DRESS — AND FANCY FEATHERS : A FAMOUS DANCER.

AN OBJECT - LESSON IN THE ART OF WEARING FANCY DRESS : NEW PORTRAITS OF MRS. VERNON CASTLE.

Fancy dress, to be effective, needs to be worn with an appropriate air. It is not enough merely to don fantastic garments. The character represented must also be studied, and likewise the art known to Mr. Turveydrop as that of "deportment." That worthy would hardly be the best mentor, perhaps, for the modern devotees of fancy dress. The feminine among them who wish to shine could not do better than study the methods of Mrs. Vernon Castle, who is seen here as she appeared at the recent Victory Ball.—[Photographs by Malcolm Arbuthnot.]

Always exquisitely dressed, Irene Castle's appearance in costume at the Victory Ball held at the Royal Albert Hall on 27 November 1918 was no exception. The cream of society attended the event with 4,000 tickets sold to raise money for the Nation's Fund for Nurses. (Illustrated London News/ME)

CANDIDATES FOR PARLIAMENT : PROMINENT POLITICAL WOMEN.

INDEPENDENT CANDIDATE FOR RICHMOND (SURREY) : MRS. DACRE FOX.

WOMEN'S PARTY CANDIDATE FOR SMETHWICK : MISS CHRISTABEL PANKHURST.

LIBERAL CANDIDATE FOR MANSFIELD, NOTTS : MRS. CARRUTHERS (MISS VIOLET MARKHAM.)

LABOUR CANDIDATE FOR STOURBRIDGE : MRS. W. C. ANDERSON (MISS MARY MACARTHUR).

Continued.]

Miss M. Carney, Sinn Fein Candidate for the Victoria Division of Belfast ; and Mme. Markievicz, Sinn Fein Candidate for the St. Patrick's Division of Dublin City. It should be mentioned that Mrs. F. A. Lucas was adopted as Unionist Candidate for Kennington on the death of her husband, the late Colonel F. A. Lucas, who had been nominated as the Unionist Candidate there, shortly before the election. By the time this number of " The Sketch " appears, all will know whether or not they may add the coveted " M.P. " to their names !

Photographs by Lafayette ; Underwood and Underwood, New York ; and H. Walter Barnett.

When women over the age of thirty were given the vote for the first time, opportunities also opened up for female candidates in the post-war election but the results were disappointing. These four candidates, including Christabel Pankhurst, standing for the Women's Party and Violet Markham, previously responsible for the Women's Section employment scheme during the war, all failed to win the seats they were contending. (Illustrated London News/ME)

sculptor, George Edwards. The bronze model, showing the Angel of Resurrection guarding the entrance of a mausoleum while the British lion held down the dead eagle of Prussia, was available as a replica at a cost of 100 guineas. Elsewhere, Hughes, Bolckow and Co. of Dover Street advertised their war shrines made from wood taken from the naval training ship HMS *Britannia* as a 'fitting memorial to the patriotism of Britain's sons'. For those wishing for a personal memento of the dead, Mr Hemsley's Khaki Studio at No. 22 Baker Street could recreate a likeness from a photograph and accurate particulars regarding the complexion, hair and eye colour. 'In these days of bereavements and anxious partings, Mr Hemsley's clever oil paintings come as a boon and a blessing', wrote *The Queen* in 1917.

A national museum to record the events of the war and to commemorate the sacrifices of both military and civilian sections of society was first suggested by Sir Alfred Mond MP in March 1917, and reflected a public desire to remember and connect with the conflict. The Imperial War Museum first opened at the Crystal Palace in 1920 and moved to its present home in the former Bethlem Hospital in Lambeth in 1936. The aftermath of war also saw a wave of tourists visiting the battlefields of France and Belgium, many to visit the

Demobilised men at the Demobilisation Office in Whitehall waiting to get their papers. The group here are 'pivotal' (the job creators) and 'slip' men (those who had written assurance from employers of a position after the war) – the first of the post-war workforce to be demobilised from the army. (Illustrated London News/ME)

graves, where they existed, of loved ones. Ettie, Lady Desborough, visited her son Julian's grave in May 1919 and wrote to a friend of how she 'dreaded coming back here in a way, as well as longed to' while Lady Kenmare told Ettie how she found visiting her own son Dermot's grave 'all so beyond comprehension, the wide battlefields, so awful, so terrible; the strange hush over all that devastation, the grim ruins, the piteous little crosses standing here and there in utter loneliness…'

The cenotaph in Whitehall, designed by Edwin Lutyens, was temporarily constructed in timber and plaster for the first Remembrance Day in November 1919 before being permanently built in Portland stone the following year. Almost a century on, it remains the central focus for the Remembrance Day ceremony. In Westminster Abbey is the Tomb of the Unknown Warrior, where lies the body of an unidentified soldier, brought back to England from a major battlefield on the Western Front as an anonymous representative of those who had fought and died in the First World War, especially those with no known grave. As with the war cemeteries of Northern France and the simple dignity of Lutyen's memorial, the Tomb of the Unknown Warrior and its inscription ('They buried him among the Kings, because he had done good toward God and toward his house' – 2 Chronicles 24:16) is powerful and moving in its quiet simplicity. In 1923, as the new Duchess of York, the former Lady Elizabeth Bowes-Lyon, left Westminster Abbey following her marriage to Prince Albert, Duke of York, she spontaneously placed her bouquet on the tomb. One of her brothers, Fergus, had been killed at the Battle of Loos in September 1915.

A staggering 722,785 British soldiers died in the Great War, added to which were over 15,000 war-related deaths in the merchant and fishing fleets, 1,266 civilian deaths through air raids and bombardments, and more in munitions factories. The death toll was unprecedented, the resulting grief unimaginable and, after the passing of a century, the First World War refuses to loosen its grip on the popular imagination. Though the conflict is barely now within living memory, the voices of the men and women whose views, opinions and experiences form the basis of this book remain as fresh, witty and moving as ever. For the most part, the privileged society they so often describe (and occasionally criticise) rose to the challenges of war remarkably well, showing impressive reserves of resourcefulness, energy and courage, and in so doing made a significant contribution towards eventual victory. Certainly, though their actions are no more or less valuable than thousands of others who worked towards the same goal, their lives, told through the buzz and gossip of society magazines, are a particularly fascinating and compelling aspect of the Great War story.

The First World War changed Britain, and for many people, whatever their class, the experience irrevocably altered them. Eve, in a moment of contemplation, summed it up for readers of *The Tatler* in October 1915:

Truly, we've been so near, we are so near to death in these days that life can't ever be quite the same again, can it? There are some experiences one may pass through perhaps unchanged. But I don't think this is one of them.

INDEX

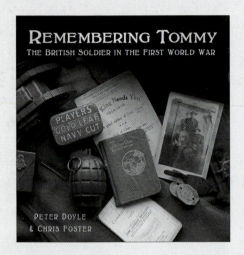
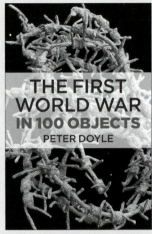
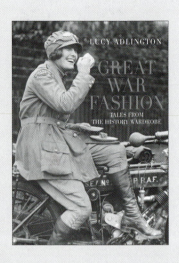
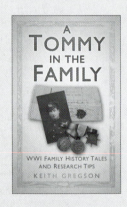
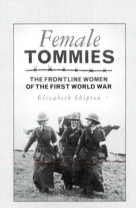
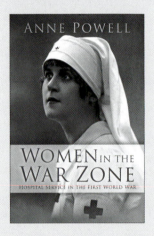
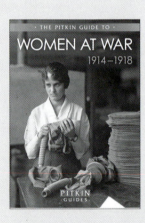

BARKERS of KENSINGTON

ROYAL WORCESTER CORSETS

The New Military Curve

TO-DAY Fashion presents a delightful surprise—the new Military vogue. Already it is becoming the rage. Its freshness, its vivacity, its freedom, are captivating the entire world of dress. The new Royal Worcester Kidfitting Corsets, which we are now featuring in our Corset Department, have caught the elusive spirit of this bewitching new mode with striking fidelity. Every model has the new Military Curve, upon which the present vogue entirely depends for its perfect expression. As these Corsets are designed by the foremost Parisian Corsetry artists in collaboration with the recognised Ateliers of creative fashion, their authenticity is beyond question.

The British lady is fast beginning to realise what her Parisian sister has always known by instinct—the economy of paying a fair price for her corsets and getting the best. The small saving one might possibly make by buying a lower-priced corset than the "Royal Worcester" would be worse than wasted; it might mean the ruination of your gowns, because no dressmaker could give you Fashion if your corsets were unfashionable.

To buy corsets without investigating the merits of the "Royal Worcester" is to set at nought the experienced judgment of the world's greatest authorities on Fashion, who practically without exception pronounce for Royal Worcester Kidfitting Corsets. We cordially invite you to call and have a pair fitted, or to send for a selection on approval, for nothing so quickly and completely establishes the superiority of these Corsets as an actual comparison.

A large Showroom is now devoted exclusively to Corsets.

MODEL 977. WITH THE NEW MILITARY CURVE.
Very chic new style. Silk elastic gore below hip. Average Figure. Sizes 20-35.   In white fancy broché.   Price **52/6**

The NEW MILITARY CURVE HAS TAKEN THE TOWN BY STORM

All the best & latest shapes can be found at BARKERS who have been appointed sole agents for a very large part of London, W. Prices from 4/11 to 4 Gns.

Ladies who cannot favour us with a visit, should write for the beautiful Illustrated Catalogue which shows styles suitable for every type of figure.

MODEL 507. Petite Figure. Height of bust from waist, 4 ins. Height of back below waist, 10 ins. Length of back below waist, 10½ ins. Chic new model designed especially for the little lady. In white coutil. Sizes 19-26   Price **8/11**

MODEL 5820. Average Figure. Height of bust from waist, 5 ins. Height of back below waist, 6½ ins. Length of back below waist, 11 ins. Free hips, stretchy skirt, good shoulder support. In white broché. Sizes 19-26   Price **12/11**

MODEL 9038. Average Figure. Height of bust from waist, 4½ ins. Height of back below waist, 13 ins. Length of back below waist, 13 ins. Given the very straight, flat appearance so much desired for back and hip. 6 bone supporters. In white coutil. Sizes 20-30   Price **25/9**

MODEL 843. Full Figure. Height of bust from waist, 5½ ins. Height of back below waist, 5½ ins. Length of back below waist, 12½ ins. Gives fulness over diaphragm. 6 bone supporters. In white. Sizes 22-30   Price **16/11** (Sizes 31-36, 2/- extra.)

JOHN BARKER & CO. LTD., KENSINGTON HIGH ST., LONDON, W.

LORD KITCHENER AS ORNAMENT FOR A LADY'S GARTER! PATRIOTIC FERVOUR IN ITS LATEST FORM.

ADMIRAL JELLICOE AS ORNAMENT FOR A LADY'S PATRIOTIC FERVOUR IN ITS LATEST FORM.

MACONOCHIES

WORLD-FAMOUS RATIONS.

A DELICIOUS STEW

A SUSTAINING AND ECONOMICAL MEAL FOR A FAMILY. COOKED READY FOR USE ONLY WANTS WARMING.

Per 1/6 Tin

3/4 lb. of the Finest Beef, without bone, (equal to 1 lb with bone), with Potatoes, Haricots, Carrots and Onions Nett Weight of contents about 22 ozs.

ON SALE EVERYWHERE.
MACONOCHIE BROS. LTD., LONDON.

CARTERS'

Telegrams: "Entubchair, Wesdo, London."   "The Alleviation of Human Pain." (ESTABLISHED OVER 60 YEARS.)   *Telep. 1040 M*

SELF-PROPELLING CHAIRS

FOR IN OR OUT-DOOR USE.

Ball-bearing wheels and pneumatic tyres if desired. The lightest, easiest self-propulsion. The "Wiesbaden" 1915 model has caned seat, adjustable back, and sliding leg-rest for either or both legs.

Over 30 designs, at all prices from 42/-

SPECIAL TERMS HOSPITAL SUPPLY

The "WIESBADEN."
"Modern Comfort Furniture" (600 Illustrations) post free.

CARTER 2, 4 & 6, NEW CAVENDISH LONDON, W.

"They 'jazz,' 'hesitate,' 'canter' and 'glide,' while the gramophone plays the latest revue melodies and 'rags.'"—vide DAILY MAIL.

The compactness and portability of the "Decca" make it ideal for the Dance. It will play the appropriate needle record perfectly ; loud enough, yet always musical. It can be carried with ease anywhere.

THE DECCA
THE PORTABLE GRAMOPHONE

In Leather Cloth	Compressed Fibre	Solid Cowhide
£7 15 0	£8 15 0	£12 12 0

Of Harrods, Army and Navy Stores, Whiteley's, Selfridge's, Gamage's, and all leading Stores and Music Dealers.

ILLUSTRATED FOLDER, and name of nearest agent, free on application to the Manufacturers—
THE DULCEPHONE CO., 32, Worship Street, London, E.C. 2.
(Proprietors: BARNETT SAMUEL & SONS, Ltd.)

MANY NUTRITIOUS DISHES CAN BE PREPARED WITH POTATOES, ONIONS AND OTHER VEGETABLES AND OXO

A handbill containing recipes for OXO and vegetable dishes, etc., will be sent free on receipt of a postcard addressed to—
OXO Limited, Thames House, London, E.C.4.